THE SPIRIT IN CREATION AND NEW CREATION

The Spirit in Creation and New Creation

Science and Theology in Western and Orthodox Realms

Edited by

Michael Welker

WILLIAM B. EERDMANS PUBLISHING COMPANY

GRAND RAPIDS, MICHIGAN / CAMBRIDGE, U.K.

© 2012 Michael Welker

Published 2012 by
Wm. B. Eerdmans Publishing Co.
2140 Oak Industrial Drive N.E., Grand Rapids, Michigan 49505 /
P.O. Box 163, Cambridge CB3 9PU U.K.

Printed in the United States of America

18 17 16 15 14 13 12   7 6 5 4 3 2 1

Library of Congress Cataloging-in-Publication Data

The Spirit in creation and new creation: science and theology in Western
    and Orthodox realms / edited by Michael Welker.
        p.   cm.
    Proceedings of a dialogue held in the fall of 2009 at the Internationales
    Wissenschaftsforum, University of Heidelberg.
    ISBN 978-0-8028-6692-9 (pbk.: alk. paper)
    1. Religion and science — Congresses.   2. Creation — Congresses.
    3. Spirit — Congresses.   I. Welker, Michael, 1947-
    II. Internationales Wissenschaftsforum.

    BL240.3.S69 2012
    261.55 — dc23

                                        2011043530

www.eerdmans.com

Contents

Contents

Acknowledgments

This book documents a dialogue about the SPIRIT — divine and human. It reflects on the nature and the workings of the Spirit in creation, which we can experience, and in new creation, the universal renewal, for which many people hope. Participants in this dialogue were scholars from the fields of physics, biology, mathematics, psychology, sociology, and systematic and historical theology, and from such diverse countries as the USA, Great Britain, Germany, Greece, Russia, and the Ukraine. Insights from the Russian and Greek Orthodox traditions as well as from Roman Catholic, Lutheran, Reformed, Anglican and Pentecostal backgrounds come together with perspectives from the wide range of academic disciplines mentioned above.

This multi-perspectival approach was taken in order to plumb more deeply an area of faith and knowledge which has been dominated by vague notions and much guesswork, the area of "spiritual realities." For a critical and self-critical exploration of this field the fact that the different academic disciplines have different modes of thought proved as advantageous as the diversity of perspectives provided by the faith traditions represented in the discourse.

The dialogue was made possible by the John Templeton Foundation and its "Humble Approach Initiative," and organized by Dr. Mary Ann Meyers. It took place in the Internationales Wissenschaftsforum of the University of Heidelberg, Germany, in the fall of 2009. As Dr. Meyers noted, it was held at the end "of a millennium of which the world has taken little notice" — and which began with the election of pope Sergius II in 1009, a date important as a step "towards the insertion of the filioque clause in the Nicene Creed, the theological event leading to the first major

Acknowledgments

division in Christendom." Divisions often cause conflict and pain. However, they can also generate fruitful and creative differences and contrasts of perspectives from which we profit, as is obvious in the differentiation of the academic disciplines today. Similarly, building on the differences among the religious traditions can lead to a more nuanced and deeper understanding of the nature of the Spirit — human and divine.

We thank the John Templeton Foundation for its generous support of the symposium and the publication of its results. We are most grateful to Dr. Mary Ann Meyers and her staff on the American side, and Frau Sabine Wagner and the Heidelberg Internationales Wissenschaftsforum on the German side, for the circumspect organization of the event and for collecting the contributions. Herr Henning Mützlitz has assisted us with the technical details of the publication. Our special thanks go to Eerdmans Publishing House. A Russian translation will follow in 2012.

MICHAEL WELKER

Introduction

Michael Welker

This book explores a vast field of experience, knowledge, curiosity, wonder, and awe. It aims at a better understanding of and respect for the Spirit — divine and human, for its working in creation and its striving towards new creation, a process in which human beings are transformed and ennobled. How does the Spirit relate to the world in which we live, and how does it lead to "the world to come"? The contributions from different academic fields and different faith traditions collected in this volume approach these questions in a number of ways. While some authors endeavor to cross the boundaries between the areas attributed to religion and theology on the one side and the natural sciences on the other side, others demand that their separation be respected and cultivated, and thus emphasize the differences between cognitive, emotional, and prayer-based approaches towards spiritual realities. Some contributions attach strong importance to contemporary research, while others primarily seek to preserve the continuity of current knowledge with grand traditions of faith and spiritual learning. All contributions, however, agree in their estimation that the dialogue among the different academic disciplines and different faith-traditions is fruitful and even needed, when we want to gain new and deeper insights into the working of the Spirit in creation and new creation.

I

The first four contributions relate insights from physics, biology, and mathematics to biblical, patristic, and modern theological perspectives on the Spirit. John Polkinghorne (The Hidden Work of the Spirit in Creation) draws attention to the fact that the working of the Spirit in creation is discreet and even hidden, and he tries to identify the character of this working from a scientist's perspective. After the displacement of the materialistic and mechanistic worldviews from the scientific agenda, and on the basis of observations such as the fact that as far as the atoms are concerned, our actual bodies are distinct from our bodies several years ago, we can develop perspectives on the role of the Spirit even in natural and material creation. Polkinghorne speaks of the role of "active information" in the physical world. He suggests that the Spirit creates highly complex "information-bearing patterns" and acts by inspiring and guiding all creatures in the unfolding work of continuing creation. Several contributions take up his insight that the Spirit is active "at the edge of chaos," that is, "in situations in which order and openness, regularity and contingency, necessity and chance, interlace each other."

Denis Alexander (The Spirit of God in Evolutionary History) gives an impressive picture of correlations of order and disorder, chance and necessity, the impersonal and the personal in evolutionary history. He observes a very early "tendency towards increased complexity in specific evolutionary lineages" and systems of sociality. This constellation already hints at the development of personality and "orders of intentionality." Many of these observations are in line with the insights and wisdom of the biblical traditions: ". . . the characteristics of the work of the Spirit known to us through revelation can provide a magnifying lens through which the biological story can provide a richer theological narrative."

Jeffrey Schloss (Hovering Over Waters: Spirit and the Ordering of Creation) takes up the biblical claims that "the dynamically creative and life-giving energy of spirit is associated with the purposeful ordering of word or wisdom." He shows how scientific enquiry can be inspired by this insight, but also how scientific enquiry can "inform belief by both affirming and challenging it." He illuminates the relation of the Spirit as "life-force of created beings" and "living space in which they can grow and develop their potentialities." He deals with the highly disputed question whether there are "directional trends" in evolution, and makes out tendencies towards "goal-oriented functionally purposive aspects of living systems" and "biotic intensification through progressive escalation of cooperative interdependence." He does not claim that this leads to a (quasi)scientific demonstration of the role of the Spirit in creation. More modestly, he sees an impressive concordance of these observations with ancient insights into the meaning and work of the Spirit in creation.

The philosopher and mathematician Vladimir Katasonov (Mathematics of Infinity and the Orthodox Name Worshipping Spiritual Tradition) evokes the world of spirituality and mathematics in early 20th-century Russia. He outlines "the Name worshipping theology" of a spiritual movement (palamitism and hesychasm) which sees God's presence in the world in and through His energies. Famous Russian theologians (such as P. A. Florensky) and famous mathematicians (such as N. N. Luzin) interact in shaping a post-materialistic worldview, which can embrace mathematical thought about the infinite and a spirituality which tries to relate to the divine in prayer and spiritual insight.

II

Jürgen Moltmann (The Spirit of Life) sets out with a Trinitarian perspective on creation and proposes to read the biblical creation accounts in a broader biblical perspective. The Spirit — as the "Spirit of the Earth" and the "New Earth" — is at work in creation and new creation. Righteousness and justice are indispensable for "endurance and peace" on earth. The prophetic traditions of the Old Testament and the life, cross, and resurrection of Jesus Christ unfold both the tensions and the relation between the old creation and the new. With the help of the theologies of Paul and Luke (esp. the Pentecost account), Moltmann illuminates the work of the Spirit in both domains. His contribution ends with reflections on the limits of a merely scientific approach to these matters.

Vladimir Shmaliy (Spirit or/and Spirits in Creation: Recalling the Seventh Assembly of the World Council of Churches in Canberra) argues for a fine balancing of the doctrines of creation, Christology, and pneumatology in a Trinitarian framework. Constant theological watchfulness is required to discern helpful theological rebalancings (such as overcoming the attempt to neglect or downplay the work of the Spirit in creation) from new disbalances or misbalances. He accentuates the need for a "discernment of the spirits," so that the Holy Spirit will not be confused with all sorts of spirits. This is a prerequisite in the search for understanding and truth in meaningful dialogues with other Christian faith traditions, with other religions, and with philosophy and science.

Sergey Horujy (How Exactly Is the Spirit Present in Creation? The Hesychast Reception of Natural Theology and Its Modern Implications) offers such an attempt to discern the spirits. He turns to Orthodox ascetic traditions (hesychasm) which over against pre-modern and modern types of "natural theology" emphasize that "knowledge of God . . . (has to be) converted from the purely intellectual cognitive paradigm to the integral, holistic paradigms of love and communion." The Holy Spirit is the power that effects a spiritual transformation which enables and ennobles the human being to attain knowledge of God and of God's creation. Horujy recommends a strong anthropological concentration of the science and theology discourse in order to foster their rapprochement. His contribution leads to the question which guides the third part of this book: "Convergence between Theology and Science?"

III

Cyril Hovorun (Convergence between Theology and Science: Patterns from the Early Christian Era) argues that we should think in broad time-spans and should learn from the 'Cappadocian Synthesis' which focuses on the human being, located between the created and the non-created world, in constant movements from non-existence to existence, from existence towards God and to perfection. From Gregory of Nyssa we should learn not to confuse theology and technology and to base theology more strongly on spiritual experience than on intellectual exercises.

Friederike Nüssel (Challenges of a Consistent Christian Language for the Creativity of God's Spirit) invites us to consider "the unity of the one spirit of God active in creation and granting righteousness in new creation." She reconstructs the intricate theological history in which the working of the Spirit became disconnected from cosmological perspectives. Taking up insights from Wolfhart Pannenberg, she argues that we should unfold pneumatology in the framework of a Trinitarian theology in order to illuminate the whole spectrum of workings of the Spirit in creation and in new creation. She concludes with reflections on how we could meet current challenges from the so-called New Atheism in the neurosciences.

Michael Welker (The Human Spirit and the Spirit of God) illuminates the dimensions of human mind and human spirit, which are often confused. The admiration for the enormous powers of the individual and above all the communal human spirit often blurs the fact that the human spirits and the "spirit of the world" can generate all kinds of self-endangerment and destruction. It is thus crucial to clearly differentiate the human spirit in its many forms and the divine Spirit. Here Paul's insights are most helpful. Welker shows how the "pouring" Spirit of God constitutes the "new creation" in the midst of the "old creation." The belief in the transformation and renewal of creation gains a clear form when it focuses on the life and lordship of the resurrected and elevated Jesus Christ who wins his witnesses in the power of the Spirit to participate in his kingly, prophetic, and priestly offices.

Renos K. Papadopoulos ('Keep Thy Mind in Hell and Despair Not': Implications for Psychosocial Work with Survivors of Political Violence) makes use of these Christological and pneumatological insights and differentiations in order to deal with pressing issues in the social sciences, namely work with survivors of political violence and traumatized victims of natural disasters. He further uses a saying of the famous Russian monk called Silouan which he quotes in the title of this contribution. The trauma grid in clinical and field work cannot be addressed, named, and opened up with the help only of symbolic forms from religious wisdom and pneumatological insight. Rather, trust in the working of the divine Spirit can open up persons to a renewal of their personality out of the depths of despair. The search for theological and socio-scientific insights and the search for spiritual renewal should not be disconnected or even become opposed to each other.

IV

The last part focuses on the work of the Spirit in new creation. Marcus Plested (Pneumatology and the New Creation in the Macarian Writings: An Ecumenical Legacy) deals with insights of Macarius-Symeon (Pseudo-Macarius, fourth century) in his work on mysticism. Macarius describes ways to a union with the Spirit which opens up the soul in compassion and love. Insights into the ambivalence of nature which can mirror the divine reality but also the powers of evil lead to the search of "active information" (John Polkinghorne) which opens the soul to the search for truth, compassion, and salvation, for the light of new creation "here and evermore."

Andrew Louth (The Holy Spirit in Creation and Re-Creation: The Byzantine Fathers) supports and unfolds these insights on the basis of further writings of the Church Fathers. From the Byzantine Fathers we can learn that we should not translate "our hopes and expectations, as well as our fears, into a theological vein." Openness to the Spirit results from prayer and discernment; it is a fruit of an ascetic struggle and a gift of the synergy between the human and the divine. Only an attitude of "humility and watchfulness" can open the eyes and our hearts for the work of the spirit in creation and new creation.

The Pentecostal theologian Frank D. Macchia (*Justified in the Spirit: Implications on the Border of Science and Theology*) offers a surprising perspective on Luther's explanation of the first article of the Creed (God as Creator). Following Oswald Bayer, he sees that Luther underlines the immense spiritual grace of God already in creation. In his *Small Catechism* and other writings, Luther says that we receive even the most basic gifts of nature "without our merit or worthiness." Macchia argues for a deep and realistic understanding of justification which encompasses the breadth of the working of the Holy Spirit and the depths of the basic processes of creaturely life. In this perspective we reach an area where concerns of theology and science can and must overlap. We also see how closely old and new creation lie together and how badly the powers of new creation are needed in each step of our earthly life.

The social scientist José Casanova (*Human Religious Evolution and Unfinished Creation*) warns against ideological contaminations in the study of socio-cultural developments such as "methodological individualism, methodological racism, and methodological nationalism and now methodological evolutionary theory." He argues for a nuanced view which differentiates humanity's natural evolutionary development as a species, its socio-cultural development, which culminates in the current phase of globalization, and the radical moral and religious predicament, which indeed challenges us to search for a deeper understanding of the spirit in creation and new creation. He also argues for a differentiated perspective on "the dyadic analytic categories sacred/profane, transcendent/imminent, and religious/secular" which are often confused with one another and with the dual of "creation and new creation." With these insights and with his provocative proposal that we might need "a new de-secularization of nature and of the earth," he demonstrates that the voice of social theory is needed in the theology and science dialogue on the spirit in creation and in new creation, and that social theory can as well profit from this dialogue.

I. THE SPIRIT IN CREATION: SCIENTIFIC PERSPECTIVES

The Hidden Work of the Spirit in Creation

John Polkinghorne

Western iconography of the Holy Trinity represents the Father as a kingly figure and the Son as the crucified Christ, but the Spirit is represented only by the modest figure of a dove. Eastern Orthodoxy, with the three angelic figures of the Old Testament Trinity, is much more even-handed in its iconic treatment of the divine Persons. Yet in that tradition also there is the recognition of a certain degree of hidden character in the work of the Spirit. Vladimir Lossky wrote:

> The divine persons do not assert themselves, but one bears witness to another. It is for this reason that St John Damascene said that 'The Son is the image of the Father, and the Spirit is the image of the Son.' It follows that the third Hypostasis of the Trinity is the only one not having His image in one of the Persons. The Holy Spirit, as Person, remains unmanifested, concealing Himself in His very appearing.[1]

There is, it seems, a kenotic self-effacement present in the activities of the Spirit, whose full revealing is awaiting fulfilment in the eschatological assembly of the community of the redeemed. To which we must surely add, awaiting also the total transformation of this suffering world into the world of God's new creation, for the Spirit is not concerned with the redemption of humanity alone. The Spirit hovered over the waters of chaos (Genesis 1:2) and participates in the travail of creation (Romans 8:26; the word translated 'sighs' derives from the same Greek root as the creaturely 'groaning' of vv. 22-3). The seed event from which the whole new creation

---

1. V. Lossky, *The Mystical Theology of the Eastern Church,* James Clarke, 1957, p. 160.

grows is the Resurrection and Romans 1:4 tells us that Christ was 'declared to be Son of God with power according to the Spirit of holiness by resurrection from the dead.'

This hidden character of the Spirit appears to be reflected in much contemporary Christian understanding and practice. Outside of the charismatic movement, many believers may seem to have only rather vague notions about the Holy Spirit. Pentecost is the Great Festival that probably attracts the least attention in the Church and it is often referred to simply as 'the birthday of the Church,' rather than as the day of the 'Pouring of the Spirit.'

If this is the case within the community of the faithful, what help could pneumatology hope to receive from the outside by way of scientific insight? The method of science is to view the world from a single perspective, focused on the physical and biological and framing its discourse in terms of the unfolding of impersonal processes, while at the same time bracketing out questions of the presence of meaning and value in what is going on. The narrowness of this view has enabled science to make great progress within its self-limited domain of understanding, but it leaves scant room, one might suppose, for any discernment of a spiritual dimension of reality, let alone the recognition of the work of the Holy Spirit. The founding figures of modern physics, such as Galileo, Kepler, and Newton, certainly believed in a spiritual dimension to reality. Newton was happy to suppose that if there were instabilities in the solar system, they would be corrected by angelic action. Yet, by the middle of the eighteenth century science appeared to have banished all notion of spirit from a world whose true character seemed to be that of clockwork mechanism. Books were written with titles such as *Man the Machine* (de la Mettrie). This situation was not significantly altered by the nineteenth-century discovery of field theories, made at the hands of Michael Faraday and James Clerk Maxwell (both sincere Christians). Despite what some theologians seem to suppose, there is nothing intrinsically spiritual about classical fields. They are carriers of energy and momentum and their equations are as rigidly deterministic as those of Newtonian particle dynamics. Another misapprehension with some currency in the theological world is that somehow the notion of energy itself has a spiritual character. This is not the case. Einstein's celebrated equation, $E = mc^2$, can be read in both directions, as much asserting the materiality of energy as the energetic character of matter. The nineteenth century's picture of the physical world was as aridly spiritless as that of the eighteenth century.

However, reality fights back against a crass physicalism and the twentieth century saw the death of a merely mechanical way of viewing the universe. At the beginning of the century, the discovery of quantum theory showed that the subatomic world is cloudy and fitful, with intrinsic unpredictabilities present in it that serve to imply that it is something more subtle than a realm of mere mechanism. In the middle of the century, the discovery of the intrinsic unpredictabilities of chaos theory showed that even the macroscopic world of classical physics, and everyday experience, is not a world of mere mechanism either. The word 'intrinsic' is important here. These unpredictabilities are not ones that could be removed by more precise measurement or more exact calculation. They are properties inherent in nature itself.

This fact immediately raises the question of whether these limitations are epistemological or ontological, matters of unfortunate necessary ignorance or signs of an actual openness to the future present in the process of the world. It turns out that this is a question that physics cannot settle on its own, since answering it calls also for an act of metaphysical decision. For example, quantum physics can be interpreted either as indeterministic (following the ideas of Niels Bohr) or as deterministic (following the ideas of David Bohm). Either option leads to the same empirical consequences and the choice between them has to be made on the basis of such metaphysical criteria as naturalness of explanation and lack of contrivance.[2] Our understanding of the nature of causality is certainly constrained by physics, but it is not determined by it, rather as the foundations of a house limit, but do not specify, the nature of the edifice that can be erected upon them. Causality is a metaphysical issue which has to be settled on metaphysical grounds, resulting in a kind of discussion in which it is perfectly proper for theological insights and constraints to play their appropriate roles. The choice of an open interpretation of unpredictability does not need to imply that future behaviour is a kind of random lottery, for the interpretation simply allows the presence of causal principles additional to those described by the conventional scientific picture of energy exchange between constituents. We shall return shortly to the consideration of that possibility.

Another comparatively recent development has further enriched our scientific understanding of the nature of the physical universe. It has be-

2. See, for example, J. C. Polkinghorne, *Quantum Theory: A Very Short Introduction,* Oxford University Press, 2002.

come possible to study the behaviour of some mildly complex systems treated as totalities, without their having to be reduced to their constituent bits and pieces. Some of this work has been based on computer models[3] and some of it has involved dissipative physical systems held far from thermal equilibrium by the exchange of energy and entropy with their environment.[4] None of these systems is anything like as complicated as even a single living cell, but even so both kinds of system display quite astonishing powers of spontaneous self-organisation, leading to the generation of patterns of overall dynamical behaviour that are of remarkable complexity and which are quite unforeseeable in terms of the properties of the individual constituents. For example, Stuart Kauffman studied a logical model called a Boolean net of connectivity 2. If there are 10,000 elements in the net, the number of different configurations in which it might in principle be found is about 10^{3000}, an absolutely huge number, vastly in excess of the total number of particles in the observable universe. Yet, as the system evolves, according to its simple rules and starting from an arbitrary initial configuration, it soon settles down to circulating through about only 100 configurations, an act of the self-generation of an astonishing degree of order. As a physical example of the spontaneous generation of remarkable order, one can consider the phenomenon of Benard convection. Fluid is confined between two horizontal plates, the lower of which is maintained at a higher temperature than the upper. In certain well-defined circumstances, the heat transfer from bottom to top is found to take place by convective motion confined within an orderly network of hexagonal convection cells. This involves the correlated motion of trillions upon trillions of fluid molecules. These examples of holistic behaviour are truly astonishing. As the saying goes, it has turned out that 'More is different,' the whole exceeds the sum of its parts.

At present this work is at the natural history stage consisting of the study of particular examples, and it has not yet attained the status of a mature science by discovering an underlying general explanatory theory covering all these individual behaviours. Yet such a theory must surely exist and when it is discovered it will have a profound effect upon our picture of the process of the world. One may venture to conjecture the general shape that this future theory may reasonably be expected to take.

The constituent laws of conventional physics (which will, of course,

3. S. Kauffman, *At Home in the Universe*, Oxford University Press, 1995.
4. I. Prigogine and I. Stengers, *Order out of Chaos*, Heinemann, 1984.

continue to be important) will have to be complemented by holistic laws, concerned with systems treated in their totalities. The prime concept of these laws will not be the exchange of energy between constituents, but the specification of the dynamical patterns in which total energy flows. We could call the specification of these dynamical patterns 'information,' and it is becoming increasingly clear that contemporary science is on the cusp of developing some well-defined concept of information that is required as an essential concept in its thinking.[5] We may expect that by the end of the twenty-first century, information will stand beside energy as an indispensable category for our understanding of the physical world.

Information in the sense of the specification of dynamical pattern is only very faintly reminiscent of spirit, but there is at least the modest hint of a promise of some useful sort of connection. Certainly the spiritless world of mere mechanism has been displaced from the scientific agenda. In assessing this development one must note an important distinction between the case of physical systems and the case of computer models. The latter are logical systems whose deterministic character means that all structure derives solely from the bottom-up influence of interactions between the individual units of the system, even if it requires the use of holistic concepts for its effective description and understanding. In the case of physical systems, however, the metaphysical possibility of a genuine ontological openness to the future, offered by the presence of the intrinsic unpredictabilities previously noted, means that information can be held to be more than simply a useful concept for thinking about holistic behaviour. Instead, it may play a genuinely causal role, exercising a top-down influence complementary to bottom-up constituent causality. One might call this role 'active information.'[6] Here could be a glimmer — I say no more than that — which might help us to begin to understand how human beings (ultra-complex systems of immense intricacy) are able to act as agents in the world. When I decide to raise my arm, of course there is a bottom-up story of currents flowing in nerves and muscles contracting, but it is *I*, the personal agent, who makes that decision. There is a holistic story to be told of my willed action.[7] If there is some truth in the approach that is being suggested, that would prove to be a gain for *science*. At last it

5. H. C. von Baeyer, *Information*, Weidenfeld and Nicholson, 2003.

6. J. C. Polkinghorne, *Belief in God in an Age of Science*, Yale University Press, 1998, ch. 3.

7. There is a connection here with the ideas of Donald Mackay, an early pioneer of research into artificial intelligence; see D. M. Mackay, *Brains, Machines and Persons*, Collins, 1980.

would begin to describe a world of which we could fittingly consider ourselves to be inhabitants, in contrast to the lunar landscape of its present account, which describes a world populated by replicating, information-processing systems, but one that has no persons in it. There was always something highly implausible in a merely mechanical view of reality, the claim that we are automata, yet somehow engaged in rational arguments capable of demonstrating our strictly deterministic nature. What could validate the 'programmes' running on this hardware? If the world were clockwork, would not these human clocks just tick away regardless?

Of course, the application of these speculative ideas to entities as immensely complex as human beings would require a correspondingly immense enrichment of the concept of information, carrying it far beyond the naïve levels suggested by examples drawn from the consideration of logical networks and dissipative physical systems. The point can be made by asking how one might think of the human soul in an anthropology that takes seriously the psychosomatic unity of human beings. The soul is, presumably 'the real me,' the carrier of the continuity of my human personhood. At first sight, one might be tempted to interpret this basic human conviction of personal continuity in terms of the apparent physical continuity of the body. However, this continuity is, in fact, an illusion. The atoms that make up our bodies are changing all the time, through wear and tear, eating and drinking. We have very few atoms in our bodies that were there even a few years ago and we are atomistically distinct from ourselves as children. What carries the continuity is not human flesh itself but the almost infinitely complex 'information-bearing pattern' carried at any one time by the material of the body. Of course, in our present state of knowledge such a statement is wildly imprecise, no more than hand-waving but (the ideas we have been discussing suggest) waving in a promising direction. The 'pattern that is me' must be rich enough to include my character and my memories. It is not contained wholly within my skin, for it must surely include those relationships with others that do so much to constitute me as a person. One might add that this embodied 'pattern' possesses no intrinsic immortality, for it will be destroyed at death by the decay of the body that carries it. However, it is a coherent Christian belief that the faithful God will not allow the pattern to be lost, but will retain it in the divine memory and reembody it in a new environment through the eschatological act of resurrection.[8]

8. J. C. Polkinghorne and M. Welker (eds.), *The End of the World and the Ends of God,*

The concept of active information offers a way of thinking about the providential action of the Spirit, guiding the unfolding work of continuing creation. If we, through our chosen acts, play our part in bringing about the future, surely the Creator of the world will not be without the power of providential agency to act within its history also. In the terms that we have been exploring, we can picture this as arising through the input of pure (that is, disembodied) information. Here is a faint, but suggestive, image that has some resonance with theological belief in the Spirit at work, subtly and patiently, on the inside of creation. That working is not contrary to nature but takes place within the divinely ordained open grain of nature. The Spirit acts by inspiration and guidance, not by interference.

According to this picture, agency, whether human or divine, operates in regimes characterised by the cloudiness of intrinsic unpredictability, an insight that is in accord with the theological insight of the hidden character of much of the work of the Spirit. The processes of the world cannot be analysed with complete clarity and decomposed into distinct and separate components, as if one could assert that nature did this, human agency did that, and the Spirit did the third thing. Causal powers are inextricably entangled. The working of the Spirit may be discernable by faith, but it can never be unambiguously demonstrated by experiment. The issue of the balance between what the Spirit does and what is the work of creatures is the familiar issue of grace and free will, now written cosmically large.

Scientific insight suggests that this discrete veiling of developing change within the unpredictability of process is intrinsically linked with the fruitfulness of the Spirit's working. Science has discovered that the regimes in which truly novel possibilities are realised are always to be found at 'the edge of chaos,' that is to say in situations in which order and openness, regularity and contingency, necessity and chance, interlace each other. If things are too orderly, they are too rigid for more than the possibility of the rearrangement of already existing elements. If things are too haphazard, any novelty that emerged would fall apart too quickly to be able to persist. Only at the edge of chaos can the really new both come to be and continue to be. If there were no genetic mutations, there would be no new forms of life to be sifted and preserved by natural selection. If genetic mutations were too abundant, no new species could become established long enough for natural selection to act upon them. The 3.5 billion-

Trinity Press International, 2000; J. C. Polkinghorne, *The God of Hope and the End of the World,* SPCK/Yale University Press, 2002.

year history of life on Earth, turning a world that initially was populated only by bacteria into one with persons in it, was enabled by just the right rate of genetic mutation.

Before leaving the topic of the Spirit and modern science, we should note a quite different point that remains to be made. In the Gospel of John, Jesus speaks of the Spirit as the 'Spirit of truth' (14:16; 16:13). We must, therefore, believe in the presence of the Spirit within all truth-seeking communities, including the community of science. The hidden character of the Spirit means that many in these communities, including many scientists, will be unaware of His presence, but I believe that the Spirit has been at work, and God has been glorified, in all new acts of scientific discovery that reveal the wonderful order with which the universe has been endowed by its Creator. The very existence of pure science depends upon the human recognition of the intrinsic value of knowledge for knowledge's own sake and the Spirit of truth grounds and endorses that value. The activity of science takes place within a community of mutually interacting seekers after truth and one of the gifts of the Spirit is *koinonia,* fellowship. The intellectual health of the scientific community depends upon the practice of virtues such as honesty in reporting results, generosity in sharing insights with others, and a just recognition of the achievements that individuals have attained. These are gifts that the Christian believes are ultimately enabled by the Spirit of truth.

The Spirit of God in Evolutionary History

Denis Alexander

The *ruach* of God is a dominant theme in the Old Testament — God's atmosphere, wind breath — providing the context in which God gives and takes away life from humans (Genesis 2:7; Job 33:4; Psalm 146:4; Isaiah 42:5) and animals (Psalm 104:29-30; Job 34:14-15), maintains the normal rhythms of the created order (Ecclesiastes 1:6; Psalm 135:7), and brings new life to people, such as the exilic community in Babylon (Ezekiel 37:4-5; 7-10). Wind *(ruach)* in the Old Testament is always God's wind (e.g. Exodus 10:19; Numbers 11:31; Psalm 148:8; Hosea 13:15). *Ruach* and wisdom are often tightly associated (Deuteronomy 34:9; Isaiah 11:2; Daniel 5:11). It has even been suggested that any translation of *ruach* in the Old Testament as Spirit or spirit is inappropriate, given its intimate association in Hebrew thought with the sheer monistic physicality of God's created order.[1]

In the New Testament the *ruach* of God 'crystallises out,' as it were, and continues to give life, this time the transforming life of the third person of the Trinity who empowers and enlivens the founding and expansion of the early Church. The focus of the New Testament Spirit is on the giving of spiritual life (John 3:5; Acts 2:38), the bestowal of gifts (1 Corinthians 12:4-11), empowerment for service (Acts 1:8), leading (Luke 4:1; Romans 8:14; Galatians 5:18), the producing of fruits in the life of the believer (Galatians 5:22-23), speaking to churches (Revelation 2:7, 11, 17, 29; 3:6, 12, 22), and calling believers forward to the *eschaton* (Revelation 22:17).

Specific references to the work of the Spirit in creation in either Tes-

---

1. T. Hiebert, *'Air, the first sacred thing: the conception of ruah in the Hebrew Scriptures,'* in N. Habel and P. Trudinger (eds.), *Ecological Hermeneutics,* Atlanta: Society of Biblical Literature, 2008, pp. 9-19.

tament are relatively rare, but by no means absent. To reflect on the work of the Spirit in evolutionary history, we will here draw on two theological starting points. The first is provided by Colin Gunton: "When in the ancient creeds the Spirit is celebrated as the Lord and giver of life, he is seen as the one who enables created things, and particularly living created things, to be what they truly and variously are in their manifoldness. The world does indeed cohere in the Son, but is diversified and particularised as the second hand of the Father enables things to be what they are created to be in the Son, even before the end and even despite the chaos and disorder inserted into the general order of things by sin and evil."[2] "In turn, that means that everything looks — and indeed, is — different in the life of the Trinity."[3] The second is provided by Jürgen Moltmann, who points out that "the divine Spirit *(ruach)* is the creative power and the presence of God in his creation. The whole creation is a fabric woven by the Spirit, and is therefore a reality to which the Spirit gives form."[4] Moltmann goes on to argue that "we must start theologically from the revelation and experience of 'the Holy Spirit' in the church of Christ, and from this deduce the presence and the mode of efficacy of 'the Spirit' in creation."[5]

Going much further back in Church history, we can draw on the perceptive insights of Basil of Caesarea, who wrote that "God, before all those things which now attract our notice existed, after casting about in his mind and determining to bring into being that which had no being, imagined the world as it ought to be, and created matter in harmony with the form which he wished to give it,"[6] so that "The Spirit . . . prepared the nature of the water to produce living things."[7]

The approach here will therefore be to take three sets of contrasting modes of action of the *ruach* of God in the Old Testament, or of the 'crystallised out' Holy Spirit in the New Testament, and to determine what resonances these modes might find in evolutionary history. This approach is not suggesting that the characteristics of the work of the Spirit can be derived by a kind of 'bottom-up approach' from the data of evolution *per se,* but rather the reverse, that the characteristics of the work of the Spirit

2. C. Gunton, *The Triune Creator,* Eerdmans, 1998, p. 161.
3. C. Gunton, *The Promise of Trinitarian Theology,* Edinburgh: T&T Clark, 1991, p. 4.
4. J. Moltmann, *God in Creation,* SCM Press, 1985, p. 99.
5. Moltmann, op. cit., p. 99.
6. Basil of Caesarea, *Hexamaeron* I:10.
7. Basil of Caesarea, *Hexamaeron* II:6.

known to us through revelation can provide a magnifying lens through which the biological story can provide a richer theological narrative.

1. Unity and Separation

One of the most evocative phrases in the whole Bible is provided by Genesis 1:2 with the *ruach* of God "hovering over the waters," or in Hiebert's memorable translation, far from being the hovering of a bird, the *ruach* becomes the wind sweeping in on a storm from the Mediterranean: "God's *ruach* swept over the surface of the water."[8] The immediate consequences of that sweeping are informative, and shape the first of the two contrasts.

'Separation' is a key thread running through Genesis 1: light is separated from the darkness (verse 4); the waters of the sea and sky are separated (verse 6); the lights separate day and night (verse 14); yet all diversify from the same amorphous 'formless and empty' creation (verse 2). Humankind is separated off from the rest of the created order by, uniquely, being made in God's image (verses 26-27). Everything comes from the same single created source, but is diversified, separated, into components that provide the created order with its distinctive interrelatedness. Just as separation characterises the work of God in creation, so it is a mark also of his work in redemption, as the people of God are called to separate themselves from things that make them unclean (Leviticus 15:31; Ezra 10:11; Nehemiah 9:2; 2 Corinthians 6:17). As the Spirit works in the Church, so unity is expressed through the diversity of the Spirit's gifts, working together for the good of the whole body (1 Corinthians 12:4-31).

The theme of diversity in unity is likewise a striking feature of evolutionary history. All living things are united by sharing the same chemistry, the same genetic code, the same cellular structure, the same kinds of biochemical pathways. It was Darwin's brilliant insight to bring history into biology and show how the tree or bush of life connects up all living things in one great systematic history. As the late evolutionary biologist Ernst Mayr remarked: "The theory of evolution is quite rightly called the greatest unifying theory in biology. The diversity of organisms, similarities and differences between kinds of organisms, patterns of distribution and behaviour, adaptation and interaction, all this was merely a bewildering chaos of facts until given meaning by the evolutionary theory."

8. Hiebert, op. cit., p. 15.

The theological resources were already available long before Darwin to take his theory of natural selection and baptize it into the traditional Christian doctrine of creation. John Wesley, Anglican founder of the Methodist movement, wrote a century before Darwin in his 5-volume work, *A Survey of the Wisdom of God in Creation:*

> There are no sudden changes in nature; all is gradual and elegantly varied. There is no being which has not either above or beneath it some that resemble it in certain characters, and differ from it in others. . . . From a plant to man . . . the transition from one species to another is almost insensible. . . . The ape is this rough draft of a man; an imperfect representation which nevertheless bears a resemblance to him, and is the last creature that serves to display the admirable progression of the works of God! There is a prodigious number of continued links between the most perfect man and the ape.[9]

We do not need to make John Wesley into a crypto-evolutionist to see that these comments are remarkably prescient of Darwin's theory, showing in great detail how the whole of God's great 'chain of being' demonstrated connections and similarities, since all stemmed from the creative handiwork of the same creator God. All Darwin needed to do was join up the dots, as it were, demonstrating that the great ladder of life had important vertical struts holding all the steps together and giving them a unified history.

All living things have one common source, sharing the same genetic code, universal except for the occasional minor differences, and are structured on a common cellular unit, displaying a remarkably similar basic molecular machinery, with biochemical pathways that are common to all. None of this makes any sense without a shared evolutionary history. But at the same time the evolutionary diversification, the separation of living forms into a myriad manifestations of liveability, is equally remarkable. No one actually knows the exact number of species on earth. The number already classified is around two million. There are 4,629 mammalian species, about 10,000 species of birds, 15,300 fish species, 250,000 flowering plants, 69,000 species of fungi, and 50,000 species or groups of species of tree. Yet all of these numbers fade into insignificance compared to the 850,000 insect species named so far, of which 300,000 are beetles, and it has been es-

---

9. J. Wesley, *A Survey of the Wisdom of God in Creation, Vol. II,* N. Bangs and T. Mason, New York, 1823,[3] pp. 192ff.

timated that 80-95% of insect species have yet to be named and classi-fied.[10] So the final tally of species in the world could be nearer 20 million than 2 million, especially if the proportion of cryptic species turns out to be as high as some people think. And all of this remarkable diversity is gen-erated by an elegant combinatorial genomic system of variant genes num-bering in the tens of thousands or less. The living world is one of impres-sive unity, but also of exotic evolutionary diversification.

2. Order and Disorder

The second impact of God's *ruach*, sweeping across the waters, is to bring order out of the *tohu vebohu* ('formless and empty' or 'waste and void') world portrayed by Genesis 1:2. The literary structure of Genesis 1 in which Days 1-3 provide the form and Days 4-6 the fullness of living things that fill the form has often been described. God's creative work through the power of his *ruach* is linked to his wisdom (Proverbs 8:22-31), and his judgment in the Old Testament on those who display a lack of wisdom is frequently associated with a reversion to *tohu vebohu* (Isaiah 34:11; Jeremiah 4:23). The order brought to church life by the work of the Holy Spirit is contrasted with the disorder that arises from an undisciplined use of the Spirit's gifts (1 Corinthians 14).

At the same time the work of God's *ruach* is portrayed as unpredict-able, producing unexpected consequences. Saul's sudden change of heart in response to God's *ruach* must have seemed startling and unexpected for those who knew him (1 Samuel 10:9-10), and the consequences grave when the *ruach* departed (1 Samuel 16:14). Indeed the wind blows wherever it pleases (John 3:8). The disorder was so great at Pentecost that drunkenness seemed the only reasonable explanation (Acts 2) and the work of the Spirit so dramatic that money was on offer in a mistaken attempt to buy the same results (Acts 8:18-19). Guidance by the Spirit was sometimes quite unexpected, even bizarre, yet ultimately fruitful (Acts 8:26-40; 16:6-7; 20:22).

Evolutionary history displays a similarly creative display of order and disorder, of chance and necessity, random genetic variation creating the raw materials on which necessity, in the guise of natural selection, exerts its stringent choice. Overall the process is constrained and tightly regulated:

10. N. E. Stork, *'World of insects,' Nature* 448: 657-658, 2007.

necessity has the upper hand. Evolution provides the search engine that explores design space. The history is marked by repeated convergence as identical or very similar solutions are found to the same biological challenge, as necessity paves the way.[11] With hundreds of genome sequences now available from different organisms, and with the 3-D structures of thousands of proteins now solved, it is a striking fact that if we examine all the known proteins in the world, and their structural motifs, based on all the genomes that have been sequenced so far, we find that the great majority can be assigned to only 1,400 protein domain families. About 200 of these domains are common to all kingdoms of life. The evolutionary search engine has uncovered an elegant but very limited repertoire of structures that underlie all of life's complexity.[12]

Further underlying biological complexity are networking principles that are turning out to be fewer and simpler than they might have been. Given that in every cell complex networks of interactions occur between thousands of metabolites, proteins, and DNA, this is quite surprising. As Uri Alon from the Weizmann Institute comments: ". . . Biological networks seem to be built, to a good approximation, from only a few types of patterns called network motifs. . . . The same small set of network motifs, discovered in bacteria, have been found in gene-regulation networks across diverse organisms, including plants and animals. Evolution seems to have 'rediscovered' the same motifs again and again in different systems. . . ."[13]

Proteins appear to be highly constrained in the evolutionary pathways that they can follow. A research group from Harvard published a paper in 2006 entitled 'Darwinian evolution can follow only very few mutational paths to fitter proteins.'[14] It is intriguing to read the final sentence of their abstract: "We conclude that much protein evolution will be similarly constrained. This implies that the protein tape of life may be largely reproducible and even predictable." As our scientific understanding of the molecular mechanisms underlying the evolutionary process increases, so the language of order, constraint, and even predictability has become more common in the literature.

11. S. Conway Morris, *Life's Solution — Inevitable Humans in a Lonely Universe*, CUP, 2003.

12. For more examples see D. Alexander, *Creation or Evolution — Do We Have to Choose?* Monarch, 2008, ch. 15.

13. U. Alon, 'Simplicity in biology,' *Nature* 29: 497, 2007.

14. D. M. Weinreich et al., *Science*: 111-114, 7 Apr 2006.

A further example comes from a consideration of 'fitness landscapes,' which play an important role in evolutionary discourse. These traditionally represent topographical pictures of the adaptation of different populations of living organisms to local ecological niches, but the idea of fitness landscapes can also be applied to enzyme structure and function. Again it turns out that the evolutionary pathways to arrive at a particular function of a particular enzyme are remarkably constrained. As the authors of a recent paper on this topic conclude: "That only a few paths are favoured also implies that evolution might be more reproducible than is commonly perceived, or even be predictable."[15] The point is that there are only certain ways of getting from A to B. If you want to climb the Matterhorn in Switzerland, you cannot climb it randomly, there are certain preset routes that constrain your ascent.

As with proteins, so with genes, there are underlying biological principles that constrain the location and type of gene evolution. The 'raw material' for evolution is provided by 'random' mutations, gene flow, and the genetic recombination that occurs during the generation of the germ-line cells. But note that 'randomness' here means only that genetic variation occurs without the needs of the organism in mind. By contrast the genetic variation that leads to evolution is not 'random' in the sense that any kind of variation in any kind of gene will do. In reality there are so-called "hotspot genes," those that are far more likely than others to play key roles in evolutionary change, such as a gene that delights in the name *shavenbaby* found in the *Drosophila* fruit-fly.[16] Such genes act as 'input/output genes,' encoding key switching proteins that integrate whole sets of information that are then mediated to downstream effectors. The *shavenbaby* gene regulates the existence and distribution of fine trichomes or cellular hairs on the surface of the larvae of *Drosophila*, so that mutations in *shavenbaby* lead to a lack of trichomes — hence the name.

It is genes such as *shavenbaby*, "hotspot genes," that render evolution possible because they regulate an integrated programme of events, in this case converting cells into hair-making cells. The mutations that occur are in the regulatory sequences of this gene that control how much of the protein is actually made. So far about 350 of these kinds of "hotspot genes"

15. F. J. Poelwijk et al., *'Empirical fitness landscapes reveal accessible evolutionary paths,'* *Nature* 445: 383-386, 25 Jan 2007.

16. D. L. Stern and V. Orgogozo, *'Is genetic evolution predictable,'* *Science:* 746-751, 6 Feb 2009.

have been identified in plants and animals. As the authors of a recent review entitled 'Is genetic evolution predictable?' comment: "Recent observations indicate that all genes are not equal in the eyes of evolution. Evolutionarily relevant mutations tend to accumulate in hotspot genes and at specific positions within genes. Genetic evolution is constrained by gene function, the structure of genetic networks, and population biology. The genetic basis of evolution may be predictable to some extent. . . ."[17]

Yet also along with this highly constrained evolutionary history comes a striking contingency. There is no linear increase in complexity from the origin of life about 3.8 billion years ago up to the present. Instead life's trajectory has been marked by periodic flowerings of novelty that have led to completely new phases in evolutionary history. During the first 2.5 billion years of life on earth (approximately), things rarely grew bigger than 1 millimetre across, about the size of a pin-head.[18] Not until the advent of multicellular life did living organisms start to get bigger, although even then they were generally on a scale of millimetres rather than centimetres. With the flourishing of the late Ediacaran fauna during the period 575-543 million years ago, we move into the centimetre scale. Only in the so-called 'Cambrian explosion' during the period 505-525 million years ago did sponges and algae grow up to 5-10 cm across, and the size of animals began to increase dramatically from that time onward, providing the new life-forms and body-plans for virtually all the animals with which we are familiar today.

Novel contingent breakthroughs in evolutionary history are exemplified by the first cell that acquired a nucleus (about 1.8–2.2 billion years ago), the first cells that started living symbiotically with the bacteria that eventually became the organelles that we now know as the mitochondria and the chloroplast, and the advent of multicellular life from 1.2 billion years ago. It was cyanobacteria that were able to obtain energy from the sun by photosynthesis that came to live inside other cells, a process known as endosymbiosis, and then became permanent residents, giving rise to the organelles we now call chloroplasts, responsible for the photosynthesis of the plant cells that pump out oxygen into the earth's atmosphere. A similar endosymbiosis took place for the bacteria that became the cells' mitochondria, which are the power-generating organelles of our cells, that have their

17. D. L. Stern and V. Orgogozo, op. cit.

18. S. Carroll, *'Chance and necessity: the evolution of morphological complexity and diversity,'* Nature 409: 1102-1109, 2001.

own separate DNA. In this way an enormous influx of useful genetic information took place into cells, with a huge impact on evolutionary history — a contingent and unpredictable event if ever there was one.

Contingent events in evolutionary history open up whole new landscapes of opportunity in which new ecological niches can be explored once certain novel adaptations are acquired. This has been demonstrated in the laboratory by tracking the evolution of strains of bacteria over a period of more than twenty years.[19] On 24th February 1988, Rich Lenski, then at the University of California, Irvine, started a series of 12 populations growing of the bacteria *Escherichia coli,* fed using glucose, all derived originally from a single bacterium. Each day about half a billion new bacteria grow in each flask, involving the replication of the same number of bacterial genomes, and in total about a million mutations occur in each flask as the bacteria divide. Since there are only about 5 million base-pairs in the bacterial genome, this means that every few days virtually the whole genome will be subject to genetic 'analysis' to see whether any of the new mutations might be useful. In practice the vast majority are not, but occasionally new mutations come along that provide some growth advantages.

Every night the bacteria run out of their glucose food source and become dormant, so bacteria that could cope best with this changing environment have a big advantage. The next day about 1% of the culture from each flask is used to start a new culture with a new supply of glucose. Most of the mutations that occur provide up to a 10% growth advantage, and such mutations spread rapidly through the population as the progeny carrying the mutation have the growth advantage. In fact what Lenski found was that the evolution of the different flasks of bacteria, as measured by their growth, developed not in a smooth trajectory, but in a series of abrupt jumps as advantageous mutations 'took over' the population.

After more than a decade of sub-culturing the 12 flasks, something rather extraordinary happened at generation 33.127. One of the cultures 'discovered' how to use citrate as a food source, a chemical used to buffer the pH and so always present in all the flasks since the beginning. This of course gave this population a huge growth advantage as it was no longer dependent upon glucose as a food source. This critical event happened in only one of the 12 flasks and it took more than ten years to show up. Further analysis revealed that the capacity to use citrate could not evolve all in one step, but took three different mutations to achieve. The two 'back-

19. T. Chouard, *'Revenge of the hopeful monster,' Nature* 463: 864-867, 2010.

ground' mutations had to occur first, and it was the third critical mutation that then enabled the complete ensemble of three mutations to allow the use of citrate, thereby opening up a whole new way of living for the colony. In fact what has happened in practice is for 99% of the colony to use citrate, whereas about 1% of this bacterial culture have become 'glucose specialists,' stubbornly refusing to forsake their original food source.

God's *ruach* sweeping over the waters certainly brought order out of *tohu vebohu,* just as Genesis 1 depicts. But God's *ruach* also brought creativity, unpredictability, and incredible variation, so that "from so simple a beginning endless forms most beautiful and most wonderful have been, and are being, evolved."[20] The Spirit in creation blows where He wills. Evolution is nothing like a human engineering project. There is no fixed blueprint for evolution, although in the dynamic relationship between chance and necessity, it is clear that ultimately necessity has the upper hand. If it were not so, then from a biological perspective the earth would forever have remained in a state of *tohu vebohu.*

3. Personal and Impersonal

The images of God's *ruach* in the Old Testament — mostly breath or wind — do not convey a strong sense of personhood, although God's *ruach* certainly interacts repeatedly with human individuals, especially to generate creativity (Exodus 31:3; 35:31; Numbers 11:25; Deuteronomy 34:9 etc). In the New Testament the personhood of the Holy Spirit begins to come through more explicitly, now portrayed as the one who leads (Matthew 4:1), who anoints (Luke 4:18), who gives birth and life (John 3:6; 6:63), the Counselor who teaches and testifies (John 14:26; 15:26), and who encourages (Acts 9:31) and speaks (Acts 28:25).

The emergence of personhood in evolutionary history requires that there be an arrow of evolutionary time marked by a dramatic increase in complexity. Without a tendency towards increased complexity, there would have been no hope of personhood arising from simple single-celled organisms. But increased complexity is precisely what evolution delivers. As Sean Carroll from the University of Wisconson–Madison remarks in a review in the journal *Nature:* "Life's contingent history could be viewed as an argument against any direction or pattern in the course of evolution or

20. C. Darwin, *On the Origin of Species,* 1872, 6th edn.

the shape of life. But it is obvious that larger and more complex life forms have evolved from simple unicellular ancestors and that various innovations were necessary for the evolution of new means of living."[21] Carroll chooses his words carefully, but if pressed every biologist has to admit that multicellular organisms *are* more complex than bacteria, that mammals *are* in some sense more advanced than yeast, and that the human brain has more capacities than that of a shrew. So it is perverse to deny some form of directionality to the arrow of biological time.

Much recent data support the idea of a tendency towards increased complexity in specific evolutionary lineages. For example, there is a remarkable and pervasive trend for increasing morphological complexity in multiple parallel lineages of the Crustacea, the major arthropod group with the longest and most disparate fossil record throughout the geological era known as the Phanerozoic.[22] Such examples do not imply that increased complexity is an inevitable outcome in every evolutionary lineage: environmental constraints and contingent events play critical roles, in addition, to limit or even reverse such trends. But if we stand back and look at evolutionary history as a whole, as Carroll points out, then the overall trend towards increased complexity becomes obvious.

Early evolutionary history does not, at first glance, look very personal. But even there, in the intensely communal lives of bacteria and the archea, the seeds of communal living are beginning to be sown. The very earliest fossils dating from 3 to 3.5 billion years ago consist of fossilized mats of photosynthesising cyanobacteria known as stromatolites, ranging in size from a few millimetres to more than 10 metres. Stromatolites are layered structures that are formed when bacteria grow in giant colonies on the surface of water and sediments are deposited above or among the cells, building up many mineralised layers. This is far from personhood, but it does underline the fact that the earliest known life-forms were communal.

Later, multicellularity was a new exercise in a related kind of communal living. As complexity of life-forms increased following the Cambrian explosion, around half a billion years ago, so new modes of living were marked by higher levels of cooperation, sometimes known as biological altruism. Sociality increased in parallel as an emergent property of brain

21. S. B. Carroll, *'Chance and necessity: the evolution of morphological complexity and diversity,'* Nature 409: 1102-1109, 2001.

22. S. J. Adamowicz, A. Purvis, and M. A. Wills, *'Increasing morphological complexity in multiple parallel lineages of the Crustacea,'* Proceedings of the National Academy of Sciences USA 105: 4786-4791, 2008.

size, complexity, and role identification in social structures. Some remarkable examples of cooperation may be found in the social insects.

Social insects, which can engage in tournament-based warfare (honeypot ants), agriculture (fungus-growing ants and termites), and complex symbolic communication systems (honeybees), are found mainly amongst the termites, ants, bees, and wasps, and represent the most structured animal societies on earth.[23] The last three of these groups are known as the Hymenoptera and some species of Hymenoptera can form huge colonies containing millions of individuals, each belonging to a caste with specialised duties and functions, generally divided into queens and workers. It is not for nothing that they are often dubbed 'superorganisms,' so intricately are the different social roles linked together for the good of the colony.

The queens focus on reproduction whereas the workers are involved in colony maintenance, growth, and defence. A colony of social insects may contain just one or a few queens, but from tens to millions of workers. Queens have huge ovaries and can lay thousands of eggs per day, whereas workers may lack ovaries completely. There is a further division of labour amongst the workers. Amongst the ants the smaller workers care for the brood, whereas the larger workers can specialize as soldiers with large jaws and painful toxins (as anyone who picnics in the wrong spot often finds out to their cost). Once the individuals in the different insect castes have been established, there are massive differences in the sets of genes that are switched on in one caste rather than another. For example, in honeybees, out of the roughly 10,000 protein coding genes in their genomes, no less than 2,000 are expressed differently in the brains of queens rather than those of the workers. Amongst the workers, there are also differences, such as those between honeybees that forage and those involved in 'nursing,' looking after the young.

The social insects may have warring ants with fiery bites, and queens that get killed if they don't have the 'correct' genetic profile, but there are also some ant colonies that can become quite tolerant of intruders. The Argentine ant *(Linepithema humile)* provides a nice example.[24] It's a spe-

23. G. E. Robinson, *'Sociogenomics takes flight,'* Science 297: 204-205, 2002; G. E. Robinson, C. M. Grozinger, and C. W. Whitfield, *'Sociogenomics: social life in molecular terms,'* Nature Reviews Genetics 6: 257-270, 2005.

24. T. Giraud, J. S. Pedersen, and L. Keller, *'Evolution of supercolonies: the Argentine ants of southern Europe,'* Proceedings of the National Academy of Sciences USA 99: 6075-6079, 2002.

cies that back in its native South America defends its colonies against other competing ants' nests, rather typical insect behavior. But after its emigration to Europe this creature has adopted a more laid-back approach to life, becoming much more tolerant of visitors from other nests. In fact the species in Europe has formed two immense super-colonies stretching over 6,000 kilometres from the Adriatic Coast of Italy to the Atlantic Coast of Spain: a Catalonian super-colony, and then the other main super-colony consisting of all the other nests. The main super-colony comprises millions of nests consisting of billions of workers. Individuals from either of these super-colonies visit other nests freely, provided only that they belong to the same super-colony. Even after the two colonies were established in the laboratory for 18 months, representative workers from either super-colony would still kill each other, whereas if workers came from nests of the same super-colony but 6,000 kilometres apart, they would be nice to each other. Aggression never occurred between members of the same super-colony.

These examples of sociality and cooperation are provided not because they provide examples that should be followed in human ethics, but because they demonstrate how such systems evolved very early in evolutionary history, representing (with the benefit of hindsight) hints of what was to come. Indeed, cooperation appears to represent a fundamental output that keeps reappearing in different shapes and forms during evolutionary history. Cooperation is of course not personhood, but personhood is difficult to imagine without cooperation. Personhood is not some idealized abstraction that exists immaterially in a world of platonic ideas, but rather is rooted in the very material world of biology, and emerges with sociality and cooperation.

Personhood further develops in evolution with increased self-awareness and a 'theory of mind,' in turn dependent upon the rapid increase in brain size that has taken place in the hominin lineage over the last two million years of evolution. Only two million years ago did hominin brain size begin to seriously surpass that of our nearest living cousin, the chimpanzee, which has a brain volume of about 400 cubic centimetres. Bipedality does not appear to be the critical factor that has driven this rapid cultural evolution, for there is reasonable evidence that putative hominins such as *Sahelanthropus* were bipedal around 6 million years ago, and certainly the hominins (most likely *Australopithecus afarensis*) who left their fossilised footprints in the volcanic ash at Laetoli in Tanzania, 3.5 million years ago, were bipedal. Furthermore, the first stone tools do not start appearing until 2.6 million years ago, so bipedalism and tool use may be necessary but not sufficient to explain the rapid brain evolution that occurred later. A more likely explanation is the increasing complexity of hominin social life over the past two million years, in which the need for cooperativity in hunting and other social activities gave significant evolutionary advantages to those with larger brains.

Tracking the hominin lineage over the past two million years is informative. *Homo habilis* was alive in Africa up to about 1.6 million years ago and had a brain somewhat larger than that of *Australopithecus,* up to 680 cubic centimetres, nearly half the size of the human brain. *Homo ergaster* began to appear in the fossil record about 1.8 million years ago, growing as tall as six feet with long legs, narrow hips, and a barrel-shaped rib-cage in place of the funnel-shape that characterised *Australopithecus.* The skull also began to look much more like our own and the brain size was also increased to about two-thirds that of today's humans. One possibility is that *Homo ergaster* emerged as a rather successful long-distance runner, natural selection operating to favour that repertoire of characteristics that would give reproductive success to groups of hunters on the African savannah. The appearance of *H. erectus* from 1.8 million years ago was associated with the development of more sophisticated tools. Instead of simply chipping rocks to make a sharp edge, tools were now cut into predetermined and more versatile shapes, the so-called Acheulean technology after the town of St. Acheul in France where such tools were first discovered. This more advanced technology was again associated with increased brain size, now in the range 850-1,100 cubic centimetres. Then *Homo heidelbergensis,* sometimes known as archaic *Homo sapiens,* appeared in Africa about 600,000 years ago with anatomical features distinct from *H. erectus,* not least a further increase in brain size to 1,200 cubic centimetres, only 200 cc short of the average size of modern humans. Only with the appearance of anatomically modern humans *(Homo sapiens sapiens)* from 200,000 years ago do we find our present brain size of 1,400–1,600 cc.

Increasing brain size was characterized by an increase in the numbers of 'orders of intentionality.' The idea of 'orders of intentionality' comes from the 'theory of mind,' the ability of our own minds to realise that there are other minds that think like ours and that have intentions and purposes that may be similar to or even quite different from ours. We take this 'mind-reading' completely for granted but it is in fact a crucial aspect of our identity as humans. To engage in communal religious beliefs, for example, several different orders of intentionality are required, in fact four and perhaps as many as five. In an example given by Robin Dunbar, with each level of intentionality underlined and numbered: 'I suppose [1] that you think [2] that I believe [3] that there is a God who intends [4] to influence our futures because He understands our desires [5].' There appears to be an approximately linear relationship between brain size and the number of orders of intentionality in the hominin lineage. Dunbar speculates that 4th-order intentionality would not have appeared until about 500,000 years ago, about the time of the emergence of archaic *H. sapiens*, with 5th-order intentionality appearing with anatomically modern humans, perhaps along with language.[25]

So it seems that personhood was incipient all along, waiting, as it were, for the *ruach* of God, that nascent understanding of the Holy Spirit, to keep blowing, until the inevitable happened: personhood emerged out of lifeless matter, a 3.8 billion-year-old narrative. With the benefit of hindsight, knowing now that the Holy Spirit is the third person of the Trinity, the emergence of personhood through the Spirit's immanent work in the created order is precisely what one might expect.

4. Conclusions

Had we started with the evolutionary narrative alone, without any other inputs, we would have been forced to the conclusion that "something very organized and special is going on here." We might have concluded that there was some force, impersonal, or perhaps even personal intelligence or power, that had brought about such a remarkable history.

Starting with the known work of God's Spirit in both the created order in general, and in human history in particular, however, provides a much richer narrative, one in which the resonances can be more finely nuanced. The work of the Spirit in evolutionary history in unity and separation, order and yet disorder, and in both the impersonal and the personal, increases our hope and expectations for our new life in the *eschaton*. If things get this good in the present evil age, then how good must they be in the age which is to come? The Spirit and the bride say, "Come!" (Revelation 22:17).

25. R. Dunbar, *The Human Story,* London: Faber, 2004.

Hovering Over Waters:
Spirit and the Ordering of Creation

Jeffrey Schloss

1. Science and Spirit

A. *Spirit*

"The Spirit in Creation" is an especially formidable topic around which to attempt a science and theology dialogue for at least two reasons. For one thing, at first appearance (and this is an appearance I shall argue against), it seems to embody the quintessential tensions between science and religion, involving oppositional dualisms of matter and mysticism, natural and supernatural, efficient and final causes. For another thing, unlike some concepts that both science and theology may engage, and for which exists some modest clarity about conclusions (though by no means agreement about conclusions) — like design, or biogenesis, or even the plausibility of raising the dead — it is not altogether clear what we mean by "spirit." Theologians differ, and most scientists not only ignore, but actively shun the notion.

But the notion and terms used to designate it in various traditions do seem fundamental.

Every year I bring students into the laboratory to measure their "vital capacity" (VC). Although this does not refer to a life force or vitalistic potential, it is by no means unrelated. VC is the volumetric difference between fully expired and inspired lungs, and is assessed by means of a "spirometer." Etymologically, the instrument quite literally "measures spirit" or breath (Lat. *Spiritus,* from *spirare,* to breathe). And as spirit derives from the word for breath in Latin, so spirit in the New Testament derives from the Greek *pneuma* for breath, and in the Old Testament, Hebrew *ruach* for breath or wind.

As a starting point then, I want to take spirit to refer simply (though far from unambiguously) to the distinguishing principle of life. Culturally, this distinction predates theological discourse.[1] And individually, it seems to arise very early (maybe even prelinguistically) in cognitive development, as seen in native abilities to distinguish animate from inanimate, agency from physical causation.[2]

The brilliant move of biblical monotheism is not to invent but rather to employ and subsequently reformulate the notion of spirit in several ways. First, the dynamically creative and life-giving energy of spirit is associated with the purposeful ordering of word or wisdom. In Genesis 1 God's *ruach* moves over the face of the waters, and God's word successively orders the formless then blesses what emerges. Psalm 33 maintains that "by the word of the Lord the heavens were made, their starry host by the *ruach* of his mouth." It is this God who "watches all who live on earth — who forms the hearts of all. . . ." The magisterial creation account of Proverbs 8 depicts wisdom as the master craftsman of creation, both setting boundaries and playing in the earth, and in Isaiah the "spirit of wisdom" is also the "spirit of power."[3] In the New Testament the spirit is both spirit of power and spirit of truth, quickening presence and teacher-guide.[4]

Second, the one God who through his spirit creates, creates all things in "heaven and earth." In a Trinitarian view, what is true of the Word is also true of the Spirit: "All things came into being through Him" (John 1:3). The point here is that all things (and not just living beings) have their origin in spirit; but contrary to the promiscuous attribution of spirit at early stages of both cultural and cognitive development, all things are not spirit. Moreover, living beings — who have spirit (breath) — do not generate or possess it autonomously, but have it only from God, and return it to God (Ecc 12:7; Ps 31:5). The radical dualism that posed is not just matter and

1. W. Pannenberg, *"The Doctrine of the Spirit and the Task of a Theology of Nature,"* in T. Peters (ed.), *Toward a Theology of Nature,* John Knox Press, 1993, pp. 123-138. Indeed, this concept appears to be a cultural universal.

2. E.g., P. Bloom, *Natural born dualists,* Edge, http://www.edge.org/3rd_culture/bloom04/bloom04_index.html.

3. Indeed, not only is God's spirit associated with wisdom, but this is the source of human understanding as well: "It is the spirit in a man, the breath of the Almighty, that gives him understanding" (Job 32:8).

4. There is also tension here, as Paul distinguishes between the ineffable utterances of spirit and comprehensible instruction — worshipping in spirit and understanding. Christian traditions appear to emphasize different aspects of "spirit," from the emphasis on ecstatic charisms of Pentecostalism to Origen's equating of spirit with *Nus,* or reason.

spirit, not living and non-living, not gods versus mortals, but creator and created. Importantly, the former is both transcendent from (calling into existence) and immanent in (breathing into) the latter.

It is this de-deification of the world along with attributing its origin to the ordering activities of a single, transcendent, free, but rational mind, that has — as least in part — funded the empirical and mathematical inquiries of natural science into a world presupposed to be intelligible by such probings. But as with the separation of soul from body, so the disjunction of spirit from world entailed by divine transcendence can end up leaving little work for the former to do in our quest to understand the latter. Pannenberg speaks of relinquishing this quest as leaving us ". . . no longer clear to what extent the biblical creation faith applies to this world in which today's humanity lives, and to the world described by the modern natural sciences. The proposition that the world was created by the God of the Bible then becomes an empty formula, and the biblical God himself a powerless specter, since he can no longer be understood to be the origin and perfector of the world as it is given in our experience."[5]

But what would it mean to develop an alloyed understanding of the world, involving scientific accounts of its workings along with theological notions of spirit? At a coarse-grained level, the work of the spirit can be differentiated in fundamental activities.[6]

Creating, Animating, and Imbuing Life The Holy Spirit is the "Lord and Giver of Life" in the Nicene Creed (as revised in the second council at Constantinople). In the prominent priestly account of humankind's creation, "God breathed into his nostrils, the breath of life, and the man became a living being." Job affirms "The Spirit of God has made me; the breath of the Almighty gives me life." It is God who both "created the heavens and stretched them out" and "who gives breath to its people."[7] But this entails no privileged status for humankind as the only ones to derive breath from God. All living creatures with *ruach* receive it from God (and all with *ruach* are invited to praise God — Ps. 150:6). "In his hand is the life of every creature and the breath of all mankind" (Job 12:10) and the earth is full of God's creatures who die when He takes away breath but are made living

---

5. W. Pannenberg, *The Historicity of Nature: Essays on Science and Theology,* Niels Gregersen (ed.), Templeton Press, 2008, p. 25.

6. Pannenberg (1993, ibid.); J. Moltmann, *God and Creation,* Fortress Press, 1993, p. 12.

7. Job 33:4; Isaiah 42:5.

"when you send your Spirit" (Ps 104). This entails the astonishing elevation of all life to the status of vital commerce with the divine, along with
the humbling (Lat. *humus,* earth) recognition that apart from such commerce, there is no life.

**Preserving Life, Providing Nurture, and Sustaining the Bio-Friendly
Stage on which the Drama Unfolds** It is God who both fans the internal
fire and provides the fuel for life: He sustains breath of all creatures, and
provides food to the lions, garb to the lilies. But before there even was life,
God's spirit was moving over the chaos and creating of it conditions that
would support life. This is not just an isolated depiction in Genesis 1. After
a stunning account of the God who measures the waters, marks off the
heavens, weighs the mountains, and counts every star (fine tuning if ever it
existed!) — Isaiah affirms "he who fashioned and made the earth, did not
create it to be empty, but formed it to be inhabited" (Is 40; 45:18). And not
only does God form the earth, but as he sends his Spirit, the face of the
earth is renewed (Ps 104:30).[8] Thus the Spirit is not only the animating
force of life itself, but also the orchestrating presence — the gardener, as it
were — arranging the conditions, providing nurture, pruning development to promote flourishing. Of course John explicitly develops this in an
instructively ambiguous image — suggesting we derive our life by drawing
directly from the divine vine, while being pruned by the divine vine-
dresser. It is a sublime irony that the first Adam was a gardener, and the
second Adam was mistaken for one — though one he truly is. As we partake of his spirit, we too have the privilege of being gardeners, "keeping
and tending" the matrix of care into which the beloved may grow.

Renewing and Consummating Life and the Creation Although the Old
Testament seems to emphasize the spirit of Yahweh's fundamental role in
creating the world and in conferring life, it also describes soteriological renewal (e.g., new or renewed hearts in Ps 51, Ezek 34; reanimation of dead

---

8. I do not wish to be overly sentimental here. There are also numerous places in the
Old Testament where God withdraws his spirit and life is lost. Or even more disparately, it is
not always the withholding but the very conferral of God's breath that makes life tenuous: "a
blast of breath from your nostrils" may represent not blessing but divine rebuke (Ps 18:15).
Indeed, the breath of God can actually dry up life: "The grass withers and the flowers fall,
because the breath of the Lord blows on them" (Is 40:6). What is important is that even these
negative influences of the spirit are not represented as chaotic or capriciously destructive,
but as reflecting the administration of justice.

bones in Ezek 37; vibrant ecological renewal in Is 55). The New Testament and ensuing Christian tradition dramatically emphasize this salvific activity over creative activities of the spirit. Indeed, as a parallel to God's *ruach* blowing over the chaos on the first day, the age of the church is inaugurated with God's *pneuma* "blowing like a violent wind from heaven" and filling the believers. This spirit raised Christ, gives a new kind of life to our own mortal bodies, will one day raise our bodies to immortality, and in the interim both guides us and testifies to us that we are beloved of God. There is a promise and a peril here. The promise is that this theological imagery represents the expression of powerfully transformative experience — undergone by the writers and presumed accessible to readers — of healed lives, of acceptance prevailing over shame, of unimagined sense of intimacy with God himself. The peril is that the expression of this experience becomes incommensurable with what we know of the rest of life, and hence does not enable us to make sense of or value the world in which God has placed us or, indeed, the God who framed it and called it good.[9] To continue with the metaphor developed above, we lose touch with the earth — the humus that is the source (in both an etymological and an evolutionary sense) of our very humanity.

> This redemptive Spirit is cut off both from bodily life and from the life of nature. . . . If redemption is placed in radical discontinuity to creation, then 'The Spirit of Christ' has no longer anything to do with Yahweh's ruach. . . . This brings us up against the question about the continuity and discontinuity of the redemptive and the newly creating Spirit on the one hand, and the creative and all-animating Spirit on the other — the relation between the Spiritus santificans and the Spiritus vivicans.[10]

In ways I shall only hint at in this brief overview, I believe scientific reflections on the latter can inform and be informed by theological reflections on the former.

9. "Although the emphasis of the New Testament writings concerning the spirit is on the new life of faith communicated by the spirit and on the spirit's charismatic presence, the deep meaning of those affirmations and their particular logic and rationality is accessible only if one takes into account the basic convictions of the Jewish tradition concerning the spirit as the creative origin of all life." Pannenberg, 1993, p. 125.

10. J. Moltmann, *The Spirit of Life: A Universal Affirmation,* Fortress Press, 2001, p. 9.

B. Interactions with Science

There are several ways the sciences may interact with these issues. Of course one is natural theology, which employs observations of the natural world in support of (or even to attempt demonstration of) theological conclusions. A strong version entails arguing for divine causation from the insufficiency of natural regularities to account for what we observe. While there are no in principle grounds for rejecting the possibility of causal gaps mediated by divine action — and there may even be room for this without violating regularities or the laws posited to underlie them in the underdetermined (e.g., quantum events) or in singularities to which natural regularities may not apply (like the origin of the cosmos) — there are also scientific and theological risks to this move.[11] Notwithstanding, Paul seems to be making this kind of a claim by affirming that Christ "was declared with power to be the Son of God by his resurrection from the dead" (Rom 1:4). Ezekiel might seem to be doing something similar with the exhortation that, after the dry bones are miraculously raised, "Then you will know that I am the Lord" (37:6). Contemporary versions of this strong approach include widely criticized arguments that the origin of life, or even the origin of specific components of living systems (like the bacterial flagellum), are inexplicable by natural causes and thus testify to "intelligent design" — the causal intervention of divine *ruach.*

A more modest approach involves viewing not the abridgement, but the very character of natural regularities as being pointers to or even demonstrative of divine reality. Some fine-tuning arguments involve this, as does the dramatic change in natural theology since Darwin, which appeals to the natural regularities that endowed the progressive history of creatures' arisal rather than the purportedly supernatural instantiation of individual creaturely attributes.[12] Darwin's contemporary, Frederick Temple, is well known for advocating this: "Instead of insisting wholly or mainly on the wonderful adaptation of means to ends in the structure of living animals and plants, we should look rather to the original properties im-

11. E.g., the discovery that a singularity isn't singular. This is what happened both with the special creation of species and more recently with the special creation of cellular structures like the bacterial flagellum. It is also what is attempting to be asserted, though with vastly less success, in arguments against fine-tuning by multiverse theory.

12. This change has been widely discussed, and involves arguing for the hand of God not in the products, but in the process of evolution. See, e.g., Michael Ruse's *Monad to Man: The Concept of Progress in Evolutionary Biology* (1996, Harvard) and *Darwin and Design: Does Evolution Have a Purpose?* (2003, Harvard).

pressed on matter from the beginning and on the beneficent consequences that have flowed from those properties."[13]

However, a different approach from natural theology entails starting with theologically infused notions as fundamental precommitments rather than seeking to infer them from the "ground up" as it were. Newman's often cited though by no means original aphorism applies equally well (perhaps more) to spirit than to design: "I believe in design because I believe in God; not in a God because I see design."[14] We may find ourselves at this starting point through the aegis of intuition (as in basic or non-reflective beliefs),[15] or revelation, or primary experience. Indeed, the above example from Ezekiel actually seems to be a case of the latter. Far from urging us to inductively posit the presence of the divine from the abridgement of natural regularities, the spirit of Yahweh claims "I will put breath in you, and you will come to life. Then you will know that I am the Lord" (37:4). It is the experience of being revived that generates the conviction of God's presence in the world. The direct experience of being enlivened by God's breath changes perspective on reality. But of course the task still remains to make sense of the world in light of this perspective.[16]

---

13. R. Temple, *The Relations Between Religion and Science,* London, Macmillan, 1884, pp. 118-119, cited in M. Ruse, *Darwin and Design: Does Evolution Have a Purpose?* Harvard University Press, 2004, p. 301. However, although Temple and others are often held up as exemplars of this more modest natural theology, he was in fact quite ambivalent about fully endorsing evolution. He was, for example, uncertain that human origins reflected common descent, and was convinced that evolution could not account for human moral capacities (discussed in the above work, in the chapter on "Apparent Collision between Religion and the Doctrine of Evolution," http://anglicanhistory.org/england/ftemple/bampton/06.html).

14. J. H. Newman, *The Letters and Diaries of John Henry Newman,* C. S. Dessain and T. Gornall (eds.), Oxford, Clarendon Press, 1973, p. 97.

15. Although there is a long tradition of affirming the epistemic necessity of fundamental intuitions or basic beliefs about God and moral reality, going back to Thomas Reid and even Pascal, William Whewell seemed to endorse this approach to design itself: "How then can we . . . infer design and purpose in the artist of the universe? On what principles, on what axioms can we proceed. . . . When we collect design and purpose from the arrangements of the universe, we do not arrive at our conclusion by a train of deductive reasoning, but by the conviction which such combinations as we perceive immediately and directly impress upon the mind." (W. Whewell, *Astronomy and General Physics,* Bridgewater Treatise 3, 1833, pp. 343-344. Cited in Ruse, 2004, ibid., p. 77.)

16. In his introduction to Pascal's Pensees, T. S. Eliot comments that the task of the Christian intellectual is not to develop arguments for the virgin birth by calculating the odds of conception by spontaneous parthenogenesis, rather it is to develop a coherent understanding of our beliefs and their relation to the world.

This spirit-breathed perspective may interact with science in complementary ways. First of all, as with all background beliefs, those that are spirit-breathed influence the plausibility criteria by which we both assess evidence and — perhaps even more important — formulate hypotheses for investigation. In one sense then, theological precommitments may serve as treasure maps for where to do exploratory digging. Or to use an example from the gospels, they may suggest where to throw our nets of inquiry. Presumably, there was nothing in the prevailing fishing science of the day to endorse going out again after a night of failure (Luke) or throwing nets onto the right rather than left side of the boat (John). "But I will do as you say and let down the nets." Some of my scientist colleagues may object to this notion, but there are numerous hypotheses in evolutionary theory — involving proposals of directionality, progress, even purpose; irreducibility; self-organizing generativity; altruism — that are not suggested by the dominant (though by no means uncontested) paradigm, but may be suggested by revelation and Christian experience, and that are empirically assessable. The goal of fishing on the spirit-breathed side of the boat is not to develop an argument, but to seek to engage and understand the world in light of the spirit's invitation. Whatever the rationale for where nets are cast, however, it is essential not to tell "fish stories" about the data we pull up, so that the world may push back against and help shape our most fundamental beliefs.

This brings up the complementary mode of engagement: scientific inquiry may not only be informed by, but may also inform belief by both affirming and challenging it. When Peter saw the load of fish, he "fell down at Jesus' feet . . . for amazement had seized him" (Luke 5:8-9). One can be powerfully gripped by the concurrent ramifications of what one has already nasciently believed. Conversely, our experience of the world can generate appropriate doubt. One wonders what a Cornelius might have thought if in response to a spirit-encounter, messengers were sent to Joppa to look for a man named Peter in the house of Simon the tanner — and were informed that Simon had died two years ago, and there was nobody named Peter in town. We are invited to test the spirits. Even if one is skeptical of natural theology's attempt to fish for facts in order to support the conclusions of faith, the alternative extreme (critiqued in Pannenberg's response to Barth quoted above), is a faith that no longer engages the world of fish. It is difficult to see how faith in a biblical creator can escape the risks of fishing. If it can be shown that living systems are adequately explained without any reference to function or teleology, if it can be shown that the history of life has no progressive or even thematically coherent directional trends — then the notions of a divine spirit infusing life and providentially superintending, much less entering, history — would seem to be vacuous.

> The rejection of a creation mysticism by no means excludes a creator and governor of the world. . . . [But] [e]ither one says no to a primal ground, primal support, and primal goal of the whole evolutionary process, in which case one must take account of the meaninglessness of the whole process and the forsakenness of the human being . . . [o]r one says yes to a primal ground, primal support, and primal goal. In that case, while one may not base the fundamental meaningfulness of the whole process and one's own existence on the process itself, one may still trustingly presuppose it.[17]

2. Origin and Nature of Life

"It is an unfounded assumption," says Küng, "to postulate the existence of God on the basis of the transition from the inanimate world to the biosphere . . . this would merely be a pernicious God of the gaps."[18] But I am interested in the complementary enterprise: to postulate (or more deeply to appreciate) the transition to animacy on the basis of God's existence. Indeed, with the rise of mechanism and the complete extrusion of spirit from the vocabulary with which the world is described, it is tempting if not inevitable to conclude, as Haeckel did, that "the distinction between living and dead matter does not exist."[19] [It is interesting that this may give rise to an error that is the inverse of and far less defensible than the explanatory gap ? God move of gap theology: i.e., no gap ? no God. Haeckel concludes, "The (cell's) component parts properly united produce the soul and body of the animated world. . . . With this single argument the mystery of the universe is explained, the Deity annulled. . . ." And "design does

---

17. H. Küng, *The Beginning of All Things: Science and Religion,* J. Bowden (trans.), Eerdmans, 2007, pp. 144-145.

18. Küng, ibid., p. 142.

19. E. Haeckel, *Natürliche Schöpfungsgeschichte,* Zweite Auflage, Berlin, 1873, p. 21, (translation cited in C. Hodge, *What is Darwinism,* Scribner & Armstrong, 1874, p. 95, http://caliban.mpiz-koeln.mpg.de/haeckel/natuerliche/kapitel_01.html accessed 10/20/09).

not exist, any more than the much vaunted goodness of the Creator" (die vielgerühmte Allgüte des Schöpfers).][20]

While the tradition represented by Haeckel may have overestimated the metaphysical implications of accounting physically for the nature and origin of life, it vastly underestimated the difficulty of actually developing such accounts. As Nobel laureate Christian de Duve aptly observes: "How did life arise? The answer to this question is clear: We don't know."[21] In fact, we lack not only a solution, not only a generally accepted hypothesis, but even agreement about what the exact nature of the problem is that must be solved. De Duve believes that the natural world was "pregnant with life" and "life was bound to arise under the physical-chemical conditions that prevailed at the site of its birth."[22] Harvard chemist and Joseph Priestly Award–winner George Whitesides takes a different view. He agrees with de Duve on the answer to the question: "But where did the cell come from? How did this wonderfully, astonishingly complex system come into existence? We do not know." But he disagrees on the challenges that an answer must solve, "The central conundrum about the origin of life — that, as an accidental event, it seems so very improbable — is not one that science has yet resolved . . . we have (in my opinion) no idea how these simple reactions might have blundered together to make the first protocell. Monkeys at typewriters pecking out Shakespeare seems child's play by comparison."[23]

I am neither scientifically nor theologically predisposed to take sides on this issue. The interesting thing is that here — as with other topics I will take up in more detail shortly — each position on the inevitability versus contingency debate has been used both to bolster and to critique postulations of providence:

- wild improbability: God must have intervened (e.g., William Dembski)
- wild improbability: what the world contains could never have been intended by God (e.g., Stephen J. Gould)

---

20. First quote cited in L. Eiseley, *Darwin's Century*, Garden City, NY, Doubleday, 1958, p. 346. Second, Hodge (ibid., p. 17).

21. Ibid., p. 97.

22. Ibid., p. 97.

23. G. Whitesides, *"The Improbability of Life,"* in *Fitness of the Cosmos for Life: Biochemistry and Fine Tuning*, J. Barrow et al. (eds.), Cambridge University Press, 2008, pp. 11-19. Quotes pp. xix and xvi.

- inevitability: God's agenda is built into nature (e.g., S. C. Morris)
- inevitability: no need, or even room, for God to act (e.g., Daniel Dennett)

These arguments against providence, no matter what the case is, seem reminiscent of the children in the marketplace calling out to each other, "We played the flute for you, and you did not dance; we sang a dirge, and you did not cry" (Luke 7:32). The creative instantiation of purpose requires an interplay of both contingency and constraint, and recognition of this dialectic seems to have been anticipated in the biblical insight of creation occurring by the blowing of the spirit and the ordering of the word.

While the physical-chemical steps leading to life are presently inscrutable, I want to comment briefly on two issues that reflect progress in understanding.

A. Necessary Preconditions

A fascinating surprise in the recent physical sciences entails now widely accepted discoveries that the conditions necessary for life to emerge are prescribed with extraordinary specificity. There are at least three areas in which this is true. At the cosmic scale, what has come to be the classical recognition of "fine tuning" involves the precise values of fundamental constants and the initial conditions on which they acted, so that the necessary preconditions for life were able to emerge — cosmic bodies rather than on the one hand a giant undifferentiated mass or on the other hand dispersed, unconcealed matter; a range of elements rather than simple hydrogen or, conversely, only heavy metals, etc. Though not a theist, Royal Society President Martin Rees speaks of "a providence-like physics which has led to galaxies, stars, planets, and the 92 elements of the periodic table . . . the recipe [for this] seems to be a very special one."[24]

At the level of chemistry, the particular way the elements interact to yield the distinctive and seemingly necessary properties of the molecules constitutive of life seems unusually fortuitous. Just the properties of water alone — its specific heat, thermal conductivity, polarity, differential solubility of oxygen and carbon dioxide, expansion near freezing — have been

---

24. M. Rees, *"Andere Universen — Eine Wissenschaftliche Perspektive,"* in *Im Angang War (K)ein Gott,* T. D. Wabbel (ed.), Düsseldorf, 2004, pp. 47-51; cited in H. Küng, *The Beginning of All Things: Science and Religion,* Grand Rapids, MI, Eerdmans, 2007, p. 67.

the subject of much commentary by physiologists and ecologists. At the turn of the last century, Lawrence Henderson developed a seminal treatment of nature's chemical suitability for life. He proposed "the fitness of the environment" as a complement to the Darwinian account of how life becomes fitted to that environment.[25] Henderson was widely read through the mid 20th century, but fell out of favor, not because his observations were overturned, but perhaps because of the way his work was amenable to, and at times overtly endorsing of, teleology.

Finally, moving from physics to chemistry to geoscience (a continuum not only of scale but also of controversy on this topic), we have the biophilic properties of earth itself. The size and age of our sun, and the location of the solar system in the galaxy influence the availability and proportion of life-essential elements; the size of earth influences the ability to retain an atmosphere and what kind of atmosphere it is; the distance from the sun determines the possibility of liquid water — too close, vapor, too distant, ice; the moon and Jupiter influence earth's vulnerability to cataclysmic collision; the existence and rate of geoconvection replenishes crustal material upon which life depends; the percentage of earth's surface that has been dynamically allocated to land and water influences its thermal range and stability, etc. "He fashioned the earth to be inhabited" (Is 45:18)? The properties of our planet surely do seem astonishingly well-suited not just for the emergence of life, but more important, for its ongoing sustenance and its interaction with lithosphere, hydrosphere, and atmosphere — to form an evolving, quasi-homeostatic biosphere.

Notwithstanding the remarkable attributes of our planet, there is not agreement about how rare such a planet is given the probabilistic resources of the cosmos (the contingency/inevitability issue again). Even if taken to be rare, there is disagreement about whether this is suggestive of divine preparation for life.[26]

Two observations are in order. First, the attribution of spirit-tended suitability of the cosmos and of garden earth for the flourishing of life is,

25. L. J. Henderson, *The Fitness of the Environment: An Inquiry Into the Biological Significance of the Properties of Matter,* Cornell University Press, 2009 (1918).

26. An interesting debate on this topic exists between astronomers Donald Brownlee and Guillermo Gonzalez, both of whom agree that earth is rare and cite one another's scientific work with approval, but disagree on the implications. E.g., Ward and Brownlee, *Rare Earth: Why Complex Life is Uncommon in the Universe* (Copernicus Books, 2004); Gonzalez and Richards, *The Privileged Planet: How Our Place in the Cosmos is Designed for Discovery* (Regnery, 2004).

strictly speaking, based on assessing precision and not calculating probability of fit between conditions and need. When my toddler son used to
climb into the bath after I'd adjusted the temperature for him, he would
say "Thank you, Daddy — just the right size!" Notwithstanding the cute
misnaming of the relevant parameter, he nevertheless appropriately in-
ferred my care — not by an estimate of likelihood but by a recognition of
anthropic precision — "just right for me!" Whether or not there may be
other suitable baths elsewhere is not relevant. The English hymn "Great is
Thy Faithfulness" captures this with "all I have needed Thy hand hath provided . . . blessings all mine, with ten thousand beside." One thing the sciences may do is increase conceptual resources for recognizing and then expressing gratitude for the way the spirit tills the soil of our existence.

Second, the "just right for me" claim is nevertheless vulnerable both to
errant assertion and to errant dismissal. Whewall is taken to have argued that
God's design is evident in the fact that the seasons are perfectly fitted to cycles
of plants and animals, and even day length is suited to the duration of human
sleep. Darwin derided the notion that the whole universe is adapted to our
needs, rather than our being adapted to the structure of nature, as an "instance of arrogance!!!"[27] This is an anthropocentrism rightly to be avoided.
But there is a complementary and equally arrogant anthropocentrism, perhaps idolatrous in character. This posits that the fundamental correspondence between organismic need and features of the environment, so condu-
cive to our flourishing, can be understood as resulting from our capacity to
develop adaptive fit — without recognizing features of the environment, perhaps remarkable features, that make possible any life at all and especially the
unique requirements of conscious life. Rival anthropocentrisms.

Thus, while the biblical revelation clearly emphasizes that "God's Spirit
is the life-force of created beings," the spirit is also "the living space in which
they can grow and develop their potentialities."[28] It may even be that the
term, *ruach,* is "related to *rewah* — breadth. *Ruach* creates space. It sets in
motion. It leads out of narrow places into wide vistas, thus conferring life."[29]

---

27. C. Darwin, *Notebook D, Transmutation of Species,* note 49, Aug 27, 1838 (http://
darwin-online.org.uk/content/frameset?viewtype=text&itemID=CUL-DAR123.-
&keywords=arrogance&pageseq=47). Actually, it is not clear where the arrogance lies. In
reading the original reference in Whewell's 3rd Bridgewater Treatise (and not the secondary
commentator who provoked D's response), Whewell does not unambiguously make the
claim that Darwin attributes to him.

28. Moltmann, 2001, p. 83.

29. H. Schüngel-Streamann, *"Ruach (Geist, Lebenskraft) im Alten Testament,"* in

B. The Nature of Life

The question of whether "spirit" — as a literal substance, or as an animating teleological principle — is in any way important to the understanding of life has historically entailed protracted debates over a variety of issues: vitalism vs. mechanism, spontaneous generation, and morphology (emphasis on structure) vs. physiology or teleology (emphasis on function). Darwin profoundly influenced these debates. Interestingly, however, his influence was ambiguous.

Because of Darwin's emphasis on adaptation, Asa Gray took him (rightly, it seems) to bolster notions of function by providing for them a naturalistic foundation: "Darwin's great service to Natural Science is bringing it back to Teleology; so that, instead of Morphology versus Teleology, we shall have Morphology wedded to Teleology."[30] By teleology Gray did not mean Final Cause, but merely organismic goals or functions [although contra Darwin, Gray believed a natural process capable of generating functions reflected a Final Cause].

But Huxley saw the very opposite. He claimed that what struck him "most forcibly" in the *Origin* "was the conviction that Teleology, as commonly understood, had received its deathblow at Mr. Darwin's hands."[31] Huxley did not just mean the demise of Paleyan natural theology, which Darwin did impact. As an advocate of morphology over physiology, he meant the very notion that organisms have ends: "Far from imagining that cats exist in order to catch mice well, Darwinism supposes that cats exist because they catch mice well — mousing being not the end, but the condition, of their existence." Underneath the rhetorical flourish (of course cats themselves do not exist "in order" to catch mice — no one believes that cats are means to mouse catching),[32] there are several serious questions. There is the Aristotelian question not of whether cats serve ends, but whether they have ends. I.e., do they seek, is a "goal" of their existence to catch mice? And concomitantly, do properties or characteristics of cats exist in order to attain those ends — e.g., might one say of claws, that they do

---

M. Kassel (ed.), *Feministische Theologie. Perspektiven zur Orientierung,* 2nd ed., Stuttgart, 1988, pp. 59-73. Quoted p. 61. Cited in Moltmann, 2001.

30. Gray, 1876, p. 237.

31. Huxley, 1864, p. 82.

32. Actually, some people who own cats may well believe just that. And in one sense they are right! Cats have been bred by humans, and may in fact exist "for" mouse catching as much as saws exist for cutting wood.

indeed "exist in order to catch mice well"? Evolutionary biologist George Williams affirms just this and even uses the language of functional design on this point: "Only the intellectually dead could fail to see that the snake has what are clearly weapons, precisely designed and used to produce a victim. . . . They illustrate a basic contrast between physical nature and biological nature, and one that Huxley did not fully appreciate."[33]

This is a debate that has waxed and waned in evolutionary theory. Ultimately, of course, any phenotype exists because it serves one end well: facilitating the transmission of underlying genotype. But the core of Darwin's adaptationist argument, which Huxley never fully endorsed, is that those traits that endure do have proximal ends which they perform well. In a sense, both of Huxley's (falsely dichotomized) options are true: traits are retained because they do things well, and in being retained, they are employed by organisms in order to do things well. There are some interesting and unresolved philosophical questions, not just over whether Darwin provides a causally adequate account of function, but also over whether or not, in light of this account alone, it makes sense even to speak of "function" (i.e., if one is committed to reductive, materialistic causation, are effects all we are entitled to speak of?).[34] If so, and yet we are convinced that there are functions in biology, then this could be seen as an opportunity for natural theology. However, the complementary enterprise that I have been suggesting is also in view: by starting with a precommitment to spirit-breathed character of life (i.e., that while it may be composed of dust, it may not be reducible to the properties of dust), we might cast our nets on the function side of the boat — seeing if biological inquiry that employs the concept yields a catch that we otherwise miss.

This indeed seems to be the case. Biologists find it very difficult to describe, much less explain, living systems without utilizing teleological language. While some have tried to soft-pedal the implications of this by employing notions of teleonomy to avoid the implications of teleology, Robert Brandon and others have argued persuasively that what we see in biology is plain teleology, and we just should use that term.[35] One is re-

33. G. C. Williams, *Huxley's Evolution and Ethics in sociobiological perspective*, Zygon, 1988, 23: 383-438. And given the abundance of organismic traits clearly designed for such purposes, Williams emphatically rejects the idea of a benevolent God being behind the process.

34. Theist Alvin Plantinga and non-theist Jerry Fodor agree that only language of effect, not of function, makes sense in the context of mechanistic explanation.

35. R. Brandon, *Adaptation and Environment*, Princeton University Press, 1995.

minded of Whewell's Bridgewater affirmation, cited earlier, that views design as a "conviction which such combinations as we perceive immediately and directly impress upon the mind."

Although biologists do not agree on a definition of life, the attributes widely agreed to characterize it (some since the time of Aristotle) cannot be construed apart from goal orientation. Motility as opposed to mere movement: boulders roll down hills and living things walk up. Responsiveness as opposed to mere reactivity: ice melts in the sun, plants follow solar angle with their leaves. Development as opposed to change, even directional change: mountains erode and stalagmites lengthen, but vertebrates "mature." Homeostasis as opposed to passive steady state: a cave is isothermal because it is thermally buffered, a bird holds a constant temperature because it has a thermostat and heater that actively monitor and regulate internal conditions. Self-replication as opposed to . . . (there does not appear to be an abiotic analogue to this phenomenon, with the possible exception of autocatalysis, or the propagation of certain chemical reactions). Each one of these is a goal-directed phenomenon that involves an organismal "target" and the ability to generate and respond to feedback on the trajectory toward the target. Moreover, organisms have both structural and behavioral adaptations that are clearly designed to operate along with feedback mechanisms for achieving these ends, and they have discernable strategies or "energy budgets" for employing these adaptations.

With characteristically unabashed candor, in his seminal treatment of adaptationism George Williams asserts, "Whenever I believe that an effect is produced as the function of an adaptation perfected by natural selection to serve that function, I will use terms appropriate to human artifice and conscious design. The designation of something as the means or mechanism for certain goals or function or purpose. . . ."[36]

The implications of this for spirit (or spirit for this) are twofold. First, regarding our construal of life itself. Haeckel's dictum — "the distinction between living and dead matter does not exist" — involved a precommitment-driven casting of nets on one side of the boat as much as anything ever has. We have made tremendous strides in describing the physical chemistry of living systems, and their material constituents indeed obey the same laws as all other matter does. [But this is no news — dust is dust.] Collectively however, in becoming "living matter" and evidencing the above activities, molecules do what no dead matter does. Even

---

36. G. Williams, *Adaptation and Natural Selection*, Princeton University Press, 1966, p. 9.

the behavior of molecules themselves incorporated into living systems require teleological language to describe, from "scavenging" or "repair" enzymes to chemical messengers to "regulatory" genes. Examining life down to its very molecular components seems to have deepened rather than supplanted the need to ascribe teleological processes unique to organisms.[37]

Second, regarding our construal of Spirit in the emergence of spirit: It is indeed striking that our very best descriptions not only of how things work, but also of how they came about, "use language appropriate to human artifice or conscious design." By citing this, I am not at all suggesting the inadequacy of secondary causes. Rather, I am confirming that the functional character of their effects is concordant with (though not demonstrative of) their construal as secondary causes.

Centuries before both Williams and Darwin, in his *Religio Medici*, Thomas Browne concluded: "In brief, all things are artificial, for nature is the art of God."[38]

3. The History of Life

One of the long-standing and common understandings of "spirit" is that it is the very breath of creativity, that which inspires art itself. If nature is the art of God, what are its themes? If history is the superintended process of its development, what is its trajectory? The debate over the relationship of these questions of telos to evolutionary change has been even more significant than the question of telos to organic function. But if there is a God who not only created the stage for historical drama, but in some sense both directs the play and has joined the cast, there must be a discernable (though by no means unambiguous) plot.

37. This comment could mean two different things. One is the question of whether we will ever have an adequate causal account of life in terms of physical-chemical principles. George Whitesides acknowledges that we are far from having one, but believes we will; Robert Rosen believes this task is not possible in principle (*Life Itself: A Comprehensive Inquiry into the Nature, Origin, and Fabrication of Life*, Columbia University Press, 2005). But the other question is whether, even if we can account for the behavior of living systems in terms of material or efficient causes, we will have fully explained, much less understood their livingness apart from teleology. I argue no.

38. T. Browne, *Religio Medici*, 1643 1862 edition, pp. 28-29, Boston, Ticknor & Fields (http://books.google.com/books?id=ZR9KhmhppfsC&dq=%22Thomas+Browne, +Religio+Medici%22).

A. Purpose

Discussion of providence in history has often been subverted by the red herring of purpose in evolution. While Darwin believed and many other biologists have since believed that evolution is thematically coherent or even progressive, virtually none believe that it is purposive, goal oriented, or regulated in a way comparable to the workings of physiological or intentional systems. Therefore, there is understandable resistance to suggestions that evolution has a "purpose." And although there are currently some proposals of this nature, neither do I wish to assert there is a kind of self-regulated purpose "in" evolution.

But there is another sense in which something may have a purpose, which involves not purpose "in" but purpose "for," i.e., purpose conferred by employment rather than attained by functional capacity. Such purpose exists not in virtue of possessing features designed to monitor and achieve an internally specified end (like a thermostat, the purpose of which is to maintain temperature), but simply in virtue of being utilized by an external agent in the achievement of ends to which it is suited but may not be designed to target (like a rock that is used for a door stop). Any process or entity — including evolutionary change — may be employed by something that transcends or lies outside it, for an end that it is competent to serve but does not itself seek or monitor.[39]

Setting aside then the issue of whether evolution is itself purposive or functionally regulated, the question remains of whether it seems fit to the purposes attributed to the spirit by the biblical narrative. That is, even if the mechanisms of evolutionary change are non-teleological, is the observable nature of that change concordant with the providential outworking of God's purposes throughout history? Three debates exist on topics relevant to this question. All involve scientific disputes, but each also is explicitly influenced by theological or atheological concerns.[40]

39. Pannenberg himself seems to conflate these issues, as well as the relationship of contingency and determinism to purpose, by pitting them against each other: "the basic contingency of each and every event in the world of creation, including the occurrence of order and uniform pattern in the sequence of events, is much more fundamental concerning the task of a theological interpretation of the natural world in terms of creation than the idea of purpose is" (op. cit., p. 63). But if contingency is necessary for the realization of God's purpose for, or the instantiation of, his purposes in the world, it is not clear how the importance of purpose and contingency can diverge.

40. For a fuller account see J. Schloss, *"Divine Providence and Evolutionary*

B. Progress

One question concerns whether evolution is progressive — in the standard sense of ongoing, directional change toward a valued end. Darwin thought it was: ". . . as natural selection works solely by and for the good of each being, all corporeal and mental endowments will tend to progress towards perfection."[41] Monod argued passionately against the idea of a force toward progress as "an animist projection . . . incompatible with science."[42] More recently Stephen Gould famously decried it as a "noxious, culturally embedded, untestable, nonoperational, intractable idea that must be replaced if we wish to understand evolutionary history."[43] Note that these objections do not themselves claim that progress doesn't occur, but only that it is unscientific to ask whether it does. In one sense, this objection is correct: if progress is change along an axis of valuation, since science cannot tell us what to value, it cannot adjudicate the question of progress. But given any specified evaluative precommitment — say, to the value of love or attachment, or the capacity to feel joy, or the ability to reason or to employ if not choose a widening range of behaviors, or even just the capability to sense and respond to the external world or homeostatically control the internal environment — the question of whether there is "progressive change" toward these ends over evolutionary history is fully addressable by empirical means. The crucial empirical issue then becomes whether or not there is thematically coherent directional change.

C. Directionality

The second question, and the one underlying issues of "progress" if not Spirit in creation, is whether there are any directional trends at all in evolution. Although in his first major contribution to evolutionary theory, Gould argued for a profound trend in fundamental strategies of living or-

---

Directionality," in J. Cobb (ed.), *Back to Darwin: A Richer Account of Evolution*, Grand Rapids, Eerdmans, 2005, pp. 330-350.

41. C. Darwin, *On the Origin of Species by Means of Natural Selection*, New York, Gramercy Books, 1995, p. 459. [Reprint of 1859 first edition.]

42. J. Monod, *Chance and Necessity*, Vintage Books, 1972, p. 40.

43. S. J. Gould, "*On Replacing the Idea of Progress with an Operational Notion of Directionality*," in M. Nitecki (ed.), *Evolutionary Progress*, Chicago, University of Chicago Press, 1988, pp. 319-338. Quote p. 319.

ganisms,[44] he later changed his views and argued there were "none worth speaking of." There are a number of reasons he and others expect this. It could be that contingencies overwhelm the action of natural selection: à la Gould, replay the tapes of evolutionary history a thousand times over, and we will never get humans again. It could be that the environment lacks the requisite structure to allow ongoing directionality — either because its structure is ephemeral or because its stable structure is sufficiently shallow that organisms quickly achieve adaptive equilibrium. Both these issues have to do with "possibility space," and are relevant to the question of endowment of the garden by the gardener. Still another possibility arises from the fact that, at face value, natural selection itself does not entail any directionality — not even that things shall get absolutely better at reproducing but only that those organisms that are relatively worse shall be weeded out. Speaking of progressive (i.e., in the sense of cumulatively increasing) change, George Williams says, "I would maintain, however, that there is nothing in the basic structure of the theory of natural selection that would suggest the idea of any kind of cumulative progress."[45]

All of these issues are empirically assessable by examining the long-term history of life, and there is ample evidence that with respect to numerous organismal characters evolution is directional and even functionally progressive. In a benchmark treatment, Geerat Vermeij argues that the fossil record demonstrates progressive directional change in a variety of features: locomotor ability, metabolic rate, body size, parental care, body temperature, dental specialization, shell-breaking ability (and shell-repair ability). This reflects a selection-driven process he calls evolutionary escalation, involving measures and countermeasures of interacting species.[46] Richard Dawkins and John Krebs provided a seminal overview of such coevolutionary arms races that drive "progressive trends in response to the selection pressures set up by the progressive improvements in other lineages."[47] The question also turns out to be addressable experimentally. Richard Lenski and coworkers have conducted the longest-term evolutionary experiment ever undertaken — 40,000 generations in 12 different lines of bacteria. In every line, he found increased growth rates, increased size,

44. S. J. Gould, *Ontogeny and Phylogeny,* Harvard University (Belknap) Press, 1977.

45. Op. cit., 1964, p. 34.

46. G. Vermeij, *Evolution and Escalation,* Princeton University Press, 1993. Also *Nature: An Economic History,* Princeton, 2006.

47. Dawkins and Krebs, *"Arms Races Between and Within Species,"* Proc Royal Soc Lond, B. 1979, 205 (1161): 489-511. Quote p. 492.

increased specialization. Moreover, many changes were shared in all or the majority of lines — suggesting selection and not contingency. And in some cases where genetic changes were not shared, lines had achieved similar function by another route — suggesting a remarkable capacity for convergence.[48]

This wide range of directional and convergent trends evident across evolutionary history appears to be characterized by at least two general themes. The first is that the goal-oriented or functionally purposive aspects of living systems — temperature and osmotic regulation (homeostasis in general), sensory acuity, metabolic scope, locomotor ability, behavioral plasticity — increase in sophistication. In a sense, there is an intensification of the very distinctives and potencies of life itself. Indeed, even *spiro* — the literal breath of life — gradually appears and then amplifies over many millions of years with the arisal and elaboration of aerobically respiring creatures.

The second theme involves a series of major evolutionary transitions in structure that foster the above biotic intensification through progressive escalation of cooperative interdependence at the molecular, cellular, organismal, and populational levels. Functional "individuals" cross thresholds of reorganization into higher scales of individuality: prokaryotic → eukaryotic → multicellular → social organisms. These major evolutionary transitions involve not just cooperation but obligate interdependence.[49] And having crossed such thresholds, the nature of interdependence then progressively intensifies (e.g., increased multicellular specialization, parental care, social attachment, etc.).

Neither of these general themes is prima facie predictable by the mutation/selection mechanism. I should be quite clear that I am not suggesting, because they are unanticipated, that they are inexplicable and require something beyond natural processes in the form of intervention by spirit. But both themes — intensification of biotic potency and the expansion of functional integration or unity — are concordant with the notion of God's immanence: the Spirit breathes life into creation, sustains and renews the breath and flourishing of all creature; the Word sequentially brings order out of chaos. And both represent surprise catches on a side of the boat

48. N. Philippe, E. Crozat, R. Lenski, and D. Schneider, *"Evolution of Global Regulatory Networks during a Long-Term Experiment with Escherichia coli,"* BioEssays, 2007, 29: 846-860.

49. J. Maynard Smith and E. Szathmary, *The Major Transitions in Evolution,* New York, Oxford University Press, 1998.

underfished by nets cast according to the prevailing wind of scientific fashion, if not theoretical entailment.

D. Active vs. Passive Trends

Finally, there is a debate over whether — even if there are directional trends — they are "active" or "passive," "biased" or randomly diffusional.[50] This entails the question of whether there is something in life itself that favors or gravitates toward certain ends. Is there, in one sense, a telos to natural selection? Like Williams, Gould argues against any selective directionality, employing the rhetorically powerful and justly famous image of a drunk stumbling down the street, with a wall on one side and the gutter on the other. If he starts out at the wall and walks randomly forward until he eventually collapses in a stupor, he is likely not to be at the wall.[51] Thus we may see some trends, but they reflect nothing about what life "seeks" or where it is externally channeled to go.

Curiously, although Gould has advocated no conflict between science and religion in his prominent ideas of non-overlapping magisteria (NOMA), the way he achieves no contest is by removing from religion any factual claims about the world. This is akin to what Pannenberg criticizes as emptying religion of value. Indeed, Gould concludes — and here he echoes George Simpson, Richard Dawkins, Thomas Huxley, Ernst Haeckel, and countless others — that evolution is incommensurable with the notion that providence had humans in mind. "By taking the Darwinian 'cold bath,' and staring at factual reality in the face, we can finally abandon the cardinal false hope of the ages. . . ."[52]

I should point out two aspects of this interesting scientific dispute. One, even if the drunk has no preference for the gutter, this is still not unbiased change, since there is a wall on one side and a gutter on the other. Possibility space itself is structured to bias the outcome and facilitate directionality. [Directional change away from the wall could be prevented by having walls on both sides, or no minimum wall, or no street at all.]

50. D. McShea, *"Mechanisms of Large-Scale Evolutionary Trends,"* Evolution, 1994, 48 (6): 1747-1763.

51. S. J. Gould, *Full House: The Spread of Excellence from Plato to Darwin,* Three Rivers Press, 1997.

52. S. J. Gould, *"Introduction to Carl Zimmer,"* in *Evolution: The Triumph of an Idea,* HarperCollins, 2001.

Moreover, possibility space alone is necessary but not sufficient for the outcome. Something must keep the drunk walking: even for diffusion, there must be a driving force. Perfume will not diffuse out of a bottle into a room unless (a) there is a room and (b) the concentration gradient provides a driving force favorable for diffusion to occur. We do not fully understand what the "driving force" is for evolution. Evolution involves generative and filtering components, and while we have made much progress in understanding the latter (primarily selection), the former (involving mutation, but many other proposals as well) needs more study. To describe directional change as "passive" — even if there is no selective bias in a particular direction — is open to misconstruing the importance and character of evolutionary driving forces or generative mechanisms. It may well be that generative mechanisms, while entirely random with respect to the needs of the organism, are non-random with respect to the phenotypic features most readily generated. Proposals for symbiosis as a generator of novelty or cooperation as an evolutionary force are examples, and are concordant with just those thematic trends described above.[53]

Second, in addition to the biased (active) versus random (passive) dichotomy being somewhat oversimplified, it turns out that there is considerable evidence — from both experimental and fossil data — for the existence of active trends as strictly defined by biased or directional selective advantage.[54] Thus, certain features of the physical environment and/or forms of organismal interaction are structured in way that selectively filters or promotes progressive change in hallmark characteristics and competencies of life.

It would be wrong to suggest that these themes of evolutionary history and the causal structure underlying them constitute demonstrations of the Spirit's role in creation — in virtue of either the inadequacy of natural regularities to explain, or the remarkable improbability of natural regularities that do explain historical progression. But it would be equally wrong to reject as incommensurate with or dismiss as irrelevant to theology the

53. B. Kozo-Polyhansky, *Symbiogenesis: A New Principle of Evolution*, L. Margulis (ed.), Harvard University Press, 2010.

54. E.g., John Alroy's benchmark demonstration of biased replacement in mammalian body size. Karl Niklas's studies of what he calls "homeomorphy" — biased directional changes in body shape that are due to selection and not just random diversification. ". . . evolutionary history was shaped (literally) far more by the operation of natural selection than by random events." R. Lenski, "*Life's Evolutionary History: Is it Determinate or Indeterminate?*" in S. C. Morris (ed.), *The Deep Structure of Biology*, Templeton Press, 2008, pp. 32-46, quote p. 43.

themes or the causal structure of life's history. These notions of the progressive intensification of life, of fecundity and constraint, of generative and filtering interplay are concordant with ancient insights into the meaning and operation of Spirit in animating and ordering, in nourishing and pruning, in expanding the possible and bringing the actual to pass.

Mathematics of Infinity and the Orthodox Name Worshipping Spiritual Tradition

Vladimir Katasonov

The problem of the interaction of science and religion is one of the most acute problems of the modern philosophy of science, theology, and culture as a whole. We Christians of the 21st century live in a world created by God, but in a civilization constructed on scientific technologies. There is no concept of God in science, but almost no fragment of reality has been left untouched by scientific analysis, which pretends to be a complete world-outlook — a secular, materialistic one. Two different outlooks cannot simply coexist; inevitably they come into conflict. This conflict certainly has very unpleasant aspects, but nevertheless, if it proceeds long enough, nolens volens, it shows the nature of each of the conflicting parties and slightly opens more Truth to us. . . .

Name worshipping is one of the most interesting and "not too frequently turned" pages of Orthodox theology. Having a basis in the centuries-long practice of "Jesus prayer," confirmed by the authority of many Athos' monks, incurring severe persecutions in the beginning of the 20th century and attempted destruction during the Soviet time, this current of ascetic practice and theology, simultaneously, now draws the special attention of professionals of theological studies and wide orthodox circles in general.[1] In fact, it is no wonder that discussions of this question, planned during the Council of the Russian Orthodox Church in 1917-1918, did not happen because of the Bolshevik revolution. And the

---

1. See Episkop Illarion (Alfeev), *Sviatschennaja taina Tserkvi*. T.1, 2. Spb. 2002 (in Russian); Prot. Dmitriy Leskin, *Metafizika slova i imeni v russkoi religiozno-filosofskoi misli*. Spb. 2008 (in Russian). There are few Western books on the subject; see L. Graham and J. M. Kantor, *Naming Infinity. A True Story of Religious Mysticism and Mathematical Creativity*. Harvard University Press. Cambridge, London. 2009.

next Councils of the Russian Orthodox Church did not come back to this theme. . . .

1. Name Worshipping

The Name worshipping movement arose in 1909-1912 in the Russian monastery of St. Panteleon on Athos. Among the leaders of the movement were spiritual authorities such as Fr. Antony Bulanovich. It is his confessor, St. John of Kronshtadt, who proposed the formula "God's Name is God."

Reverence for the Divine Name is a characteristic feature of the Bible. In the Old Testament we have, truly, a cult of the Divine Name. Here are some examples only from the Psalms:

O Lord, our Lord, how majestic is thy name in all the earth! (8:1)

The name of the God of Jacob protect you! (20:1)

I will thank thee forever. . . . I will proclaim thy name, for it is good, in the presence of the godly. (52:9)

We give thanks to thee, O God, we give thanks; we call on thy name and recount thy wondrous deeds. (75:1)

Let them praise thy great and terrible name! Holy is he! (99:3)

In the New Testament the Christ quite often says that he has opened the Name of God the Father to his followers: "I have manifested thy name to the men whom thou gavest me out of the world. Holy Father, keep them in thy name, which thou hast given me, that they may be one, even as we are one" (Jn. 17:6, 11). The Gospels tell of the working of miracles in the Name of Jesus Christ. The Apostle John tells Jesus: "Teacher, we saw a man casting out demons in your name, and we forbade him, because he was not following us." And Jesus answers: "Do not forbid him; for no one who does a mighty work in my name will be able soon after to speak evil of me" (Mk. 9:38-39).

Name worshipping theology was connected with the tradition of Palamitism, with recognition of God's presence in the world through His energies. In hesychast spiritual practice through the so-called Jesus prayer, centered on God's Name, monks comprehended this Divine presence experientially. Byzantian hesychasts Simeon the New Theologian, St.

Nicephorus of Mt. Athos, St. Gregory Palamas, Nicholas Cabasilas, Simeon of Thessalonica, etc., have given detailed descriptions of a prayer technique which, having cleared and prepared the soul of man for meeting with God, then conducts man to theosis, to connection with God through His energies. In the 14th to 15th centuries, the hesychast tradition was absorbed into Russian Orthodoxy and has borne plentiful fruits. Through St. Sergius of Radonezh and his pupils, hesychast practice has become the basic prayer method in Russian monasteries. The writings of St. Nile Sorsky, St. Paisy Velichkovsky, St. Philaret of Moscow, St. Ignatius Brianchaninov, St. Pheophan the Hermit, and St. John of Kronstadtsky discuss hesychast practice deeply. But at the beginning of the 20th century the question of the theological sense of reverence for the Divine Name arose again.

In the monastery of St. Panteleon, conflicts arose regarding the understanding of Name worshipping. The minority of monks resisted Name worshipping, but it was supported from the outside. Two members of the Holy Synod, archbishops Nikon Rozhdestvensky and Antony Khrapovitsky, were opponents of Name worshipping. In 1913 the Government Synod of the Russian Church condemned Name worshipping as a heretical doctrine. Constantinople Patriarchs Ioakim III and Herman V condemned it, too. After physical altercations in the monastery, armies were called in, and about thousand Name worshipping monks were arrested and taken back to Russia. They were disseminated to various monasteries; some of them disappeared in the Caucasus Mountains. After the Bolshevic revolution of 1917, the Soviet authorities considered the Name worshippers to be the "Jesuits of Orthodoxy." These Name worshippers were carefully watched and in every possible way pursued. Many Name worshippers were taken to the Gulag and shot.

But already during the tragic events in 1913 Russian religious philosophers P. A. Florensky, S. N. Bulgakov, V. F. Ern, A. F. Losev, and others were involved in protection of Name worshipping and considering its problems. Within the limits of Russian religious philosophy the theme of Name worshipping has been closely connected with the problem of the philosophy of the Divine Name in general. We shall return to this below.

2. Infinity: Mathematics and Theology

The close relationship of mysticism and religion with mathematics is a well-known topic of the history of science and the history of culture. Rapprochements of mathematics and mysticism in the thought of the Pythagoreans is only a small fragment of this big theme. By the end of the 19th century, one more example of the meeting of mathematics and mysticism came to light: the problem of infinity. The idea of infinity came to European science through Christian theology.[2] Ancient mathematics, faced with paradoxes of actual infinity, banned its existence in science. "There is (actual) infinity neither in Cosmos nor in mind," Aristotle taught. There is no infinity in the ancient idea of the cosmos, because in it all things and space are final. And there was no abstract consideration of the actual infinite in the mind — for example, all natural numbers — because this would infringe on fundamental axioms of knowledge;[3] thus it could not be accepted by Greek science built on a strict philosophical base. Roughly speaking, ancient thought had no actual infinite object to build any theories about infinity. Infinity in ancient thought was permitted only as something potential: infinity as a process, either infinite increase of natural numbers or an infinity of divisions of a segment.

But with the arrival of Christianity, such an infinite "object" appeared. In Christian theology, God was understood as actually infinite in power, in knowledge, in clemency. Interestingly, this understanding did not occur all at once. Still, Origen was very dependent on ancient interdictions that considered God as final. According to Origen, God could not be infinite because otherwise He could not comprehend Himself: infinity is inconceivable. . . . But already Augustine challenged the thesis that God cannot think all the numbers (actual infinite set): ". . . We should not doubt that He knows all numbers. Great is our Lord, and abundant in power; His understanding is beyond measure, they sing in the Psalm (Ps. 147:5). Therefore infinity of numbers, even if there was no number of infinite numbers, cannot be uncomprehended for One, Who does not have measure to His reason."[4] Gradually, the idea of the infinity of the Christian God became standard in divinity. Since the 14th century, the natural philosophy of scholasticism started to build speculative constructions about the infinite,

---

2. See in my book: V. N. Katasonov, *Borovshiisia s beskonechnim. Filosofsko-religiozni aspekti genezisa teorii mnogestv G. Cantora (He who strove with the infinite. Philosophical and religious aspects of genesis of G. Cantor's set theory)*. M., 1999 (in Russian).

3. Namely, the axiom: *the part is less than the whole.* If we take all the natural numbers, then between all its members and its part, only even numbers, it is possible to establish one-to-one correspondence: the part is equal to the whole.

4. St. Augustine, *City of God*, XII.19 ("The answer to the allegations that even God's knowledge cannot embrace an infinity of things").

mainly connected with the problem of the structure of continuum. Nicholas of Cusa's speculative theology was an essential stage in the legitimation of actual infinity in European thought. As models for his theology Nicholas used infinite triangles, infinite circles, etc. He also gave the first sketches of the use of the infinitesimal in mathematics. All this resulted in the 17th century in the invention by Newton and Leibniz of differential and integral calculus, which deliberately uses concepts of the actual infinitesimal. However, even for the founders of calculus the sense of operations with the actual infinite was not clear. Leibniz made some attempts to substantiate the new mathematical method he invented, but all of them remained unpersuasive. For mathematicians and philosophers in the 18th to 19th centuries, the actually infinite remained a problem.

But by the end of the 19th century, German mathematician G. Cantor constructed the theory of sets and gradated infinities, building on the concept of infinite numbers, and thus a grandiose reorganization of all the building of mathematics began. However, soon paradoxes were discovered in the theory of sets, which could be solved neither by Cantor himself nor by his followers. So, the brightest representatives of the French school of mathematics at the beginning of the 20th century — E. Borel, H. Poincare, H. Lebesgue, and R. Baire — tried to overcome the difficulties found in the theory of sets. However, since then, actual infinity constructions have not found a serious continuation in the tradition of the French mathematical school. Most likely this is connected with the French traditional orientation of science on Descartes' scientific precepts. ". . . We never begin to trouble ourselves with reasoning about the infinite," Descartes wrote. "Really, it would be ridiculous, if we, being final, try to give it any definition and thus try to limit it and to comprehend."[5] D. Hilbert's formalism and L. Brouwer's intuitionism were not unanimously shared by all the mathematicians either. Problems of bases of mathematics generated by paradoxes in the theory of sets held mathematics in a condition of crisis all through the 20th century.

Problems of infinity, which traditionally was considered an attribute of God, naturally drew the attention of theologians. Cantor himself, a deeply believing and mystically engaged man, constantly connected his mathematical propositions with philosophical and theological theses.

Cantor understood his activity and considered himself to be a tool of the Supreme force, as an organ of revelation informing people of high divine truths. In 1883 he wrote to his friend and the publisher of mathemati-

5. R. Descartes, *Origins of Philosophy,* P.I, §26 (any edition).

cal magazine "Acta Mathematica," Swedish mathematician G. Mittag-Leffler: "My dear friends, loving to name themselves mathematicians, can think of my ideas whatever they want, they can write what seems to them correct, to London, Paris, even to Kamchatka, but I firmly know, that ideas about which I work with my weak forces, will be interesting for the thinking minds of all the generations, even when I and my kind friends, master mathematicians, have long gone the way of all mortals. I am far from attributing my discoveries to personal advantages because I am only a tool of a Supreme force which will work after me, in the same way as it did a thousand years ago in Euclid and Archimedes. . . ."[6]

Certainly, Christian philosophy, as recounted above, was earlier engaged in the question of the infinite. In the teaching of Thomas Aquinas infinity is an essential attribute of God. However, Thomas emphasized that infinity concerns only the inner divine life, the power and knowledge of God: in the created world there is no actual infinite: "There is no infinity of individual things, but even if there were infinity of them, God would know them all the same."[7] But Cantor wanted to prove the existence of actual infinity in the created world. Generally speaking, Cantor distinguished three types of the actual infinite. Actual infinity in God — Cantor named it Absolutum — is discussed in theology; actual infinity in the created world — in concreto — Cantor named Transfinitum; and actual infinity in our mind — in abstracto — was Cantor's infinite numbers. The founder of set theory focused his attention on the existence of the last two kinds of infinity. He was not stopped here either by the negative attitude to actual infinity of philosophical tradition, or by the classical theological arguments against the existence of the actually infinite in the created world. Thus, the traditional theological understanding of the verse from the book of The Wisdom of Solomon, "Omnia in pondere, numera et mensura disposuisti" (Wis. 11:20), meant that in the world there were only final numbers. Cantor objected: "Here it is not written 'in numero finito.' And inasmuch as the consistency of cardinal numbers and ordinal numbers [i.e., Cantor's theory of sets — V.K.] is proved, hence they also are meant in this place of the text and consequently it should not be used as an argument against 'numeris infinitus,' as unfortunately often occurs."[8] In this

6. Excerpt from a letter from G. Cantor to G. Mittag-Leffler. Halle, Dec. 23 // Fidelio. Journal of Poetry, Science and Statecraft. Vol. III, N. 3, Fall 1994. H.104-105.

7. Thomas Aquinas, *Summa contra gentiles*, T.I, Cap. 69.

8. H. Meschkowski, *Aus den Briefbüchern Georg Cantors*. S.512 // Archive for History of Exact Sciences. Ed. by C. Truesdell. V. 2, No. 6. Berlin, Heidelberg, New York.

sense, Cantor understood himself as a new Galileo, helping the Church to understand the Bible adequately. "Only by me," wrote Cantor, "is the true doctrine of the origins of the infinite offered to Christian philosophy for the first time."[9] However, the paradoxes which were found almost from the beginning in the bases of the theory of sets made this statement doubtful.

3. The Infinite in Russia

For Russian mathematicians interested in theology and theologians interested in science, set theory represented an extremely curious subject for reflection. Interest in set theory was assisted by the special intellectual atmosphere which developed in Moscow University at the turn of the 19th to the 20th century. Professor of mathematics N. V. Bugaev (the father of philosopher and poet Andrey Beliy) actively discussed worldview aspects of mathematics in his lectures. P. A. Florensky, the future priest and theologian, and N. N. Luzin, the future head of the Moscow mathematical school, were Bugaev's pupils. Then and later, after Florensky became a priest, there was an active correspondence between Luzin and Florensky. This correspondence definitely testifies to Luzin's interest in problems of Orthodox mysticism and Christian life in general. Florensky and his younger colleague on the mathematical faculty, Luzin, were interested in problems of Name worshipping already in 1906-1907. In 1907 Florensky wrote the manuscript "Holy renaming," and later, when he was a student in seminary, he read the book of monk Illarion "On the mountains of Caucasus," which told about the spiritual practice of Name worshipping. During these years Luzin was under the strong spiritual influence of Florensky (as happened with many people who came within Florensky's orbit). Meeting with Florensky led to Luzin's deep spiritual crisis — in particular, to the revision of his attitude to science which was so dear to the talented young mathematician. Conversations with Florensky led to serious questioning about his worldview, about the religious worldview. From his scientific business trip in Paris Luzin wrote to Florensky: "You found me a mere child at University, knowing nothing. I don't know how it happened, but I cannot be satisfied any more with the analytic functions and Taylor series. . . . To see the misery of people, to see the torment of life . . . — this is an unbearable sight. . . . It is painful for me to live! Those worldviews which I earlier knew (materialistic

9. From letter to Fr. Th. Esher. S.513. Op. cit.

worldviews) absolutely do not satisfy me. . . . Yes, now I understand that 'science,' in essence, is metaphysical and based on nothing. . . . In science I am interested now only in origins, symbolical logic and theory of sets. But I cannot live by science alone. . . ."[10] It is probable that, through Florensky, who in 1912-1913 began to defend Name worshipping publicly, Luzin himself entered into the sphere of this theological problem. This was assisted also by the influence of D. F. Egorov, the well-known mathematician, professor of Moscow University, and teacher of both Florensky and Luzin, who was a deeply believing Orthodox man.

Florensky undoubtedly assisted Luzin's conversion to God and Church, helped him to find a religious worldview, and was always an authority for him on questions of spiritual life, divinity, and philosophy. But Florensky also influenced Luzin in his understanding of philosophy and theology of science. To find a complete worldview was, according to Florensky himself, the central task of his scientific work and life.[11] This remarkable Russian thinker was strong precisely on questions of the philosophical and theological interpretation of science and culture in general. Like no other, he was able to open the great philosophical prospects quite often hidden behind specific scientific problems. Under the influence of his teacher, N. V. Bugaev, Florensky's interests in mathematics soon moved to the area of discontinuous functions (Bugaev's "arithmology"). Continuous and analytical functions were for Florensky a symbol of a worldview in which there is no place for breaks, jumps, unexpectedness — for a miracle, in the end — and so there is no place for God.[12] Therefore, it is no wonder that it was Florensky who first printed the paper about Cantor's theory of sets: Cantor, in particular, tried to construct a continuity from discrete sets. It is this symbolism of mathematical ideas that Luzin learned through close relations with Florensky.

As we have noted above, up to the beginning of the 20th century the theory of sets faced fundamental paradoxes, which, practically speaking,

10. Letter of N. N. Luzin to P. A. Florensky, 1.05.1906 // Istoriko-matematicheskie issledovanija. Vipusk XXXI. M., 1989. Pp. 135-136 (in Russian). The analytical functions were continuous, but *continuity* was an unfamiliar word for both friends at that time (see below about Prof. Bugaev's arithmology).

11. "His life objective Florensky sees as the building of the ways to a future integral worldview," wrote Florensky in his *Autoreferat* (*Sviatsch.Pavel Florenskiy*. Sochinenija v chetireh tomah. T.1. M., 1994. P. 38) (in Russian).

12. See Florensky's paper "Ob odnoi predposilke mirovozzrenija" // *Sviatsch.Pavel Florenskiy*. Sochinenija v chetireh tomah. T.1. M., 1994. Pp. 70-78 (in Russian).

have not been overcome even today. The problem of continuum, the Burali-Forti paradox, the Russell paradox, and later the problem of axiom of choice — the best mathematicians of the world were puzzling to find solutions to these problems, but they could not achieve the goal. Sometimes their hard intellectual work led to a loss of mental health: first of all, this was the destiny of the founder of the theory of sets, G. Cantor himself:[13] ". . . The most difficult was just the initial concept of the actual infinite set. In fact all our sensual experience is final, and if we speak about actual infinity in our mind at once we face Zeno's aporia as Greeks have opened it already in Antiquity. . . . Therefore all the constructions in the theory of sets, which has been created just, so to say, 'to reckon' actual infinity, appear extremely abstract. They can be based only on definitions for there is no other support for intuition. . . ."

Owing to Florensky's influence, the idea of Name worshipping was known in the circle of Moscow mathematicians. Florensky was an open supporter of Name worshipping.[14] Professor Egorov may have been as well. Through dialogues with Florensky, Name worshipping ideas became known also to Luzin and, later, his pupils from well-known "Luzitania" (in particular, P. S. Aleksandrov, A. N. Kolmogorov, P. S. Novikov, etc.). However, what could be the tie between Name worshipping theological doctrine and the fundamental problems of the theory of sets? This is the main question of our paper. This is just a point of special approach to the problems of infinity in the Russian scientific tradition at the time under consideration. Sometimes it is rather difficult for scholars of the Western tradition to understand, just because of the specific distinctions in the base of spiritual experience. So the authors of *Naming Infinity* wrote: "In the early twentieth century mathematicians were perplexed by the possibility of new kinds of infinities. Georg Cantor suggested these new infinities and made them seem real by assigning them different names. For some people the very act of naming these infinities seemed to create them. And here the

---

13. Beginning in 1880, Cantor spent time almost every year in a psychiatric clinic. Then he left, taught, wrote his books and papers on the theory of sets. . . . He died in a psychiatric clinic in 1918. For more details see J. W. Dauben, *Georg Cantor. His Mathematics and Philosophy of the Infinite*, Cambridge, London, 1979.

14. In 1913 Florensky together with M. A. Novoselov issued one of the basic works on protection of Name worshipping, the book *"Apologia of belief . . ." of monk and theologian Antony Bulatovich*. Florensky wrote a sympathetic foreword to this book in which he considered Name worshipping as a special case of Church doctrine about the distinction of Divine essence and energies.

Russian Name Worshippers had their opening: they believed they made God real by worshipping his name, and the mathematicians among them thought they made infinities real by similarly centering on their names."[15] Elsewhere in the book the authors link the prayer of Name worshippers with the idea of creation.[16]

First of all, it is necessary to say that the idea of creation has no relation to Name worshipping. Name worshippers do not create God by calling on His Name, and we do not know any of them who would approve this idea. Worshipping God's Name, repeating the Jesus prayer, Name worshippers come nearer to God, as if to actualize His presence for themselves. Any such statement should be understood not as a passiveness of God but rather as a human turn to God. But never is there talk of creation. One of the main apologists of Name worshipping, monk Antony Bulatovich, wrote in his "Apologia": ". . . Those names with which we call God, although we take them from human concepts and words, when we apply them to God they are immutably — God Being and Living. . . . God's Name is not only a light, but makes in us the action of light, i.e. It [God's Name] not only calls God light, but itself leads God Himself in our souls, and, hence, is God, being the verbal action of Deity and His properties."[17]

Rough enough rapprochements of ideas of Name worshipping with the idea of creation result in the book *Naming Infinity* from the authors' too-hot desire to connect Name worshipping and mathematical constructions in the theory of sets. But one should know how to do this!

It's true that in mathematics the mathematician really creates sets: he designs them, or, more correctly, creates set through definition. For example: the set of all prime numbers (i.e., those natural numbers, other than 1, divisible by no integers other than unity and itself, such as 2, 3, 5, 7, . . .); or the set of real numbers which have a square more than 2; or the set of all sets, etc. These concepts really are human mental designs and, only in this sense, real creations. It is another matter if we ask: Does something real correspond to these logical formulas? In fact, some of the formulas defining these sets can be simply logically inconsistent. So, for example, any representation about the set of all sets at once faces the contradiction that we can always increase this set by adding to it itself as its new element. And

15. L. Graham and J. M. Kantor, *Naming Infinity: A True Story of Religious Mysticism and Mathematical Creativity,* Harvard University Press, 2009. P. 96.

16. Op. cit., P. 97.

17. Ieroshimonah A. Bulatovich, *Apologia veri vo Imia Bogie i vo Imia Iisus.* P. 37 // Imiaslavie. Antologia. M., 2002 (in Russian).

behind all aporiae of the theory of sets always a simple and fundamental question was present: Are there really any other infinities, except of the infinity of natural numbers: 1, 2, 3? It is very interesting that from the very beginning of Christian theological discourse about infinity we find the idea of the different degrees of infinity. Thus, according to Dionysius the Pseudo-Areopagite, the mysterious author from the 3rd to 4th centuries, the Divine power surpasses all the degrees of infinity: ". . . if He, because of His boundless clemency, has created something possessing boundless power, even this creature of His creative power could never master His superboundless power."[18] Degrees of infinity was one of Cantor's main inventions. The theory of sets began at the moment when Cantor proved the theorem about uncountability of the real numbers set. It affirmed that there is another, greater infinity than the one of natural numbers. And though the proof of this theorem is extremely simple — it is accessible to any attentive school child of the senior classes — nevertheless, even today, this proof causes disputes and refutations. By no means all mathematicians have agreed with Cantor that his proof is logically valid. It is known that the head of the Moscow mathematical school, Prof. N. N. Luzin, despite all his interest in mysticism and Name worshipping, in his mature years did not recognize the existence of actual infinity: even actual infinity of the natural numbers, taken as a whole. In due course, it was out of opposition to the idea of actual infinity that the intuitionist school in mathematics arose and the tradition of so-called finitism.

Therefore already from the beginning of the 20th century, still during Cantor's lifetime, there was a question of principle: How to prove, justify, or even somehow to confirm the existence of actual infinity? In our opinion, in Name worshipping there is an opportunity for such confirmation.

4. Philosophy of Name and the Existence of Infinity

As a philosopher, Florensky was a convinced follower of Platonism. However, he understood Platonism rather widely: not simply as Plato's philosophy and its school but as a certain movement of thought and spirit in the history of mankind: ". . . Is it more right to understand Platonism not as a certain system of concepts and judgements always equal to itself, or as some spiritual aspiration, as a finger showing the way from earth to

---

18. Dionysius, the Pseudo-Areopagite, *Divine Names*, 8.2.

heaven? . . ."[19] Platonism was also a philosophy of mathematics for Florensky. "The number is . . . some prototype, the ideal scheme, a primary category of thinking and life. It is some clever proto-organism, qualitatively distinct from other similar organisms — numbers. And not without justification Plato almost identified the ideas with Pythagorean numbers, and Neoplatonics have merged them with gods . . . ,"[20] wrote Florensky.

But to understand the interaction of Name worshipping and mathematics one has to know Florensky's philosophy of name. This theory is by no means a nominalistic one. According to Florensky, the name is a kind of unification, a fusion (Russian "sratschenije") of object's energy and subject's essence. The name is a new entity in which both the understanding and the understandable are represented. In Florensky's own words, the name is a bridge between subject and object.[21] So in the name we have the thing itself, not through its essence, but as its energy. But essence of thing (Greek οὐσία) and its attributes (Greek ἐνέργεια) are inseparable. For Florensky this statement is one of the most important ontological laws. The highest expression of this law was St. Gregory Palamas' dogmatic statement about unseparableness and unconfusedness of God's essence and His energies. The same is true for every created thing as well: its essence and energy are unconfused and unseparable. This is the foundation both for Christian mystics and for natural ones. Because of this understanding, a believer, praying to God, has in God's Name His energies and so has God Himself.[22] Florensky didn't invent this philosophy of name. It is this philosophy of name that was implicitly and explicitly the foundation for hesychast spiritual practice.

The Name worshippers, worshipping the Divine Name, affirmed that God is present already in this Name. However, God has a lot of Names: God, the Lord, the Omnipotent, the Almighty, the Eternal. . . . Name wor-

19. S. P. Florenskiy, *Sochinenija v chetireh tomah.* T.3(2). M., 1999. P. 70 (in Russian).

20. *Pifagorovi chisla (Pythagoras' numbers)*, Pp. 637-638 // S. P. Florenskiy, *Sochinenija v chetireh tomah,* T.2. M., 1996 (in Russian).

21. In this connection, there is a problem with Florensky's philosophy of name: Is name a new *thing?* Is the naming a *continuation of creation?* For example, is Adam's naming of animals in the Bible a continuation of creation or is it only, so to say, actualization of the already created? Cf. F. Nüssel, *Challenges of a Consistent Christian Language for the Creativity of God's Spirit,* and M. Plested, *Pneumatology and the New Creation in the Macarian Writings* (both in this book).

22. See Florensky's paper *Imiaslavie kak filosofskaia predposilka (Name Worshipping as a philosophical presupposition)* // S. P. Florenskiy, *Sochinenija v chetireh tomah,* T.3(1). M., 1999. Pp. 252-286 (in Russian).

shippers emphasized Orthodox general opinion about the equal significance of these Names. So, monk and theologian Antony Bulatovich in his "Apologia" quotes Gregory of Nyssa: "A thousand other names, meaning the Height and Splendidness of God, Holy Scripture named God; and we in accuracy know from this that when one says only a name, by this one silently says all the list of names. For if He is called as the Lord, it is not supposed that other names do not belong to Him; quite the contrary, in one name He is called by all names" (St. Gregory of Nyssa, *About Beatitudes*, Word 4). Among the Names of God there is also the Infinite. Anything terrestrial does not refer to this name. Infinity is also meant in the names Omnipotent, Almighty, and Eternal. Therefore, when we speak about infinity, we nolens volens call God, and intellectually we touch Him. The reality of the Divine life turns out to be the guarantee of existence of the actual infinity. The name Infinity is a form of God's icon in mathematics. In the same way, in Orthodox iconology, our prayer before an icon is not addressed to a board; rather, it goes back to a prototype of that which is drawn, the same with the name Infinity, Infinite. Saying it, we intellectually address the infinite Source of being itself, God, for nothing from the created world answers to this name. Therefore actual infinity exists, and consequently all the immeasurable complexity of the problems arising in the theory of sets is no surprise.

From the time of Plato until today, philosophy has tried to realize the ontological status of a human idea. Anselm of Canterbury's ontological proof of God's existence tried to solve the same problem: Is there something in our thoughts that would have the ontological status of being — or, put another way, does our thought touch being itself or, just the reverse, remain closed in the sphere of subjective perception? The problems connected with actual infinity again raise this question, and Name worshipping theology gives opportunities to answer it positively.

II. THE SPIRIT IN CREATION: THEOLOGICAL PERSPECTIVES

The Spirit of Life

Jürgen Moltmann

1. Creation in God's Spirit

In modern theology, the strict distinction between God and world is put down to the biblical belief in creation. As a creation of God's, this world is not divine; it is worldly. The Israelite belief in creation stripped the world of gods and demons and, in the modern sense, secularized it. In Israel it put an end to the fertility cults and in modern times it drove the divine "world soul" out of the world picture. With this the taboos of the religions of nature fell away. Nature became the world of the human beings and was subjected to their scientific research and their technological utilization. The scientific methods were value-free, agnostically or atheistically positioned. The strict monotheism of modern times banished God into the transcendent in order to possess the world in transcendence-free immanence. In the final analysis, God was thereby thought of as world-less, so that the world could be found godless, or subjugated free of God.[1]

With these negative presuppositions, is it possible to talk about "creation" at all? The modern sciences do not answer the first metaphysical question: why is there something and not nothing? The question about the contingency of the world remains unanswered. Theology replies to this fundamental question by pointing to the creation of the world out of non-being into being through an act of God's free will. God did not have to create this world, but it was his pleasure to call into existence a reality which is neither divine nor nothingness, and which corresponds to him in its goodness. With the concept of analogy the distance between transcendence and

1. A. Gehlen, *Urmensch und Spätkultur,* Bonn, 1956.

immanence is bridged. God calls forth his external echo in the world, and through its resonances shows this world that it is a good creation of a good God. The analogy concept preserves and at the same time bridges the fundamental difference between God and world.[2]

However, there is a deeper understanding of creation. The Creator is bound to his creation inwardly, not just outwardly. According to Christian interpretation, the act of creation is a trinitarian act: God the Father creates through his eternal Word in the energies of his Spirit this non-divine reality, which though it is non-divine is nevertheless interpenetrated by God. For if all things have been created by God the Father through God the Son and in God the Holy Spirit, then they are also in God and through God and for God (1 Cor. 8:6).

In his treatise "On the Holy Spirit," Basil writes:

> Behold in the creation of these beings the Father as the preceding cause, the Son as the One who createth, and the Spirit as the perfecter, so that the ministering spirits have their beginning in the will of the Father, are brought into being through the efficacy of the Son, and are perfected through the aid of the Spirit.[3]

If we see the act of creation as being in this way a trinitarian act, then the work of creation cannot be put down simply to "God, the Father Almighty." It must be ascribed with equal weight to the Son (John 1:2) and the Holy Spirit. It is noteworthy that Basil ascribes the completion of creation to the Holy Spirit. I understand that to mean that all created beings are aligned towards their future consummation and are driven towards that through the energies of God's Spirit. The creation open to the future has to be understood as creation fashioned by the Spirit. In this direction and movement it is not merely a material reality; it is a spiritual one too. The energies of the divine Spirit come to meet creation out of their future (Heb. 6:5) and represent an "anticipation" of their completion in the glory of God.

We find a corresponding statement in Calvin's *Institutio:*

> For the Spirit is everywhere present and preserves, sustains and enlivens all things in heaven and on earth. Since he pours out his energy into ev-

---

2. For this Karl Barth's doctrine of creation is a good example. Cf. *Church Dogmatics* III/1-4.

3. Basil, *On the Holy Spirit,* ch. 38 (PG 32, 136B).

erything, and thereby for all things means essence, life and movement, this is clearly divine. (1.13, 14)

Metaphors that have to do with energy are often used for the activity of the Spirit. The powers of the Spirit are "poured out" like flooding waters on all flesh (Joel 2; Acts 2) and into our hearts (Rom. 5:5). They are like a tempest, like floodlighting, and like fire from heaven.[4]

The special thing about these metaphors is their unbroken transition from the origin to the process and its result. It is the same light in its source, in the ray, and in the radiance of things; it is the same water in the fountainhead, in the river, and in the watered earth. Here no distinction is made between the Creator and his created beings. The difference is actually bridged. Here the neo-platonic concept of emanation is appropriate, for with that qualitative differences become fluid transitions. What is strictly differentiated in the concept of creation is eternally bound together in "the outpouring of the Spirit." The Roman fountain which pours its water from basin to basin has from time immemorial been the image for the doctrine of emanation.

In the Trinitarian doctrine of creation, the work of the Father is linked with the outstreaming Godhead of the Holy Spirit, so that as a result the created world has to be viewed as divine inasmuch as it is sustained and moved by the divine energies. God does not just stand outside and over against his creation. Through the Spirit he enters into it and already "dwells" in it. The philosophical construct "panentheism" says that everything is "in God," whereas initially it is the other way round: God is already present in everything through his Spirit. The Jewish teaching about the Shekinah expresses this better. It leads to a sacramental interpretation of the world. No creations are ascribed to the Holy Spirit, as they are to God the Father, nor any incarnation, as of God the Son. The particular form of the Spirit's presence in created being is "indwelling": *inhabitatio Spiritus Sancto.*

I believe that with this we can also take further the Orthodox theological discussion about the created and the uncreated energies of the Spirit, for this alternative fails to meet the "outpouring and streaming deity" of the Spirit.[5]

---

4. For more detail see J. Moltmann, *The Spirit of Life. A Universal Affirmation,* trans. M. Kohl, Minneapolis: Fortress Press, and London: SCM Press, 1992, ch. XII. 1: *Metaphors for the Experience of the Spirit,* pp. 269-284. For the biblical theology see J. R. Levison's excellent study, *Filled with the Spirit,* Grand Rapids: Eerdmans, 2009.

5. G. Morel, ed. M. von Magdeburg, *Das fließende Licht der Gottheit,* Darmstadt, 1976; *The Flowing Light of the Godhead,* selections trans. E. A. Andersen, Cambridge: D. S. Brewer, 2003.

Between the Spirit's uncreated and created energies one must also think, as third possibility, of its creative energies. But because God's Spirit has preeminently to do with living beings, its mode of efficacy is better expressed with biological metaphors, birth, nurturing, and enlivening, rather than with metaphors drawn from physics.

2. Creation and New Creation

If for once we do not read the Bible from the beginning to the end but in the reverse order, from the end to the beginning, then Revelation chapter 21 sheds a special light on Genesis 1. Genesis 1 does not describe a perfect world, but only the beginning of a creation which just arrives at its true nature in the "new creation." Genesis 1 describes only Act I of creation, the beginning of a creation history which arrives at its goal and its perfecting in the kingdom of God's glory. The expression "new creation" can easily be misunderstood, as if the just creation had miscarried, and another, quite different one was to come about instead. What the phrase means is the rebirth of all things into their eternal form. This eternal creation, world without end, is not something lying behind us; it lies ahead of us. Creation in time is aligned towards the eternal creation in the way that mortal life is aligned towards eternal life. Then not only will death "be no more" (Rev. 21:4) but transience will be overcome as well. In this respect the "new creation" will bring not only redemption from sin, death, and chaos, but also the completion and perfecting of the first act of creation, and the fulfillment of its initial promise.[6]

Theological doctrines of creation generally depend on the two creation accounts in Genesis 1–3. These are biblical but not Christian. The starting point for a specifically Christian doctrine of creation is the Christ event: the coming of Christ into this world, his lowering of himself and his exaltation, his self-giving for the reconciliation of the cosmos, and his resurrection for the gathering together of all things *(anakephalaiosis)*. With this event the new creation of all things into their eternal form begins in the midst of this world. In the midst of transitory history eschatological history begins. In the Catholic liturgy for Easter eve, the "creation hymn" from Genesis 1 is

---

6. J. Moltmann, *The Source of Life,* trans. M. Kohl, Minneapolis: Fortress Press, and London: SCM Press, 1997, ch. X: '. . . *And thou renewest the face of the earth': The Ecology of the Creative Spirit,* pp. 111-124. Also in *Ecumenical Review* 42, 1990.

read, as being the "earliest resurrection text," so to speak: "God raises the world out of the darkness of the chaos hostile to life into the light of the life-furthering cosmos. . . . Through this, creation is given an eschatological character from the beginning, for in this way it can be perceived as God's great 'promise.'"[7] The eschatological perspective of the consummation of all things is the justification for the Christological way of reading the creation stories in the Old Testament.[8] The perspective emerges from the fact that in the Pauline epistles and in the Gospel of John the mediation in creation (which plays no special part in the Old Testament's creation narratives) is stressed and extensively presented. The reason is to be found in the incarnation of the Logos in the coming of Christ into this world, which is the starting point of these New Testament texts. God creates the cosmos through his eternal Logos: "All things were made through the Word and without the Word was not anything made that was made" (John 1:3). The Logos was with God, and God was the Logos (1:1). The creation Logos mediates between the being of God and everything that is "made." From this it follows that the cosmos has a logical structure and that in this structure it corresponds to the eternal God. This is a Christian interpretation both of the first creation account, according to which God speaks and it was so, and also of Wisdom literature, according to which Wisdom is both God's eternal beloved and at the same time "plays" before him on his earth: "He who finds me finds life . . . all who hate me love death" (Prov. 8:35-36). This means that in relation to the earth and to life, the Logos in the prologue to the Gospel of John can also be understood as the Wisdom of God. In the risen Christ, exalted over all things, the first Christians saw the manifestation not only of a savior of men and women but also of the cosmic Logos and the Wisdom of the earth. From the radiant face of the risen Christ, the light of the first creation shone on them (2 Cor. 4:6). They emphasized the Mediator in creation more than the Creator, because from him they expected the reconciliation of the cosmos and its perfecting: the cosmos was created through Christ, so it is only through Christ that it can be reconciled, brought to a unity and perfected. That goes far beyond what the creation stories in the Old Testament and the creation psalms say.

What is the relation between the Spirit of the new creation and the

7. M. Kehl, preface to P. C. Sicouly, *Schöpfung und Neuschöpfung. "Neuschöpfung" als theologische Kategorie im Werk Jürgen Moltmanns*, Paderborn, 2007, p. 14.

8. J. Moltmann, *The Way of Jesus Christ. Christology in Messianic Dimensions,* trans. M. Kohl, San Francisco: HarperCollins, and London: SCM Press, 1990, ch. VI: The Cosmic Christ, pp. 274-304.

spirit of creation? Psalm 104:29-30 distinguishes between "their breath," meaning the spirit inherent in living things, and "thy breath" which "renews" the form of the earth. The divine Spirit enters into the created spirit and "renews" it. The two are not identical, although they are alike in quality; both are called *ruach*. The renewal arises from their difference.

Romans 8:16 has a similar construction: "It is the Spirit himself who gives witness with our spirit that we are children of God." The word *pneuma* is used both times. The revelation of the divine Spirit to the human spirit brings about the new birth of human beings as "God's children" and "God's heirs," with a legal claim to the coming kingdom of glory (8:17).

The Spirit of the new creation is understood to be the anticipation of future glory, which will fulfill the promise of creation, the sighs and yearning of created being, and the human expectation of the redemption of the body from the fate of death. The spirit of creation awaits the Spirit of the new creation, and the Spirit of the new creation takes up this expectation, although this is a new entry of God into the creation process.

3. The Spirit of the Earth and the "New Earth"

The term "creation" is always somewhat too broad, because it is supposed to be the quintessence of everything that is. The Greek distinction between the "visible" and the "invisible cosmos" is also extremely comprehensive. The space of everything living known to us, and our human living space, is the earth. By "earth" we do not mean today the counterpart to "heaven," as is the case in the Bible; nor do we mean land, as distinct from water and air. We mean the "blue planet" which we call "earth." Seen from a spaceship, we do not live on the earth but in it. The earth viewed as a whole shows itself to be a living major organism which organizes and regulates itself, brings forth living things, and sustains their life. Human beings are not just "on earth"; they are also products of the earth: according to Hebrew linguistic usage, Adam (the human being) proceeded from *adama* (earth). Human beings are not just "guests on a beautiful star," to translate the title of the theologian Helmut Thielicke's autobiography. Human beings are themselves earth, which — to quote Leonardo Boff — "at a particular point in the evolution of life began to feel, to think, to love, and to feel reverence."[9] In

---

9. L. Boff, *Die Erde als Gaia: Eine ethische und spirituelle Herausforderung*, CONCILIUM 45, 2009, p. 278.

Western philosophy and theology, the concept of person for the human being went hand in hand with the development of the supremacy of human subjectivity over and above everything which the human being can make into his object. Orthodox theology, on the other hand, adhered firmly to the patristic church's concept of hypostasis: in the human being, nature coalesces into its hypostasis, so that physical human existence comprehends in itself all stages of the anorganic and the organic.[10] The distinction between body and soul is merely a differentiation within the human totality and its community with all living things and with the earth. The biblical ways of looking at the earth point in this direction:

1. The earth *(erez)* is a creative earth. It "brings forth living creatures according to their kind: cattle and creeping things and beasts of the earth" (Gen. 1:24). This creativity is not ascribed to any other created being: the earth lives and brings forth life like a mother. It has the energy for the evolution of life.[11] Darwin was right. The earth is not merely the living space for living things in all their diversity, as modern ecology teaches; it is also the creative foundation for the life of everything that lives.

2. The earth belongs within the divine covenant: after the ecological catastrophe of the Flood, God makes a covenant for life with Noah, "with you and your descendants after you, and with every living creature that is with you" (Gen. 9:9-11). But this covenant with Noah, mediated through human beings, belongs within the wider horizon of God's covenant with the earth: "I set my bow in the cloud, and it shall be a sign of the covenant between me and the earth" (Gen. 9:13). This covenant is not mediated by way of human beings; it brings the earth into direct contact with God. It embraces not just the domestic animals ("every creature that is with you") but all living things on earth. The bow — so often and so beautifully depicted as a rainbow — is a reminder to God, not human beings. For human beings, God's covenant with the earth means reverencing the divine mystery of the earth, which is God's presence in the earth, and respecting the rights of the earth as divine rights.

3. The rights of the earth in the covenant with God find their recognition in the laws about the Sabbath: "In the seventh year there shall be a Sabbath of solemn rest for the land, a Sabbath to the Lord" (Lev. 25:4). The

---

10. D. Staniloae, *Orthodoxe Dogmatik I,* Gütersloh, 1985, p. 293.

11. This is emphatically stressed by M. Welker, *God the Spirit,* trans. J. F. Hoffmeyer, Minneapolis: Fortress Press, 1994. He describes the earth as an active and energy-conferring environment (3.3).

earth has a right to rest and to be "left in peace," so that it can restore its fertility. Those who disregard the Sabbath of the earth turn the land into a desert and must disappear from the face of the earth (Lev. 26:33).

4. The spirit of the earth is the earth's creative power for life: *Spiritus vivificans*. When God's Spirit is "poured out on all flesh" (Joel 2:28) it is not just human beings who will be filled with new vitality but "all flesh," that is to say all living things. When the "Spirit from on high" is poured out, "the wilderness will become a fruitful field and the fruitful field will be deemed a forest. Then justice will dwell in the wilderness, and righteousness abide in the fruitful field. And the fruit of righteousness will be peace" (Isa. 32:15-18).

5. The earth even holds a salvific secret: "Let the earth open, that salvation may spring forth, let it call righteousness to spring up also" (Isa. 45:8). Isaiah calls God's messiah a "fruit of the land" (Isa. 4:2). It is along the same lines when Orthodox icons depict the birth of Jesus as taking place not in a man-made stable but in a cave in the earth.

The spirit of the earth is open for its renewal through the Spirit of the new earth. This will bring not just life but righteousness and justice, as Isaiah prophesies, for it is only through righteousness and justice that the earth can find endurance and peace. What distinguishes the "new earth" from the old one? The New Testament says that "according to his promise, we wait for new heavens and a new earth in which righteousness dwells" (2 Peter 3:13). Righteousness on earth is the mode of God's presence on earth, and the fact that righteousness is to "dwell" on earth signifies that it will endure. In addition, this heralds the Creator's eschatological Shekinah in his creation, the Shekinah which will refashion it into a creation that is eternal.

4. The Cosmic Christ: The Reconciliation of the Cosmos and the Restoration of All Things

Before we turn to "the Spirit in the new creation" we must consider the specifically Christian contribution to the doctrine of creation. This can be found in scattered indications in Paul, in the Epistle to the Ephesians 1:9-23, and in the Epistle to the Colossians 1:15-20. We shall begin with the reconciliation of the universe according to Colossians 1 and shall then look at the ideas about the gathering together of all things in Ephesians 1:10. For both Ephesians and Colossians, the starting point is the raising of Jesus

Christ as "the first-born from the dead," "so that in everything he might be the first" (Col. 1:18). In a similar way, the Epistle to the Ephesians begins with the raising of Christ from the dead, his exaltation to the right hand of God, and his rule over all powers in heaven and earth (1:20). The conclusion that follows is that the first-born of the new creation of all things is the first-born of creation too, and that "in him all things were created, in heaven and on earth, visible and invisible, whether thrones or dominions or principalities or powers" (Col. 1:15-16).

As the one in whom everything is created, the first-born is also, according to God's will, the one through whose self-surrender to death on the cross the universe will be reconciled (Col. 1:20). "The blood of his cross," as the symbolic expression puts it, serves not only to reconcile human beings with God, alienated from him as they are, but also to reconcile the whole God-alienated and hence evidently spoilt and disrupted cosmos. Paul had already maintained that in 2 Corinthians 5:7. If not only human beings but the cosmic forces too have to be "reconciled," this presupposes the hostility of the cosmos towards its Creator (though this is not more closely defined); otherwise it would be impossible to talk about "making peace by the blood of his cross." The cosmic order which is in harmony with the Logos must be disrupted; the thrones, dominions, principalities, and powers must have arrived at a state of rebellion and conflict with each other. These *"herrenlose Gewalten"* as Karl Barth called them, in his last words trusting that *"es wird regiert,"*[12] were apparently the cosmic problem for early Christianity, which found itself in a religious world in which the cosmic forces were deified and demonized. In this world of ancient cities, Christians came forward with the cosmic message of universal reconciliation: the risen and exalted Christ is the reconciler and peace-giver for the chaotic forces of nature too. Faith in the cosmic peace of the exalted Christ freed them from both the fear of nature and its deification. That is as up-to-date today as it was then: how should we otherwise affirm and love a life ravaged by earthquakes, tsunamis, and climate catastrophes! But it makes a difference whether human beings are delivered over to incalculable natural forces or whether the earth is despoiled, reduced to a rubbish dump through the act of incalculable human beings. Nevertheless, it is the same gospel about cosmic peace through the coming of Christ into this world and his giving of himself for their reconciliation. It goes without saying

12. See E. Busch, *Karl Barth. His Life from Letters and Autobiographical Texts,* trans. John Bowden, London: SCM Press, and Philadelphia: Fortress Press, 1976.

that this "universal reconciliation" of Colossians 1:20 embraces all human beings irrespective of their belief or unbelief. The risen and exalted Christ is universally present, even though this cannot of course yet be said of the liberating faith in him.[13]

The Epistle to the Ephesians announces Act II, which follows the reconciliation of the universe, the *anakephaleiosis ton panton:* "to unite all things in him, things in heaven and things on earth" (Eph. 1:10). Just as at creation-in-the-beginning everything was created "through" and "in" Christ, so the new creation of all things begins to arrive at its enduring form through the exaltation of Christ to be Lord over all "rule and authority and power and dominion": "He has put all things under his feet" (Eph. 1:21-22).[14] The risen Christ takes for himself all power "in heaven and on earth" until the completion of the world (Matt. 28:18), so as to lead everything into the world that is new. Because the cosmic Christ is the Christ who has been raised "from the dead," this reconciliation, this peace, and this gathering together of all things belongs not just to the future but to the past as well. The hope of resurrection is the only hope for the future for those who belong to the past. Turned into cosmic dimensions, the resurrection of the dead means "the restoration of all things." Nothing is lost, nothing is forgotten, everything that was and is and will be, will be brought again, will be put to rights, and will be gathered into the eternal kingdom. This certainly presupposes God's judgment on everything that was and is and will be, but this judgment destroys nothing, but puts right, justifies, and reconciles. It is the Judge who at the end of his judgment sets the new beginning and says, "Behold, I make all things new" (Rev. 21:5).[15]

13. J. Moltmann, *"Will all be saved or only a few? A Dialogue between Grace and Faith,"* in B. McCormack and K. Bender, *Theology as Conversation. Festschrift for D. Migliore,* Grand Rapids: Eerdmans, 2009, pp. 235-240.

14. Here we see a difference from Paul, who in 1 Cor. 15:24 talks about "destroying every rule and every authority and power." Eschatological hierarchy or eschatological anarchy? That is the question here.

15. This was always strongly stressed by Christoph Blumhardt, the inspirer of dialectical theology, religious socialism, and the theology of hope: "One thing, however, must be established over against the idea usual in pious circles:

> Judgment does not merely have a negative side; it has above all a positive one. That is to say, its aim is not merely to destroy; its purpose is above all to save; it does not desire to dissolve but above all to fulfil. It is the annihilating No to all the powers hostile to God and it is the dissolution of the world of evil, but it is the saving and fulfilling Yes of creation: Behold, I make all things new" (L. Ragaz, *Der Kampf um das Reich Gottes in Blumhardt, Vater und Sohn — und weiter I,* Zürich, Munich, and Leipzig, 1922), p. 153.

The gathering together of the cosmos presupposes the resurrection of the dead, for the cosmic Christ fills not only all the spaces of creation with his peace — the heavens, the earth, and things under the earth — but all the times of creation too. The forces of evolution in nature also need the messianic redemption, because through the process of selection they have left in their wake unnumbered victims and depredations.[16]

5. The Spirit of the New Creation

According to Christian understanding, the Spirit of the new creation is the power of Christ's resurrection and the power of the risen Christ.[17] Pentecost presupposes Easter. The "outpouring" of the Spirit, the beginning of which the community of the apostles experiences (Acts 2), is the other side of the raising of the crucified Christ: the pentecostal Spirit is the power of the resurrection. Whatever charismata and new vital energies are experienced in the community of Christ's people are the powers of the resurrection into the new life, for "the free gift (charisma) of God is eternal life in Christ Jesus our Lord" writes Paul (Rom. 6:23). The charismata are the powers of eternal life. According to the trinitarian ideas of the Gospel of John, the Spirit proceeds from the Father and rests on the Son, and from the Son radiates into the world.

Let us look at that a little more closely:

1. What the disciples experience at Pentecost as "a sound from heaven" and "tongues as of fire" is "the Spirit who is poured out on all flesh" (Acts 2:17). In the Spirit, they experience themselves as the first from "all flesh," that is to say as the vanguard of the new humanity. That means equality. Sons and daughters will prophesy — there is no discrimination, and no subordination of women to men. The young will have visions and the old will have dreams — there is no detraction because of age; no one is too young and no one is too old.[18] The Spirit is poured out on slaves; there are no longer any masters and no ruling classes; all are equally endowed with the Spirit. For Paul this equality among God's children widens out to include "Jews and Gentiles, slaves and free, men and women." They are all one

16. Cf. Moltmann, *The Way of Jesus Christ,* pp. 301-304.

17. E. Käsemann, *Essays on New Testament Themes,* trans. W. Montague, London: SCM Press, 1964, p. 68. I am following him in his Pauline doctrine of the charismata.

18. See M. Welker, *God the Spirit,* trans. J. F. Hoffmeyer, Minneapolis: Fortress Press, 1994, pp. 147-182.

in Christ and heirs of the new creation (Gal. 3:26-28). According to Hebrew usage, the phrase "all flesh," *kol basar,* does not mean just all human life but all life in general. Consequently the community that is filled with the Spirit also sees itself as the vanguard of the new creation of all things and of the new earth, on which righteousness dwells. The church's wide horizon is not defined by the world religions; its horizon is the cosmos.

2. For Paul, *pneuma* does not mean spirituality or inwardness; it means vital energy. The Spirit has physical and sensory dimensions. Through the indwelling of the divine Spirit, the human body becomes God's temple (1 Cor. 6:19). That is why God is to be praised in the body.[19] The new humanity in the Spirit is an anticipation of the resurrection and the new bodiliness which Paul talks about in 1 Corinthians 15:35-49. These bodily and sensory depths of the Spirit's indwelling lead to the social dimensions of the charismata in the community of Christ, the body of Christ. The charismatic community experiences the fullness and diversity of the Spirit's vital energies. They are as plural and as variegated as creation itself. As we said above, in the community of Christ there is no uniformity; there is plurality. The age-old basis for social life was that "like draws to like" and "dog doesn't eat dog," and that principle still seems normal today; but it does not apply in the charismatic community. Here it is rather that the differences are drawn in: "All that are sundered come back to each other, and there is peace in the midst of strife."[20] According to Jesus' Sermon on the Mount, Christian ethics is not an "ethics based on reciprocity," but an ethics of prevenience, which runs ahead to meet the other.

3. The living energies of God's Spirit are not supernatural endowments "from heaven." According to Hebrews 6:5 they are "the powers of the world to come," that is to say they are eschatological anticipations. In them God's future is already powerful in the present time of human beings, because the risen Christ, as the first fruits from the dead, has become "the leader of life." The powers of the future world in their whole breadth and depth meet the powers and powerlessnesses of this world, and awaken them to eternal life. But if the charismata are powers of the "future world," we can conclude that the "future world" is a charismatic world through and through, with an overflow of multifarious vital energies and protean forms of life. If the future world is a whole "world," then it also includes nature as we know it on earth, and the breadth of the cosmos. Hildegard of

19. E. Moltmann-Wendel, *Wenn Gott und Körper sich begegnen,* Gütersloh, 1988.
20. F. Hölderlin, *Hyperion* in *Werke II,* ed. E. Staiger, Zürich, 1944, p. 171.

Bingen called this the springtime of eternal life.[21] The earth will awaken to its true fullness of life.

6. A Postscript: Science and the Hermeneutics of Nature

As John Polkinghorne has explained, the modern sciences have emerged out of the liberation from metaphysical values and interpretations. What is investigated, measured, and described is fact. Nature is no longer read as a world of signs, in order to grasp its significance. Our knowledge of the data, for example, in genetic engineering, doubles every five years. But do we also understand what we know?[22]

Let us take an example: two years ago Craig Venter investigated his own genome completely, and published the result. It was reproduced in major newspapers. But do we now know who Craig Venter is? From his genome we do not even know his name. When I met him in Taiwan, person to person, not only genome to genome, he told me how the Vietnam war had changed his life. That could not be seen from his genome. By this I mean that the data, numbers, and images of exact research await interpretation.

Without what Jakob von Uexküll called a "doctrine of meaning" we do not understand what we know. A computer can store all the data known to us, but it cannot interpret them because it only stores them; it doesn't understand them. And at bottom, in the sciences we do not merely want to discern and know what is; we also want to understand what it means. At the end of the nineteenth century, the German philosopher Wilhelm Dilthey made the following distinction: the sciences explain, the humanities understand. But how can I explain something I have not understood? Knowing in the full sense of the word implies understanding. I understand something when I don't just know what it is, but also what it means for me, and how I should adapt to it.

The environmental researcher Jakob von Uexküll perceived the inter-

---

21. Hildegard von Bingen, *Lieder nach den Handschriften,* ed. Pudentiana Barth, Immaculata Ritscher, and J. Schmid-Gurg, Salzburg, 1969, p. 228: *Spiritus Sanctus vivificans vita, movens omnia, et radix est in omni creatura, ac omnia de immunditia abluit, tergens crimina, ac ungit vulnera, et sic est fulgens ac laudabilis vita, suseitans et resuseitans omnia.*

22. For more detail see J. Moltmann, *Sun of Righteousness Arise! God's Future for Humanity and the Earth,* trans. M. Kohl, Minneapolis: Fortress Press; London: SCM Press, 2010, ch. 16: *Natural Science and the Hermeneutics of Nature.*

action between knowing and reacting — between "noting" and "acting" as he called it — in the field of animal environment. When we investigate our human environment, we are in a similar circle of interaction. We investigate the sign cosmos of nature, and try to understand its meanings for us.

Let us take as an example the sign language of our own bodies. We recognize inner illnesses from their outward symptoms. These signs must not merely be measured and registered; they must also be interpreted. That finds expression in the diagnosis. If we have understood the symptoms correctly, the therapy can begin. And with that the hermeneutical circle of knowing and acting is closed.

But through the sciences, we perceive today much more than humanity needs to know in order to survive. John Polkinghome has pointed this out. We know the world, not just our human environment. But do we then understand "the world"? Natural theology interprets the world and the history of nature *sub specie aeternitatis.* Christian theology starts from the presence of God in Christ in order to understand the history of the world in the light of God's future. Theological interpretations do not have their place in the sciences; their place is in the hermeneutics of nature, or in the metaphysics of the science of physics. They read "the book of nature" in the light of the book of God's promises. But their presupposition and their confidence is "the readability of the world," to cite the title of one of Hans Blumenberg's books.

When genetic researchers want to "explain" what they know, in their accounts they like to draw on the metaphors of language, books, and libraries, and to talk about "the book of life." But of what use is the syntax of life if we do not know its semantics? By that I mean that no science can dispense with a hermeneutics of nature. The Christian theology of the history of nature is not the only hermeneutics of nature, but this is its useful sphere, and perhaps we must with our understanding first draw in the mass of the knowledge available to us.

The Spirit or/and Spirits in Creation? Recalling the Seventh Assembly of the World Council of Churches in Canberra

Vladimir Shmaliy

1. Why the Canberra Assembly?

The Seventh Assembly of the World Council of Churches took place from February 7 to 20, 1991, in Canberra, Australia, under the theme: "Come, Holy Spirit — Renew the Whole Creation."

The choice of pneumatology and, at the same time, creation as the theme of the WCC Assembly was very important. This theme crowned the most interesting and vivid ideas and achievements of 20th-century theological thought.

Taking up the theme of the Holy Spirit means none other than an attempt of the World Council of Churches to address the theme of the Holy Trinity.

The fact that the World Council of Churches addressed the theme of triadology was the fruit of serious efforts made by many prominent theologians of the 20th century.[1] A special emphasis placed in these efforts on the significance of the *hypostasis* of the Holy Spirit in the Holy Trinity made it possible to overcome the so-called 'Christomonism' or, rather, accentuated Christocentrism:

> In the West we think essentially in Christological categories, with the Holy Spirit as extra, an addendum, a false window to give symmetry and balance to theological design. We build up our large theological constructs in constitutive Christological categories, and then, in a second,

1. B. Bobrinskoy, *Le mystère de la Trinité, cours de théologie orthodoxe,* Paris, 1986; K. Rahner, *The Trinity,* New York, 1974; R. W. Jenson, *The Triune Identity,* Philadelphia, 1982.

non-constitutive moment, we decorate the already constructed system with pneumatological baubles, a little spirit tinsel.[2]

Christomonism seems to be a consequence of the *Filioque* insertion into the creed and the ensuing theological understanding since, as the Orthodox have repeatedly insisted, *Filioque* implies that the Father and the Son are ranked higher in the Trinity than the Holy Spirit.

The rethinking of the significance of the doctrine of the Holy Trinity and a return to the sensible triadology and hence pneumatology have important consequences for ecclesiology.

> In Trinitarian theology the Holy Spirit, although inseparably united to Jesus Christ, is not subsumed under him. On the contrary, there is a conscious effort to emphasize its distinctive role as it relates to Jesus Christ within God's salvific economy. Thus there is a conscious effort to develop a Trinitarian theology of the Holy Spirit with significant consequences for the development of an ecumenical ecclesiology.[3]

Of importance to ecclesiology and its ecumenical prospects is also the rethinking of the notion of *koinonia* of the Persons of the Holy Trinity as a paradigm for the existence of the Church. For just as the absoluteness of the divine nature of each of the Persons of the Trinity, so in the Church each local church is the Church in the full sense of the word, not belittled in its dignity by the existence of other local churches. The same concept of *koinonia* opens up the door for rethinking the nature of relations between the divided Christian communities. An alternative to the affirmation that for the sake of Christian unity all the divided communities should "relativize" themselves and consider themselves to be "parts" of united "Christianity" can be found in the assumption that divided churches can coexist in the ecumenical discourse, each continuing to regard itself as the Church in the full measure.

2. The Holy Spirit in Creation

The theme of the attitude of the Holy Spirit to creation was an essential element of the WCC Canberra Assembly. Jürgen Moltmann, in his article in

2. K. McDonnell, *The Determinate Doctrine of the Holy Spirit,* in Theology Today, No. 39, 1982.

3. E. Clapsis, *The Holy Spirit in the Church,* The Ecumenical Review, Vol. 41, No. 3, July 1989.

anticipation of the Assembly, gives this description to the shift that occurred in the theological thought:

> As Christians see it, creation is a Trinitarian process: God the Father creates through the Son in the power of the Holy Spirit. All things are therefore created "of God," formed "through God" and exist "in God." . . . Western church tradition has for long stressed only the first aspect, in order to distinguish God the Creator from the world as God's creation and to emphasize God's transcendence. In so doing it has robbed nature of its divine mystery and abandoned it to desacralization through secularization. We therefore now have to rediscover the immanence of the Creator in creation, in order to bring the whole creation into awe of the Creator. This can best be helped forward by the Christological concept of creation through the word of God and the pneumatological understanding of creation in the Spirit of God.[4]

This vision was developed in the statements of the Assembly participants and in the Assembly final documents. Thus, the report of the Assembly Section I, in particular, stated that the emphasis on the transcendence of God in relation to creation was to a great extent a source of practices leading to the relentless exploitation of creation:

> Many streams of the tradition have misunderstood dominion (Gen. 1:28) as exploitation and God's transcendence as absence. The more theology stressed only God's absolute transcendence and distance from the material sphere, the more the earth was viewed as a mere object of human exploitation and "unspiritual" reality.[5]

Placing an emphasis on the presence of the Holy Spirit in creation, the Assembly repeatedly pointed to the need for reorientation from one-sided theological anthropocentrism to a "theology of life" in which the human being is viewed as an integral part of creation.[6]

In the light of the reviewed presence of the Holy Spirit in the created

---

4. J. Moltmann, *The Scope of Renewal in the Spirit,* The Ecumenical Review, Vol. 41, No. 2, April 1990, p. 100.

5. Report of section I, in *Signs of the Spirit. Official Report of the Seventh Assembly,* WCC Publications, Geneva, 1991, p. 57.

6. Report of the Assembly, *Signs of the Spirit. Official Report of the Seventh Assembly,* WCC Publications, Geneva, 1991, p. 256.

world, the Assembly calls Christians and the entire humanity to treat the whole creation with reverence and responsibility.

> As we reflect on the doctrine of creation and affirm the Holy Spirit as the One who energizes the whole creation, we rediscover the radical interdependence of human beings and the rest of nature. . . . Humankind is not the owner of creation. It is part of it. Nature is precious, not only because of its instrumental service to humankind but also because of its reflection of God's glory. . . . The awareness that all creation is God's creation must transform our attitudes towards it. We do not contemplate it from outside it; we are part of it. We do not seek new ways to exploit it; we seek new ways to relate to it in an attitude of caring respect.[7]

This attitude is quite consonant with the thinking of the Orthodox participants in the Assembly:

> In invoking the Holy Spirit, we do not shake off our shoulders our own responsibility as human beings. The first thing, therefore, that we ask of the Holy Spirit is to create in us a state of true and genuine repentance, a metanoia, which means a reversal of our ways and attitudes so that they may be turned from self-interest and egocentrism to true love, concern and care for the others and for all of God's creation. Without this repentance God cannot intervene, for He respects human freedom and wishes to cooperate with the human being (in synergy).[8]

3. Apprehension of a Misbalance

At the same time the articulation of the role of the Holy Spirit in creation provoked fears on the part of some theologians, afraid that the new development in theological thought would bring in what they believed to be a new disbalance:

> A temptation exists to emphasize the role of the Spirit in such a way as to separate him from the work of Christ and consequently from the tri-unity

7. Report of the General Secretary, *World Council of Churches. Signs of the Spirit. Official Report of the Seventh Assembly,* WCC Publications, Geneva, 1991, pp. 152-153.

8. *Come, Holy Spirit — Renew the Whole Creation: An Orthodox Approach,* Report of the Eastern Orthodox and Oriental Orthodox Consultation, Crete, Greece, 1989. Quoted in *Resources for sections. The theme, subthemes and issues,* World Council of Churches Seventh Assembly, Geneva, 1990, p. 15.

of the Godhead. Just as earlier generations risked neglecting the Spirit with their unique stress on "Christology," in the present day the danger is that a renewed awareness of the presence and power of the Spirit, within the church and the world as a whole, will lead to a pneumatology devoid of a Christological foundation. . . .[9]

Lukas Vischer, in his article devoted to the Canberra Assembly, warns against the danger of viewing the Holy Spirit in isolation from Christ:

> The power of the Holy Spirit is not independent of Jesus Christ. The Holy Spirit effects and develops the reconciliation brought by Jesus Christ. . . . The Holy Spirit has always been a dangerous subject. Whenever the Spirit is not understood in strictly Trinitarian terms he can be made the receptacle of all kinds of contents which are alien to the gospel. Here the Spirit is used to justify the status quo; there the Spirit is identified with inspirations, dreams or visions or other liberating experiences of one kind or another. The step from Holy Spirit to the spirit of the times has never been a long one. The action of the Spirit does indeed go far beyond what is generally accepted in the churches today; but the Spirit never brings to life anything other than God's love which lived among us in Jesus Christ.[10]

Father John Breck, too, insists on the need for a solid Trinitarian foundation for the description of the work of the Holy Spirit in creation:

> (In the invocation, "Come, Holy Spirit — Renew the Whole Creation") the Trinitarian aspect of the prayer is fundamental. . . . If the Spirit is viewed as other than the Spirit of God and Spirit of Christ, personally distinct from the Father and the Son yet essentially united with them, then we do violence to God's self-revelation and offer our invocation to a "different spirit," a "spirit of error" (2 Cor 11:4; 1 John 4:6). . . . The Spirit . . . is not some independent, autonomous charismatic power, nor is his sanctifying and deifying work the product of his will alone, acting upon its own authority. His will and operation are one with the will and operation of the Father and the Son.[11]

---

9. J. Breck, *The Lord is the Spirit. An Essay in Christological Pneumatology,* The Ecumenical Review, Vol. 41, No. 2, April 1990, p. 114.

10. L. Vischer, "Giver of Life — Sustain your Creation!" The Ecumenical Review, Vol. 41, No. 2, April 1990, p. 147.

11. J. Breck, *The Lord is the Spirit . . .* , p. 115.

The participants in the consultation of Orthodox and Oriental Churches, which was held from November 25 to December 4, 1989, in Crete to consider the Assembly theme, spoke out for the Trinitarian context of pneumatology with the same certainty.[12]

4. The Development of the Theme: Discerning the Holy Spirit Working Outside Christian Communities

Having discovered anew for themselves the presence and work of the Holy Spirit in creation, many participants in the Assembly were thrilled to develop this theme, taking it beyond Christian communities. The Assembly went on to fix its attention on the question of the presence of the Holy Spirit in cultures, non-Christian religions, and ideologies and the ensuing steps.

> The Holy Spirit is at work among all peoples and faiths, and throughout the universe. With the sovereign freedom which belongs to God the Wind blows wherever it wants.[13]

> Surely the Spirit blows where it wills. We hope that the WCC as a whole will join our plea to stand in its refreshing breezes, even as we carry on the necessary task of discerning together the spirits to see if they are of God. There are new perspectives and new partners in today's world. We cannot turn our back on them.[14]

This enthusiasm was cautiously supported by the WCC General Secretary as well:

> We have gone far in dialogue with friends of other religious convictions, but now, in the perspective of the Spirit, could we not discern signs of the Spirit's actions in other people's religious experience?[15]

The theme of the inculturation of Christian faith in different religious contexts was most vividly and provocatively presented by Prof. Chung

12. *Orthodox Reflections on the Assembly theme,* The Ecumenical Review, Vol. 42, Nos. 3-4, July-October 1990, p. 302.

13. Report of section IV, *Signs of the Spirit. Official Report of the Seventh Assembly,* WCC Publications, Geneva, 1991, p. 116.

14. Report of the Assembly, p. 241.

15. Report of the General Secretary. *World Council of Churches. Signs of the Spirit. Official Report of the Seventh Assembly,* WCC Publications, Geneva, 1991.

Hyuam Kyung, a Korean feminist theologian. Her presentation represented a dramatized action with the participation of sixteen Korean dancers and two Australian aborigines, accompanied by drumbeat and the sounds of other whirring and clanging instruments. In the beginning of her presentation Prof. Chung invoked spirits:

Come. The spirit of Hagar, Egyptian, black slave woman exploited and abandoned by Abraham and Sarah, the ancestors of our faith (Gen. 21:15-21).

Come. The spirit of Uriah, loyal soldier sent and killed in the battlefield by the great king David out of the king's greed for his wife, Bathsheba (2 Sam. 11:1-27).

Come. The spirit of Jephthah's daughter, the victim of her father's faith, offered as a burnt offering to God because he had won the war (Judg. 11:29-40).

Come. The spirit of male babies killed by the soldiers of king Herod upon Jesus' birth.

Come. The spirit of Joan of Arc, and of the many other women burnt at the "witch trials" throughout the medieval era.

Come. The spirit of the people who died during the crusades.

Come. The spirit of indigenous people of the earth, victims of genocide during the time of colonialism and the period of the great Christian mission to the pagan world.

Come. The spirit of Jewish people killed in the gas chambers during the holocaust.

Come. The spirit of people killed in Hiroshima and Nagasaki by atomic bombs.

Come. The spirit of Korean women in the Japanese "prostitution army" during the second world war, used and torn by violence-hungry soldiers.

Come. The spirit of Vietnamese people killed by napalm, Agent Orange, or hunger on the drifting boats.

Come. The spirit of Mahatma Gandhi, Steve Biko, Martin Luther King Jr., Malcolm X, Victor Jara, Oscar Romero and many unnamed women freedom fighters who died in the struggle for liberation of their people.

Come. The spirit of people killed in Bhopal and Chernobyl, and the spirit of jelly babies from the Pacific nuclear test zone.

Come. The spirit of people smashed by tanks in Kwangju, Tiananmen Square and Lithuania.

Come. The spirit of the Amazon rain forest now being murdered every day.

Come. The spirit of earth, air and water, raped, tortured and exploited by human greed for money.

Come. The spirit of soldiers, civilians and sea creatures now dying in the bloody war in the Gulf.

Come. The spirit of the Liberator, our brother Jesus, tortured and killed on the cross.

After setting fire to this list and letting the ashes drift to the ceiling, Prof. Chung spoke of Korea as a land of "spirits full of Han." Han refers to the "grudge," the anguished cry, of those who have died with their misery unappeased. "These Han-ridden spirits in our people's history have been agents through whom the Holy Spirit has spoken of her compassion and wisdom for life. Without hearing the cries of these spirits," she continued, "we cannot hear the voice of the Holy Spirit. I hope the presence of all our ancestors' spirits here with us shall not make you uncomfortable. For us they are the icons of the Holy Spirit. . . ."

Prof. Chung finished her presentation with an image of the Holy Spirit which comes from the image of Kwan In.

She is venerated as the goddess of compassion and wisdom by East Asian women's popular religiosity. She is a bodhisattva, enlightened being. She can go into nirvana any time she wants to, but refuses to go into nirvana by herself. Her compassion for all suffering beings makes her stay in this world enabling other living beings to achieve enlightenment. Her compassionate wisdom heals all forms of life and empowers them to swim to the shore of nirvana. She waits and waits until the whole universe, people, trees, birds, mountains, air, water, become enlightened. They can then go to nirvana together where they can live collectively in eternal wisdom and compassion. Perhaps this might also be a feminine image of the Christ who is the first-born among us, one who goes before and brings others with her. . . . Wild wind of the Holy Spirit, blow to us. Let us welcome her, letting ourselves go in her wild rhythm of life. Come Holy Spirit, Renew the Whole Creation. Amen![16]

Prof. Chung's presentation provoked an ambiguous reaction among the

---

16. C. H. Kyung, *Come Holy Spirit — Renew the Whole Creation,* in Signs of the Spirit, Official Report of the Seventh Assembly, WCC Publications, Geneva, 1991, pp. 37-47.

Assembly participants. Some delegates deemed it possible to view this expression of Christian faith in images of Korean traditional heathen religiosity as quite acceptable, believing that Christianity embodied in a particular culture is always more or less "paganized" or, to put it better, "inculturated."

An example of this kind of reaction is given by Rev. Tissa Balasuriya written in the wake of the Assembly:

> The traditional or classical presentation of the doctrine of the Holy Spirit in the church is also in categories that are derived from "pagan" philosophies. On the one hand they say God is a mystery, but on the other they claim to know that the Holy Spirit is of the same "substance" as the Father and the Son. It is true that this is a defined doctrine of the church; but that does not prevent it from being of "pagan" origin. . . . It could be justly argued that when the ancients have recourse to their cultures to interpret the divine it is called theology; when persons of non-European cultures use their own concepts and images to speak of God, the theological establishment calls it "syncretism" and "paganization" of Christianity. A participant at the assembly asked whose paganism are we concerned about — that of the North or South, of the West or East?[17]

But even those who sympathized with Prof. Chung's presentation regarded it as syncretistic:

> As one who spent many years in the attempt to interpret Christian theology in the Hindu cultural context, I find myself sympathetic to the aim of Prof. Chung's presentation. . . . (But) . . . I was disturbed by the use of terms and names from the Korean spirit-world — Han and Kwan In — in what seems to be an implied identification with the Holy Spirit. . . . In India, for example, most Christians would agree that one can use terms like Isvara or even Bhagavan for God: but proper names like Krishna or Shiva would be avoided, because they carry with them a burden of concepts which may be difficult to reconcile with Christian faith, and will at the best create confusion in people's minds. . . . Syncretism — that effort to live and witness "among the Cretans" as the word literally implies — is quite legitimate so long as it is centred on Christology and the Trinity. But if the centre moves from that point,

17. T. Balasuriya, *Liberation of the Holy Spirit*, The Ecumenical Review, Vol. 43, No. 2, April 1991, pp. 202-203.

so that the enterprise becomes the justification of another culture (whether Korean, Hindu, Marxist, capitalist or humanist) then syncretism becomes dangerous and is to be rejected.[18]

Serious criticism of both the presentation and the tendency of some Assembly participants to give too broad an interpretation to the term "inculturation" was voiced by the Orthodox participants in the Assembly. Prof. Stanley Harakas, discussing inculturation as an embodiment of the Divine Revelation in a particular culture, insisted that it was impossible and inadmissible to relativize the historical Revelation given in concrete cultural and historical forms:

> Prof. Chung Hyun Kyung's dramatic presentation of the theme was a powerful articulation of the striving of peoples to affirm the incarnational dynamic of the Christian message. But for many, it also showed how dangerous the effort can be. Seeking to incarnate the gospel in culture can slip into the substitution of the gospel by culture. . . . The Orthodox felt that by shifting from the incarnation of the Christian message in a particular culture to the making of a particular culture a source of redemptive revelation, an important line had been crossed. . . . To equate the Christian message with every other religious affirmation and tradition is unacceptable. . . . This theology, in effect, negates the uniqueness and the necessity of the person of the divine/human Jesus Christ and his redemptive work for the world. It confuses all the "spirits" of this world with the "Holy Spirit." This confusion is not new. The scriptures describe similar confusions and reject them. Not all spirits are good. There are "demonic spirits" (Rev. 16:14). The Lord Jesus cast them out (Matt. 8:16) and he gave the disciples "authority over unclean spirits" (Mark 6:7). One of the gifts of the Holy Spirit is "the ability to distinguish between spirits" (1 Cor. 12:10). The early church was instructed, precisely, not to "believe every spirit," but "to test the spirits to see whether they are of God" (1 John 4:1). If the early church were to have followed this syncretistic approach, Apollo and Zeus and Minerva and Aphrodite would also have been accepted as Christian, and the blood of the martyrs would have been poured out for no purpose. The martyrs died precisely because they saw that offering just a little incense to the false gods of Rome was idolatry.[19]

18. R. Boyd, *"Come, Holy Spirit!" And We Really Mean "Come!"* The Ecumenical Review, Vol. 43, No. 2, April 1991, p. 181.

19. S. Harakas, *Must God Remain Greek,* pp. 194-199.

Critical response of the Orthodox participants in the Assembly to the theme of relations with other religions and the inculturation of Christian message was also given in the statement "Reflections of Orthodox Participants" presented to one of the concluding plenary sessions of the Assembly:

> It is with alarm that the Orthodox have heard some presentations on the theme of this assembly . . . they observe that some people tend to affirm with very great ease the presence of the Holy Spirit in many movements and developments without discernment. The Orthodox wish to stress the factor of sin and error which exists in every human action, and separate the Holy Spirit from these. We must guard against a tendency to substitute a "private" spirit, the spirit of the world or other spirits for the Holy Spirit who proceeds from the Father and rests in the Son. . . .[20]

It is noteworthy that the concern of the Orthodox was reflected in the statement "Evangelical Perspectives from Canberra" and in the Assembly Report:

> Spirits must be discerned. Not every spirit is of the Holy Spirit. The prime criterion for discerning the Holy Spirit is that the Holy Spirit is the Spirit of Christ; it points to the cross and resurrection and witnesses to the Lordship of Christ. The biblical list of "fruits" of the Spirit, including love, joy and peace, is another criterion to be applied (Gal. 5:22). These criteria should be remembered in our encounters with the often-profound spirituality of other religions.[21]

5. On Discerning Spirits

Thus the problem of discerning spirits became one of the most acute and key ones at the Assembly. In this process the Orthodox have encountered a serious problem. The Orthodox theology is strongly committed to its spiritual ascetic heritage as an integral element of the entire Orthodox ethos.

In the Orthodox spiritual-ascetic tradition, the theme of discerning spirits has been developed mostly in the context of struggle with demons.

---

20. Reflections of Orthodox Participants, *Come Holy Spirit — Renew the Whole Creation, Signs of the Spirit. Official Report of the Seventh Assembly,* WCC Publications, Geneva, 1991, pp. 280-281.

21. Report of the Assembly, *Come Holy Spirit — Renew the Whole Creation, Signs of the Spirit. Official Report of the Seventh Assembly,* WCC Publications, Geneva, 1991, p. 256.

That is, references to the gift of discerning spirits imply primarily the ability of an ascetic to see the machinations of demons seeking to present themselves as angels of light, saints, or God Himself and the ability to distinguish their actions from the work of the Holy Spirit.

St. Anthony the Great was an example of such an ascetic who could discern spirits.

> We have terrible and crafty foes — the evil spirits — and against them we wrestle, as the Apostle said . . . (Ephesians 6:12). Great is their number in the air around us, and they are not far from us. . . . When, therefore, they (evil spirits) come by night to you and wish to tell the future, or say, "we are the angels," give no heed, for they lie. . . . The vision of the holy ones is not fraught with distraction. . . . But it comes so quietly and gently that immediately joy, gladness and courage arise in the soul. For the Lord who is our joy is with them, and the power of God the Father. . . . But the inroad and the display of the evil spirits is fraught with confusion. . . . From which arise fear in the heart, tumult and confusion of thought, dejection, hatred towards them who live a life of discipline, indifference, grief, remembrance of kinsfolk and fear of death, and finally desire of evil things, disregard of virtue and unsettled habits . . . we ought always to pray . . . that we may receive the gift of discerning spirits; that, as it is written in 1 John 4:1, we may not believe every spirit.[22]

The Orthodox have inherited from ascetic fathers this conviction that demons often assume the guise of goodness and light. Besides, neither Holy Scriptures nor the patristic tradition give any reason to see anything positive in the pagan religious cults, much less the work of the Holy Spirit. Heathen gods are viewed at best as non-existent and at worst as demons.[23]

Natural elements are also poisoned by demonic forces. Thus, St. Athanasius the Great speaks of air devils driven away by the Cross of Christ.

> Well, by what other kind of death could this have come to pass, than by one which took place in the air, I mean the cross? For only he that is perfected on the cross dies in the air. Whence it was quite fitting that the Lord suffered this death. For thus being lifted up He cleared the air of the malignity both of the devil and of demons of all kinds.[24]

22. *Vita Antonii* 21, 35-38.
23. 1 Cor 10:20, Justin *Apol* 1.5, Athenagoras *Supplicatio* 26.1-5, Theophilus *Ad Autolicum* 1.10, Tatian *Oratio ad Graecos* 16-19, Tertullian *Apol.* 20.
24. *De incarnatione Verbi,* 25.

The prayer for the blessing and consecration of water in the Baptismal rite also refers to a presence of demons in it:

> We pray Thee, O God, that . . . no demon of darkness may conceal himself in this water; and that no evil spirit . . . may descend into it with him who is about to be baptized.[25]

So the very tradition leads to the guarded Orthodox attitude not only to all kinds of non-church spirituality but also to extraordinary forms of spiritual exaltation in Orthodoxy itself, which is seen as one form of being captured by demons. It is this tradition of guarded attitude to extra-ecclesial spirituality that is one of the reasons for the complex Orthodox attitude to the non-Orthodox, to the ecumenical movement, and, the more so, to people of other faiths.

There is a vivid example of this Orthodox attitude to the ecumenical movements, expressed by Metropolitan Vitaly (late Primate of the Russian Orthodox Church outside Russia):

> There is God, there is His One, only Holy, Apostolic Church, and there is the whole human race, all called to God through His holy Church. All other religions, so-called Christian, monotheistic or pagan, all without the slightest exception, whether it be Catholicism, Protestantism, Islam or Buddhism, all are obstacles placed by the devil as his traps between the Church of Christ and the whole human race.[26]

Thus the Orthodox theology has to respond to challenges associated with the dialogue with a reality external to the Church on the one hand and linked with isolationism and apprehensions on the other.

There are at least four spheres in the Orthodox thought in which the paradigm of Orthodox attitude to a reality external to the Church is being changed. These are:

(1) the sphere of dialogue with the non-Orthodox,
(2) mission,
(3) religious philosophy, and
(4) dialogue with science.

---

25. Baptismal rite, quoted in A. Schmemann, *Of Water and Spirit*, SVS 1974, p. 48.

26. Archbishop Vitaly of Montreal and Canada, *A Report to the Sobor of Bishops of the Russian Orthodox Church Outside of Russia*, Orthodox Life (Jordanville, N.Y.), July-August 1969.

As far as the first sphere is concerned, I would refer to the long-standing experience of the Orthodox participation in the ecumenical movement, official dialogues, and non-official contacts with the non-Orthodox. Certainly, this experience is very important.

The second sphere is also extremely important. It is in this sphere that Orthodox missionaries had to deal with heathen cults of the peoples they enlightened, to find various forms of linguistic and behavioral compromise, and to identify positive things in the culture of a people that could be used in the process of the inculturation of the Gospel. A vivid and comparatively recent example of such a missionary is St. Innocent of Moscow (Veniaminov), the enlightener of the Aleuts.

> In his attitude to the native peoples to whom he preached, whether the Aleuts or the Yakuts, he showed a remarkable breadth of vision, and he was always ready to acknowledge the positive elements acceptable to Christianity that were to be found in their customs and their worldview. "I am come not to destroy but to fulfill" (Matt. 5:17), said Jesus Christ, and Innocent agrees with Him. He found innumerable intimations of Christianity in the native cultures of Alaska and Siberia. Significantly, this was emphasized by the monastery of Valaam in the commemorative volume that it issued in 1894, on the occasion of the centenary of the mission sent from Valaam to Alaska in 1794. Appealing to Veniaminov's classic work of ethnography, *Notes on the Unalaska District,* the monks of Valaam point out that he discerned, in the moral concepts of the pre-Christian Aleuts, "elevated ideas . . . in accordance with God's Holy Revelations," and that he recognized in their traditional beliefs "the spark of God's truth." Appropriately the monks go on to quote Justin Martyr, who speaks of a belief in God that is "inborn in the nature of humankind" (2 Apology 6:3).[27]

The subject of special interest here is the effort to adapt the missionary methodology of St. Innocent to the modern analysis of the relation between Orthodoxy and Shamanism in Korea done by S. A. Mousalimas:

> Three levels of activity were analyzed in Veniaminov's affirmative pastoral work:

27. Rt. Rev. Dr. Kallistos Ware, Bishop of Diokleia, *"The Light that Enlightens Everyone": The Knowledge of God Among Non-Christians According to the Greek Fathers and St. Innocent,* The Greek Orthodox Theological Review, Vol. 44, Nos. 1-4, 1999, p. 558.

Level 1: At the initial level we find the incorporation of theology, liturgy and holy scripture into the cultures of peoples of Northeast Asia and the Arctic with steadfast fidelity to the prototypes. . . .

Level 2: At the next level, we discern whole areas within the ancestral cultures that are entirely compatible with, or neutral with regard to, the Christian faith and practices. These whole areas are maintained, transformed and even strengthened as the incorporation of Orthodoxy takes place.

Level 3: At the final level, we distinguish specific elements that are incompatible . . . the process about them may involve their reorientation more so than their wholesale suppression.

Throughout these three levels, within Veniaminov's single integrated ministry, we find a mainly affirmative and tolerant attitude without it being naive; and we find a very strongly dedicated activity without it becoming fanatic. As a result, we recognize the possibility, and indeed we see the reality, of a continuity and transformation of the ancestral cultures. As a result, the nations remain integral and distinct while unified through their essential participation in the shared faith and practices.[28]

The third sphere. Noteworthy here are the works of Archpriest Sergius Bulgakov who asserted the spiritual value of heathenism and heathen devotion and saw a special religious process in heathenism preparing to embrace the Word of God.

Revelation exists also outside of Revelation, for the Spirit of God "bloweth where it listeth." In conformity with the spiritual maturity, particular gifts, and historical destinies of paganism, the knowledge of God is realized in it in multiple and manifold ways; and this knowledge is possible only because the Holy Spirit "bloweth" also in the unrevealed (and in this sense) "natural" religions. These religions are distinguished by a special mode of knowledge, by their own gift, by a language proper to this natural Pentecost. When we are astonished by and — what is more important — are instructed by this natural revelation of different nations in the great historical religions, we directly experience this breath of the Spirit of God; and we should not shy away from this expe-

---

28. S. A. Mousalimas, *Considerations regarding Relationships between Orthodoxy and Shamanism in Korea*, in *Christianity and Shamanism: Proceedings of the First Seoul International Consultation* (25-30 June 2000, Seoul, Korea), ed. S. A. Mousalimas, online February 2001, http://www.OxfordU.net/seoul/chapter3/.

rience because of an unjustified fear that the uniqueness and truthfulness of our Revelation will be shaken. On the contrary, one should rejoice in the gifts of the Spirit of God bestowed upon these "prophets" as well, who came "from the river" like Balaam, or upon the "wise men from the east," who came to worship Christ. One should rejoice in this inexhaustible love for God and faith in Him, which does not remain unanswered, for "God is no respecter of persons, but in every nation he that feareth him, and worketh righteousness, is accepted with him" (Acts 10:34-35).[29]

And, finally, dialogue with science. It appears to be complicated and at the same time the most promising sphere. Today science itself has to overcome the grossly positivistic, scientistic, and reductionistic paradigm of the 19th century. There are efforts to overcome "objectivism" with its accent on removing from interpretation and description all that pertains to the subject and to the means of activity. Today's science has come to increasingly take into account the knowledge of an object as correlated not only with means but also value-targeted structures of activity and a broader context of culture. It is in a new paradigm of scientific study emerging today that a creative dialogue is possible between science and religion about the mystery of life and its source — the Holy Spirit.

29. S. Bulgakov; translated by B. Jakim, *The Comforter*, Eerdmans Publishing, 2004, p. 239.

How Exactly Is Spirit Present in Creation? The Hesychast Reception of Natural Theology and Its Modern Implications

Sergey Horujy

Natural theology (NT) was always one of the main Christian approaches to all problems concerning the working of the Spirit in creation. The term *theologia naturalis* originating in the Stoics and St. Augustine (in *De civ. Dei*) meant traditionally the theological discourse based on the thesis that the knowledge of the created world, natural phenomena, and laws of nature includes religious content and enables one to draw conclusions about God in His actions and His relation to the world. It is this approach that usually provided the basis for Christian understanding of the Universe, the relation of Christian theology and science, the treatment of ecological problems, etc. However, its history in the East and West of Christianity shows considerable distinctions. For the most part, its ideas were developed in the West (with the important exception of Pseudo-Dionysius) and had there much more influence, while its reception in Orthodoxy was usually more reserved. In this text, I focus mainly on the reception of NT in the Orthodox tradition of hesychasm, chiefly, in the theology of St. Gregory Palamas. I discuss the roots of the rather skeptical and critical character of this reception and try to show that the tradition in question developed a different approach to the problems of NT and the big theme of the Holy Spirit in creation. The special interest in this tradition is justified by the fact that in recent decades it was widely recognized as the core of Orthodox spirituality. Hesychasm is the school that reproduces the authentic experience of communion with Christ and union with Divine energies, and the acquisition of such experience is the aim of Christian life, in the Orthodox view.

1. Natural Theology in Orthodox Patristic and Ascetic Discourse

Be it in Western or Eastern Christian thought, the status of NT is ensured by scriptural foundations, the core of which includes one Old Testament text: *For by the greatness and beauty of the creatures proportionably the maker of them is seen* (Wisd. 13:5), and one New Testament one: *The invisible things of him from the creation of the world are clearly seen, being understood by the things that are made, [even] his eternal power and Godhead* (Rom 1:20). There are liturgical foundations as well such as the prayer to the Holy Spirit saying: ". . . the Spirit of Truth . . . that is present everywhere and fills everything." However, the immediate origins of NT are in Greek philosophy. Undoubtedly, NT belongs to those numerous elements of Christian theology that came from Greek thought and then went through the intricate process of Christianization and integration into the Christian mode of thought. This mode formed in the epoch of the Councils had two basic distinctions from the Greek mode, Person (conceived as Divine Hypostasis) and dogma. But NT was developed and took roots in Christian thought as early as in the pre-Nicaean period when Christianization was still superficial. The theses of NT can be found in the majority of pre-Nicaean theologians, and first of all in Clement of Alexandria and Origen. In Origen, the foundations of NT are brought to a very logical and systematic form. His cosmology is typical for Late Antiquity being based on the ideas of the order and law-governed nature of the world. These ideas already include the principle of hierarchy that will play such a prominent role in the future. Christianization means here essentially that the Aristotelian Prime Mover is replaced by the biblical God Creator, and this replacement implies the self-evident Christian version of Hellenic NT: "Can anything be more pernicious than contemplating the ordered structure of the world and not to think about the Creator of this world?" (*Contra Celsum,* 4). This version was adopted and developed by Pseudo-Dionysius and then accepted basically in the West. In comparison with Origen, Dionysius accentuates more strongly the hierarchical principle, turning it into the universal structural paradigm of all reality, and he formulates more precisely the basic postulate of NT: "Knowledge of existing things must make true philosophers to ascend to Him Who is the Cause of both the things and their knowledge" (Epistle 7, To Polycarp the hierarch).

NT in Western thought of the Modern Age is the direct development of Pseudo-Dionysius' position. With the progress of secularization, this thought advanced more and more to reunification with Greek philosophy.

As a consequence, in the dyad *Natural theology — Revealed theology* the second pole was more and more losing its importance and value, and the attitude of NT, i.e. the knowledge of God by means of secular science and natural reason, on the basis of general notions and logical syllogisms, was more and more accepted as self-consistent and self-sufficient. This process went through several stages. In the early modern period, Nicolas of Cusa developed panentheist ontology based on such Dionysian concepts as "world in God" and present in God images or prototypes *(paradeigmata)* of all things, and this ontology provided NT with solid ontological grounds. In the Enlightenment the prevalent position was deism which represents the relation of God to the world with the aid of the metaphor of the watchmaker and his product. At this stage NT becomes the principal content of theological discourse and the reduction of theology as such to NT is almost complete. But the course of things could not stop at this stage and in the end, with the completion of the secularization and coming of post-Christianity, in the mainstream of Western culture there comes the rejection of theological reason as such, and hence the rejection of NT as well. A new paradigm of NT has not been created so far and modern studies following the approach of NT (mainly attempts at theological interpretation of modern physical and cosmological conceptions) lack a common epistemological basis.

The history of NT in Orthodoxy is very different. Typical features of the Western and Eastern Christian cultures are such that the West cultivates the humanistic pathos of unlimited horizons of knowledge while the East concentrates on the necessity of the permanent inner work of the Christian, the work of metanoia and transformation of one's old self in striving toward union with Christ. Thus the principles of NT become subject to critical reflection already in the Cappadocian Fathers. The Cappadocians do not deny this way of knowledge of God, but they insist that it has inherent restrictions: it is incomplete and imperfect in both aspects of cognitive activity, i.e. in what can be cognized by the ways and means of NT, and how reliable and precise this knowledge can be. Both aspects are clearly seen in Gregory of Nyssa's words: "Looking at the beauty of the creation, we obtain the notion not of the essence, but only Wisdom of Him Who created everything wisely. . . . From the wisdom seen in the Universe one can see Him Who created everything only as guesswork. Similarly, in human works . . . one sees not the nature of the artist, but only the artistic knowledge that the artist put into his work."[1] This means that

---

1. St. Gregory of Nyssa, *On Blessednesses,* Moscow, 1997, pp. 88-89 (in Russian).

natural reason can cognize only the Wisdom of God, and only as guess-work. In the "Life of Moses" St. Gregory presents an even more skeptical view of the possibility for this reason to cognize God: he states that all the ideas and notions on God formed by reason acting on its own are nothing but idols that even Old Testament piety demands be destroyed. St. Gregory the Theologian always stressed that the Holy Trinity in all Its economy is inaccessible to all approaches of natural reason. Contrary to St. Augustine, he denied even the possibility of comparing or likening the Trinity to any created things and he considered only the "goodness of the Heavenly Father" as cognizable from created things.

We shall not discuss these conceptions since NT in the Cappadocians and other Eastern Church Fathers till St. John of Damascus is a well-studied subject. We only note that very often one particular conception of Greek patristics was interpreted as leading to the positions of NT: it is the conception of divine "logoses," *logoi,* present in creation. Indeed, if the *logoi* are rooted in Divine Essence, then our cognition of created things in their *logoi* would produce true knowledge of God. But, as Fr John Meyendorff shows, "a personal and dynamic understanding of God" in-herent in Byzantine thought implies the dynamic, or "energetic," under-standing of *logoi* as "energies" that "do not exist on their own."[2] Thus the conception of the *logoi* does not contradict the general skeptical reception of NT in Greek patristics. In the fundamental study by J. Pelikan,[3] this re-ception is characterized as a "metamorphosis" of the version of NT that existed in Greek philosophy. It can be added that this metamorphosis in-cludes basically reflection upon the limits of NT and giving to NT the sta-tus of a severely restricted cognitive paradigm.

The attitude of Orthodox ascetic tradition, or hesychasm, to NT is very little studied, however. One can think a priori that this tradition, be-ing practical, just did not produce any such attitude, but it is not so: in fact, the Orthodox reception of NT obtained considerable development in hesychasm, especially in the hesychast theology of St. Gregory Palamas (1296-1357). A critique of NT is Palamas' starting theme in his famous po-lemics with Barlaam of Calabria. For Palamas, Barlaam is an apologete of NT who asserts the unrestricted validity and value of "outside wisdom," or

2. Fr J. Meyendorff, *Introduction to the Study of Gregory Palamas,* St. Petersburg, 1997, p. 167 (in Russian).

3. J. Pelikan, *Christianity and Classical Culture. The Metamorphosis of Natural Theology in the Christian Encounter with Hellenism,* New Haven-London, 1993.

knowledge gained by "outside science." Following the Cappadocian Fathers, Palamas does not reject NT; but he presents a very critical estimate of it, reducing its possibilities to the extreme and stressing the deficiency of its fruits. NT can only "guess about God based on probabilistic reasoning," it provides utterly unreliable knowledge, and Palamas gives the precise verdict: "We forbid completely to expect any adequate knowledge of Divine subjects from outside science, since its teaching cannot give us anything reliable concerning God" (*Triads for the Defense of the Holy Hesychasts*, I.1, 12). What is more, in no way does Palamas confine himself to bare criticism. He points out what exactly NT lacks and why its cognition of God is just guesswork. Like other hesychast teachers, he often repeats a simple thesis, a truism for ascetic consciousness: "True knowledge, union with God and likeness to Him is achieved only through keeping to the commandments" (*Ib.*, II.3,75). What looks like a truism deserves the closest attention, however. Even if we don't know what "keeping to the commandments" means, we can see here a certain attitude to the cognition of God, or better, a certain conception of man's relation to God: we are told that for getting "true knowledge" of God *man must change himself.* True and not deficient cognition of God includes some *anthropological preconditions.*

This conclusion is of principal importance. Palamas' way of knowledge is an alternative to NT since NT means cognition which doesn't demand the change of cognizing subject. NT corresponds to the cognitive paradigm that dominated European thought during almost all its history and took its definitive form in Cartesian metaphysics as the "subject-object paradigm." In science (especially in natural sciences) it took still stronger roots than in metaphysics. In the 20th century it was rejected in philosophy (due to the processes of "overcoming metaphysics" and "death of subject"), but in scientific discourses it still continues to dominate, although some tendencies to the deconstruction of the subject-object opposition do exist at least since the discussions on the interpretation of quantum mechanics. As for the paradigm assuming the changing of the subject, it was recently studied in detail by M. Foucault. Tracing its history in the West, Foucault presents it as a sound alternative to the Cartesian subject-object paradigm that was undeservedly marginalized. Analyzing its structure, he defines the involved process of the change of the subject as "practice of the self," an anthropological practice in which man performs a transformation of himself directed to a certain goal. Thus, using Foucault's terms, we can say that the approach of NT is the (indirect and conditional) cognition of God in the Cartesian subject-object paradigm, while the approach of Orthodox ascetic thought is the direct cognition of God in the paradigm of practices of the self. This alternative paradigm was rather clearly described in hesychasm long before Foucault: in particular, Palamas, opposing it to NT, develops a full-fledged "doctrine of the two kinds of knowledge," as J. Meyendorff calls it. But hesychast practice of the self is not just another particular case of Foucault's concept. Let us describe it briefly.

2. The Hesychast Alternative to Natural Theology

The constitution of the alternative strategy starts with changing the perspective: the necessity of anthropological preconditions for the "true knowledge of God" being recognized, the consciousness focuses on these preconditions. Doing this, it has purely practical goals: to find how to meet them. How exactly should man change himself? Palamas writes only about "keeping to the commandments," but in the ascetic discourse this formula implies a complete way of life. In no way are Christ's commandments understood formally: on the contrary, their observance should direct man's consciousness and man as a whole to Christ. If the first commandment is interpreted as a precondition of knowledge of God, it adds to the cognitive attitude a very important moment: knowledge of God presupposes love for Him, and love, in its turn, presupposes striving for its object, for union with it. This striving is a deeply personal relation to God as a person, and actualization of such a relation is nothing but personal communion. Thus the cognitive attitude gets transformed and expanded: *knowledge of God is converted from the purely intellectual cognitive paradigm to the integral, holistic paradigm of love and communion.* Hence the roots of the insufficiency and deficiency of NT are revealed: "true knowledge," about which Palamas writes, is not knowledge *about* God, but knowledge *of* God as a living person that is obtained in the communion of love with Him. As for knowledge as cognitive activity, it is realized as an aspect of this communion inseparable from the whole and nourished by it. In contrast to this, NT is an isolated cognitive activity; accepting no preconditions, it disconnects itself from the economy of communion with God and tries to reach some conclusions on God by indirect ways, from knowledge of empiric phenomena. Thus, it is only some scraps of knowledge that such activity can get and they are, in addition, utterly unreliable.

Actualization of the paradigm of knowledge of God as communion with God demands the radical change of man and unfolds into a very specific practice of the self. There is a split, i.e. ontological distance, between man and God, and man must surmount this ontological split in his striving for union with God. Orthodox theology describes the surmounting as deification *(theosis)*, which means the complete union of all man's energies with Divine energies. Being an actual ontological transformation, theosis is an anthropological change of maximal, meta-anthropological scale. Orthodox ascesis identifies theosis as the final goal of its works, the spiritual state to which hesychast practice is directed. Thence the connection between "true knowledge of God" and hesychast practice is established. Hesychasm is recognized as the core of Orthodox spirituality exactly for the reason that its practice is devoted exclusively to the cultivation of communion with God, which ascends to theosis and includes knowledge of God. This connection implies also a special hesychast idea of what theology is. As seen by hesychasts, theology is not a theoretical discipline making syllogistic constructions on the basis of Scriptures and Church doctrine; it is a strictly experiential discipline that performs the direct transmission of the experience of communion with God by those who personally experienced it, i.e. ascetics reaching higher grades of spiritual ascent. "Theology is the firsthand account about that being into which man was introduced by the Holy Spirit."[4]

Clearly, hesychast practice is a practice of the self, but of a kind not described by Foucault and not considered possible by him. Here man's self-transformation is directed to a goal not belonging to the horizon of empiric being, i.e. a meta-empiric and meta-anthropological goal. Such a goal cannot be reached by man's own effort only. As higoumenos Sophrony says, it is by the action of the Holy Spirit that man is introduced into Divine being. Ontological transcending of man is performed by the grace of the Holy Spirit; it is performed, however, not without the participation of man's will and energies, but in accordance and collaboration or *synergy* with them. The transcending is the fruit of all the ascetic practice that represents a subtle spiritual-anthropological process having the form of a ladder ascending to theosis. The meta-empirical and meta-anthropological nature of theosis implies some specific features of this process, the main feature being the necessity of a rigorous method, or a complete "travel instruction" for the advancement to the goal. Since this goal is ontologically beyond-there and hence absent in our mode of being and the horizon of

4. A. Sophrony, *Starets Silouan*, Moscow, 1991, p. 153.

our consciousness, hesychast practice always risks substituting its goal and losing its way. To avoid this, it must create a complete set of rules which determine the organization, checking up, and interpretation of its experience. This set corresponds exactly to the Aristotelian notion of *organon*, and the formation of the complete organon of hesychast experience was an intricate anthropological work that took as long as 1,000 years, from the 4th to the 14th century. All the way of the ascension is structured into big blocks, each of which is devoted to a certain anthropological task: the initial block is concentrated on repentance (metanoia) and fighting the passions; the central one forms the union of the two key activities, attention and prayer (when they are joined together, their union produces the driving force for the ascension and leads to synergy, or the unlocking of human being to the contact with Divine energies); while in the concluding block, due to synergy, the first manifestations of actual transformation of human being appear (first of all, new perceptive modalities begin to form that are called "intellectual feelings," *noera aisthesis*). What is important for our theme is that all this anthropological self-transformation is not a natural process in a physical system. In this practice man realizes himself as a personality endowed with freedom and all the process follows the paradigm of personal communion representing an "ontological dialogue" between man and God. In the course of this dialogue, man in his self-transformation unlocks himself to his Interlocutor and advances to union with Him.

Now the distinctions between the "two kinds of knowledge" are seen clearly. In the hesychast view, God is not cognized as an object of study, but becomes known as a living Person, with Whom deepening communion of love springs up. Behind these distinctions of cognitive attitudes we discover essential anthropological distinctions concerning the paradigms of man's constitution. NT corresponds to the Western model of man as the subject of cognition who constitutes himself by actualizing his relation to the infinite Universe in cognizing activity (and discovering in the course of his cognition some arguments, never precise or conclusive enough, in favor of the existence of the Creator of the Universe, His wisdom and goodness). Hesychast knowledge of God corresponds to man who constitutes himself by actualizing his relation to God as Person in the practice of ontological transcending, developing as dialogue with Him, unlocking himself to Him and final complete union with His energies. In this ontological dialogue man is striving toward the horizon of personal being; and reaching union with it (in Christ's Hypostasis), he becomes himself a person (becomes hypostasized, in terms of patristic theology). The two kinds of (theological) knowledge are associated with two different types of philosophical vision of reality. Theology as NT is developed chiefly within the framework of a metaphysical vision of reality based on the oppositions of God and World, Reason and Nature, etc.; it is epistemologically correlative to philosophical discourse promoting speculative metaphysics, philosophy of nature, and theory of knowledge. Hesychast theology is developed within a Christocentric, anthropocentric, and personalist vision of reality; it is epistemologically correlative to philosophical discourse having as its core anthropology and philosophy of personality. From the viewpoint of this theology, NT is justified only as a very particular aspect of true knowledge-communion with God. In all attempts to develop it as an independent discourse it loses its foundation and distorts the perspective.

It is worth adding that the reasons for the skeptical attitude of Orthodox-ascetic consciousness to NT are completely different from those of the rejection of NT in the theology of the Reformed Churches and the dialectical theology of Karl Barth. In fact, the arguments are diametrically opposite in the two cases: in Protestant theology, which rejects synergy, NT is considered as an inadmissible exaggeration of human ability to cognize God, while for hesychast consciousness NT by itself represents rather under-estimation of this ability, the wrong way leading only to guesswork around God and diverting from the right way, in which cognition of God is part of communion with God, and man reaching synergy is favored by grace to "see God as He is," as higoumenos Sophrony puts it.

3. Some Implications for Modern Prospects of Natural Theology

Fr John Meyendorff reminds us: "The world is not Divine. . . . Secularization of the cosmos was a Christian idea from the very start."[5] The idea means essentially that the New Covenant is a bond between God and man, not the cosmos, and God's presence in the latter is actualized through the former. Yes, the prayer to the Holy Spirit tells us that He "is everywhere and fills everything," but His presence would be only implicit and hidden without man, whose mission is to actualize and reveal God's presence in creation. For Christian thought the ontological dimension of reality is generated by the relation *God-Man*, but not *God-Universe*. Philosophically,

5. J. Meyendorff, *Orthodox theology in the modern world* // Id. Orthodoxy in the modern world, New York, 1981, pp. 73-74.

it means that man is the observer and recorder of phenomena, which are endowed with ontological status and meaning only in this observing. In Heidegger's words, "Man and being are entrusted to each other. They belong to each other. . . . Only man in his openness to being lets being approach him with its presence."[6] The position described, with its concentration on the role of man, corresponds fully to that of hesychast theology. Such a position implies definite conclusions on the subject of NT, the correct way of stating its problems, and the relationship of theology and science.

In the habitual way of reasoning in NT, the stamp of God's presence in creation is seen in universal laws of nature, in the fact that the natural world in all its objects and phenomena is subject to strict laws and structures. The natural world displays striking properties of regularity and order: all processes obey definite laws, all objects and phenomena possess definite structure, and all the laws and structures are coordinated between them so that all elements involved join together into the well-organized ensemble of the Universe. However, according to the position just described, all these properties of the natural world as well as any other of its properties have no religious sense in themselves. They don't allow religious interpretation, whether in favor of God's existence or against it. The view that wants to see in the laws and structures of the natural world purposefulness and the mark of a mind, which must be introduced from without by some supernatural instance (Divine reason, God's will, etc.), is trivially unfounded. There is no purposefulness or mark of a mind in natural phenomena *taken in themselves;* they are not characteristics of phenomena as such, but the discourse used by human consciousness for their description. Consciousness arbitrarily associates its own constructions with phenomena; and what is more, the constructions in question are unfounded even as characteristics of the discourse since consciousness comes to them, tendentiously manipulating incomplete information. Using the same manipulative technology one might just as well conclude the purposelessness and absurdity of everything (diametrical opposition to NT promoted by the philosophy of the absurd).

This critical logic can be extended to a wide field of problems. As we have seen, in Christianity the *relation of the Divine and natural is necessarily mediated by the human.* In a Christian vision of reality, natural phenomena and processes acquire religious meaning and actualize their con-

6. M. Heidegger, *Der Satz der Identität,* Moscow, 1991, p. 74 (in Russian).

nection with God (the presence of the Holy Spirit in them) exclusively through man, by means of involvement in the economy of the constitutive God-Man relation. "In the Christian vision, it is impossible to speak about creation, without speaking about man."[7] Hence it follows that any discourse, all the contents of which are restricted to natural phenomena only, is devoid of religious content and has no connection with theology. This conclusion can be used as a useful criterion or test in discussions of theological problems of modern natural sciences. In many cases we find in such discussions naïve methodology of a *sui generis* "short circuit," trying to invent direct theological interpretation of scientific facts or theories in no way related to anthropological reality and hence religious reality too. In such cases what we see are illusory problems and pseudo-religious discourse in religious disguise.[8] In order to avoid the loss of a theological foundation, all considerations in this field should include as a necessary stage the disclosure of the anthropological aspect of the phenomena considered. It is via this aspect only that these phenomena can be provided with religious meaning and get involved with theological discourse.

If this criterion is taken into account, the area of direct contact, or the "interface," of theology and the natural sciences might be reduced noticeably. Pseudo-religious discourse abounds (and perhaps dominates) in discussions of problems of cosmology and quantum physics. Let me give just one small example by way of proof. When I read about the profound theological meaning of the noncommutativity of operators in quantum theory, from someone I know equally as one of the founding members of the International Association of Mathematical Physics and a member of the Theological Commission of the Russian Orthodox Church, then I know that this is a pseudo-religious discourse. The diversity of modern mathematical formalisms is such that we can formulate quantum theory (both nonrelativistic and relativistic) in lots of mathematical languages, and the choice between these languages has absolutely nothing to do with theology. The structure of such pseudo-religious discourses usually obeys a kind of Bohr's complementarity principle: If there is a combination of theological and scientific discourse, then either the first or the second of these two discourses is an imitation.

---

7. M. Stavrou, *Le mystère de la création*, Supplement au SOP, Paris, 2009, No. 339, p. 5.

8. It should be stressed here that our discussion is restricted to Christianity with its "secularized cosmos." Obviously, in Far Eastern "religions of the cosmos" or, say, magic cults, the "short circuit" methodology is fully legitimate.

But, on the other hand, an expansion of the interface of theology and the humanities should take place. The subject field *theology and science* had and continues to have an artificial configuration formed within the episteme of the Modern Age and concentrated on peripheral areas of this field. This configuration ignores the obvious and cardinal fact: first of all, theology and science meet and enter into the closest contact in the key problem of all the humanistic sphere, the problem of man. In virtue of this fact, the adequate configuration is one that focuses the main attention on the *topos of man;* and the main tasks of all the subject fields should lie in prompting the comparison and interaction of theological and scientific approaches to the phenomenon of man.

New and interesting possibilities emerge in this direction today. Both theology (Western as well as Eastern) and human sciences are now in a period of deep-going changes. The changes are caused by the coming of a sharply different spiritual and anthropological situation as well as the crisis of the classical foundations of European cultural discourse, including theological discourse, to the extent to which it also relied on the Aristotelian essentialist foundation. In the humanities the crisis manifests itself in the absence of a unifying epistemological paradigm similar to classical or structuralist paradigms in former periods. The search for a unifying ground turns to the framework of human strategies and practices and the discourse of acts and energies, to replace the old essentialist discourse. Foucault's conception of practices of the self is so far the most promising fruit of this search. As for theology, the leading strategy of renewal here is the *anthropologization of theology* based on the idea that theology must become much closer to anthropological reality and discourse. Such a strategy responds to a general trend of Christian thought which is implemented in different ways in different Christian traditions. Protestantism was the first and most active in implementing a rapprochement of theology and anthropology, creating a series of theories, of which the theology of hope by Jürgen Moltmann is the last one so far. In Orthodoxy the evident and direct way to the anthropologization of theology is to focus on the quintessential experience of Orthodox spirituality, which is the experience of hesychasm. Undergoing these discursive transformations, both theology and the human sciences take on forms that imply a new configuration of their relationship favorable to the deepening of their contacts.

The old configuration, with both theology and science using essentialist discourse and abstract categories, predisposed one to an ideological discourse that lives on oppositions and confrontations. This is reflected, in particular, in the fact that Orthodox theology used to allot its relationship with science to the sphere of apologetics, defense of faith, conceiving it in the key of defensive and isolationist reaction: in any contact with science the task was to reach as convincingly as possible the prescribed conclusion that *undisputable achievements of contemporary science don't contradict faith and theology.* In the new configuration the situation is different, however. Leaving the essentialist discourse and adopting the ground of experience and human practices, theology and science have the chance to break the deadlocks of ideological confrontation. In the paradigm of anthropologization, Orthodox theology presents itself as an experiential discourse possessing its own experiential ground. Clearly, it has no reasons to hold a defensive position with respect to scientific discourses unrelated to this ground. As for the discourses concerned with the latter in some way or other, theology can enter into a working relationship with them. Both sides can compare their concepts, methods, and standings, and if they both keep with fidelity to their experiential ground (a kind of phenomenological attitude), their common turn *zu den Sachen selbst* (Husserl's famous motto), free of ideological pressing, can be fruitful for both.

Modern studies of hesychasm present a concrete example in which the new configuration is already at work. In these studies, not only a palamitic theology of Divine energies, but all the experience of hesychast practical theologizing is used as the basis for a comprehensive modern reconstruction of hesychast practice as a spiritual and anthropological phenomenon. In our context, such reconstruction is exactly the interface *theology-science,* since it includes both theological interpretation of hesychast experience and its interdisciplinary anthropological analysis. The theological interpretation in question exploits concepts and methods of many human sciences — in particular, Foucault's theory of practices of the self. The interaction is not one-sided, however. Various aspects of the phenomenon become subjects of the analysis of various disciplinary discourses, psychology, philosophy, history, etc. And turning to the analysis of hesychast experience, for their orientation in such a specific subject all these discourses need to get some information and instructions from theology, since many important moments such as the goal of the practice, its motivation, and its inner context are adequately rendered by theological discourse only. Thus the collaboration, or "synergy," of the two sides of the interface is achieved here.

Our reasoning allows us to expect that this example is not an exception and the present-day situation is really stimulating for the rapprochement of theology and science (the human sciences, first of all). The two spheres are capable of collaborating on the crucial problem conceiving modern man in his relation to himself, the Universe, and God. The approach of Orthodox theology to this problem is aptly expressed by Michel Stavrou: "Theology of Divine energies — not as metaphysical system, but as experiential discourse of faith in God present in creation — can be fruitful, helping Christians to lend Christianity all the fullness of its cosmic dimension. Of course, it is not a question of rejecting scientific progress or turning theology against science. It is a question of combining the two fundamental human vocations with respect to the world, kingship and priesthood, domination and sanctification, without adopting one of them to the detriment of the other."[9]

9. M. Stavrou. *Loc. cit.*, p. 9.

III. CONVERGENCE BETWEEN THEOLOGY AND SCIENCE?

Convergence between Theology and Science: Patterns from the Early Christian Era

Cyril Hovorun

1. Theology and Science: Possibilities of Dialogue

The focus of the present paper is the question: *How* can any kind of mutual understanding between theology and science be achieved? By answering the *how,* I believe, we can more easily find a way to answer the question: *What* should they agree upon? In other words, by looking for the qualitative convergences between science and theology (the *how*), we will find the quantitative convergence (the *what*). When I speak of the quantitative convergence I mean absence of contradictions in interpretations of the realities which are commonly considered by both theology and science.

An obvious point of convergence between these two heterogeneous disciplines is the academic method of research, which they share. Similarly to science, modern theology applies methodologies of critical analysis and objectivisation. Another way of bringing the two disciplines closer to each other is hermeneutical. According to this methodology, either theology becomes interpreted in categories of science, or scientific data get explanations from the point of view of theology. In other words, either scientists try to speak theological language and embed theological data into the framework of their scientific thinking, or theologians try explaining the achievements of scientific research on the ground of theological axioms.

These approaches can be enriched by the methodologies extracted from the experience of the early Fathers of the Church.

2. Features of the Classical Gnoseology

A starting point for our investigation will be a challenge that the Church faced at the beginning of the Christian era: how to deal with the corpus of knowledge produced by Antiquity. This corpus did not only consist of a certain sum of knowledge. It also featured a holistic perception and practice of faith, theology, philosophy, art, science, medicine, *etc.* These disciplines were not split into distinctive activities of human spirit or branches of knowledge, as we know them now. They constituted parts of a reasonably integral phenomenon and functioned within the same epistemological paradigm. Therefore, in the period of Antiquity, a dilemma of a modern kind between science and theology simply did not exist, as they spoke similar language and reflected one holistic approach to the world.

This observation provides us with a key to a possible solution to our problem. Antiquity teaches us that theology and science should be placed into the same philosophical framework, with similar cognitive outlook. Theologians and scientists, to better understand each other, should learn and start speaking the same *philosophical* language. They have to use identical apparatus of philosophical categories, share similar perceptions of the world, and apply identical gnoseological methodologies.

Another important point is to choose a field of knowledge where theology and science can easily meet. In the classical tradition, it was primarily the issue of origins of the universe (cosmogony) and humans, including the issue of constitution of the human nature (anthropology). Apparently, cosmogony and anthropology are fields where theology and science can rediscover their integrity in the present situation as well. However, some important gnoseological and epistemological preconditions should be carefully observed.

3. Reception of the Ancient Gnosis by Christianity

As mentioned, Antiquity featured a remarkably low level of differentiation between religion, philosophy, science, and other activities of the human spirit. As a result, for early Christians, it was very hard to accept some parts of the ancient intellectual and spiritual heritage, and to reject other parts, as those parts of the whole were scarcely distinguishable. Facing this, Christianity at its initial stage had two obvious and easy ways to deal with the corpus of knowledge produced in Antiquity: either to *fully* accept or to *fully* reject it. Respectively, two parallel traditions emerged that followed these lines.

One of them, that of gnosticism, adopted Antiquity in its fullness, together with its scientific theology and theological science. Gnosticism unconditionally followed gnoseological and epistemological lines drawn by Antiquity. As a result, Gnostics ultimately rationalised Christian revelation. The very salvation of human nature they reduced to intellectual efforts. They blurred the demarcation line between the created and uncreated worlds by applying the same cognitive methods both to the visible realities and to the realm of the divine. Without any reservations, Gnostics embraced the blend of philosophical trends popular in their epoch, with Neoplatonism playing a central role among them. As a result, they produced cosmogony and anthropology which turned out to be irreconcilable with the Christian revelation. The Christian Church eventually disapproved Gnosticism, together with the methodology of unconditional adoption of Antiquity.

Another way of dealing with Antiquity consisted in unconditional rejection of anything which was not brought in by the Christian revelation and which cannot be found in the Holy Scripture. Theologians who followed this way mechanically rejected anything produced by 'pagan wisdom.' We know quite a number of early Christian writers who adhered to this tradition. One of the most prominent among them, Tertullian, articulated the credo of this group in the following words: 'What need has Athens to do with Jerusalem? What concord is there between the Academy and the Church? What between heretics and Christians? . . . Away with all attempts to produce a mottled Christianity of Stoic, Platonic, and dialectic composition! We want no curious disputation after possessing Christ Jesus, no inquisition after enjoying the gospel! With our faith we desire no further belief.' However, this tradition also did not prove its vitality, having led many of its adepts to sectarianism, including Tertullian himself.

Thus, neither of the two above-mentioned approaches was satisfactory in providing a solution to the problem of acceptance of Antiquity into the Christian tradition. Therefore, from the very beginning of the Christian literature, some writers, like Justin Martyr, Clement of Alexandria, or Origen, tried to apply a different approach. This approach consisted in acceptance of useful elements from 'pagan wisdom' and rejection of those elements which were incompatible with the Christian revelation. This methodology seems to be obvious for us, but it was not apparent in that time. One of the reasons why it was so difficult to separate wheat from weeds in the ancient wisdom was because, as mentioned, the elements of the integral tradition of Antiquity were not easily distinguishable.

4. Dialectics

An eloquent illustration of the eclectic approach to Antiquity, which eventually dominated in Christianity, is the way in which classical philosophy was integrated into the system of the Christian gnosis. Sometimes we do not realise that the entire corpus of classical literature was preserved for future generations by the Christian Church. The texts of classical wisdom were transmitted by Christian scribes, mostly monks, who carefully copied ancient manuscripts. There are no remaining pre-Christian manuscripts with the texts of Homer, Plato, Aristotle, *et al.* — all those thinkers were made known to post-Antiquity humankind owing to the Christians. This does not, however, mean that all the philosophers were read and studied equally in the Christian era. At some stage, the most popular ancient philosophical treatise appeared to be the *Categories* by Aristotle. This treatise was read and commented on more than any other philosophical treatise. An impressively large corpus of commentaries on the *Categories* became a token of the epoch of active integration of ancient philosophy into Christian theology and education. The Aristotelian *Categories* became a basis for school curriculum in philosophy, mostly through the Neoplatonic interpreters.

Thus, the Christian reception distilled from the entire corpus of ancient philosophy a dialectical apparatus of basic operational categories. The Christians were interested not in the classical philosophical interpretations of what is the world, human soul, and God, but in the technical terms by which these issues can be expressed according to the Christian revelation. This approach was symptomatic for the Christian attitude to the classical heritage. It had two basic features:

(1) Disintegration of the entirety of the ancient wisdom.
(2) Preference for the 'technical' and categorial elements of it. These elements became a fabric from which a new Christian theological language was eventually woven.

Not all attempts to select elements of 'pagan wisdom' for Christian use were successful, as it appeared to be difficult to work out the criteria for such a selection. Firm criteria were established not later than in the fourth century, owing to the theological contribution of the Cappadocean Fathers.

5. Cappadocean 'Synthesis'

What the Cappadoceans did for theology and philosophy is usually called 'synthesis,' because they managed to express axioms of the Christian revelation in philosophical language. Such purely philosophical terms as *homoousios* or *hypostasis* are rightly considered as great achievements of this synthesis. If we follow this line of thought, we may assume that the Cappadoceans also achieved synthesis between theology and science. Indeed, as we will see later, they managed to apply scientific data to theological issues, without causing any conflict either with scientific methods of their time or with Christian revelation.

At the same time, I would suggest corrections to the theory about 'Cappadocean synthesis.' In my opinion, before synthesis, there was a divorce between theology, philosophy, and science as parts of the single cognitive approach which Antiquity featured. My hypothesis is that Christianity (with the protagonistic role of the Cappadoceans) gave a forceful impulse to disintegrate theology, philosophy, and science in their classical meaning. Of course, it was not Christianity that initiated this process, because the process of separation started earlier. Nevertheless, Christianity had strong reasons to encourage divorce between the three disciplines. From the Christian point of view, the only way to preserve what was healthy in 'pagan wisdom' was to break the single tradition into pieces, and then reassemble pieces into a new tradition. It reminds us of the way in which early Christians used elements of pagan temples to build new Christian churches. Before these elements were incorporated into new buildings, old buildings had to be deconstructed and their elements separated from each other. This exactly happened to the ancient knowledge, which was first disintegrated, and then its separated elements were reassembled into new intellectual constructions.

Among the elements of classical knowledge which were acceptable for Christian use were those correspondent with science in the modern sense of the word. The Christian theologians applied these elements when exploring the origins of the world and man. Unlike Gnostics, they did not apply them to the realm of the divine. The origins of the world were explored as *hermeneia* of the six days of creation according to the book of Genesis

(Hexameron). Probably the most successful reflections on the *Hexameron* were offered by Basil of Caesarea. On the one hand, he firmly professed *creatio ex nihilo* and distanced himself from the Aristotelian affirmation that the world has no beginning. On the other hand, when speaking of the created world, he heavily relied on the scientific data of his time. For instance, in his description of the animals one can see allusions to the Aristotelian works, especially the *History of animals.* Basil affirmed the idea that when God created the world, He endowed it with its own order and natural laws. This 'order of nature, having received its beginning from that first command, continues to all time thereafter, until it shall reach the common consummation of all things.' This affirmation is very important for the dialogue between theology and science, as science is based on the idea of the autonomous order and natural laws innate in the visible world.

As for teaching about human nature, anthropology, the works of another Cappadocean Father, Gregory of Nyssa, are exemplary. Gregory developed his anthropological ideas in a number of works, among which the treatise *On the making of man* is the most important one. The paradigm in which Gregory considers man is similar to the paradigm developed by Basil of Caesarea in application to the created world. Gregory starts with affirmations of what is uniquely Christian about man. Man is created by God. His nature is created and as such is radically different from the uncreated nature of God. At the same time, human nature reflects God's nature in a unique manner, being His image and likeness. Man is a being who exists on the edge between the uncreated and created worlds *(methorios)*. Because he is not confined to this world, he cannot be considered as the world's small copy, a *microcosm,* as ancient philosophers thought. At the same time, man embodies the created world too. As such, he is subject to 'scientific' analysis and classifications which are applicable to other creatures. Classical philosophical categories are applicable to man as well. The most dear to Gregory is the Aristotelian category of movement *(kinesis),* which he widely applies to human nature as its characteristic feature. Thus, man initially moves from non-existence to existence. Then, during his lifetime he struggles to move towards God. His movement towards perfection remains endless.

Gregory of Nyssa and Basil of Caesarea also produced important clarifications about the cognitive abilities of the human mind regarding both created and uncreated worlds. Their views on these matters are crucial for understanding the epistemology of the Fathers. They articulated their views, which were eventually accepted by the Church as part of its doctrine, in reaction to the teaching of Aetius and Eunomius.

6. Limitations of Cognitivity

Aetius and Eunomius were radical Arianists who invented a specific methodology of gnosis of God in His essence. According to this methodology, the human mind is capable of knowing the essence of God. Man can know God as well as God knows Himself: 'God knows His own essence not more than we do. It is not correct to say that He knows it (= the essence) more, and we — less, but whatever we know about it, He knows the same, and vice versa' (testimony of Socrates). According to Epiphanius of Cyprus, Eunomius went as far as affirming that we know the essence of God even better than we know our own essence: 'He (= Eunomius) and those who were taught by him started saying: I know God completely. I know Him so well that I do not know myself so well.' This testimony may be a polemical exaggeration, but it reflects how confident Eunomius was about the capacity of the human mind to comprehend divinity fully and adequately.

Aetius and Eunomius affirmed that human knowledge about any essence, including the divine, can be expressed by human language. Language, for them, was a means of cognition. Language is not a human invention, they believed, but is given by God through revelation. Therefore, any name attributed to God or a creature reveals its essence. There are also other means that can express the essence of God, like, for instance, . . . geometry. There is a provocative testimony of Epiphanies of Cyprus about Aetius's approach to the cognoscibility of God: 'When he studied in Alexandria from a certain Aristotelian philosopher and sophist, having learned dialectics, he decided to present teaching about God in figures. . . . He was dealing with it and sitting on it without interruptions from morning to evening. He studied and tried to speak about God and compose definitions about Him by means of geometry and figures.' Thus, Aetius and Eunomius made language a means of adequate and complete comprehension of both the created and uncreated worlds.

This allowed Gregory of Nyssa to accuse them of turning theology into 'technology' *(technologia),* the latter word meaning 'mastery of words.' The Fathers generally rejected the Eunomian approach to cognition of God and the world. They accused Eunomius of confusing the realms of divine and created, exaggerating the possibilities of the human mind, and misunderstanding the nature of language.

The Fathers, while rejecting the ideas of Aetius and Eunomius, made a strong distinction between:

(1) the sphere of uncreated,
(2) the sphere of created,
(3) and the intellectual means that express these spheres.

These spheres touch on each other, but must not be confused. Indeed, humans can have only limited access to the sphere of the divine. The essence of God cannot be cognised by the human mind. It is only through the activities *(energeiai)* of God that humans are able to know God. Even that partial experience of the divine life that humans are capable of obtaining cannot be fully manifested by linguistic or other expressive means. Human words play only an indicative role. They cannot reveal the essence of God, but they only evoke a common experience of the divine energies that people obtain through prayer and sacraments. This applies not only to the sphere of the divine but to the visible world as well. The words and ideas about things are creatures of the human mind and the result of agreement between humans. They are not given by God.

Did these distinctions elaborated by the Fathers lead to agnosticism, as it may seem to be at first glance? Definitely no. On the contrary, they allowed Christian thinkers to develop rich theology based on spiritual experience rather than on intellectual exercises. It also allowed theologians to develop a multiplicity of theological languages, as well as absorb terms and ideas from the philosophical heritage of Antiquity.

These distinctions can also help the dialogue between theology and science. In order for this dialogue to be successful, science should not trespass the borders of the created world. Theology, at the same time, should not go too far from the world of the divine. The place where they can safely meet is on the border between the two worlds. As the human being stands on this border, science and theology should have common interest in and apply common efforts to comprehending the phenomenon of human life.

Another issue where they can collaborate is the origins of the created world, as creation is the point which in the most obvious way demonstrates the relationship between the world and God. Scientists should not give theological explanations for all the phenomena they investigate. They should be selective in this regard. In the same way theologians should realise that only a limited set of theological issues can be expressed in terms compatible with science. Both scientists and theologians need to be aware that the language they speak is not absolute, but rather conditional — it is a matter of agreement. This allows them to seek for and to find common language to better understand each other. For rapprochement between scientists and theologians, it is essential that they share the same experience of God and of the visible world. Their mindset, philosophical outlook, and categorical apparatus constitute the framework in which the dialogue between theology and science can be possible and, moreover, immensely enriching for both theology and science.

Challenges of a Consistent Christian Language for the Creativity of God's Spirit

Friederike Nüssel

While interdisciplinary discourse between theologians and scientists frequently focuses on the existence of God as the creator of the universe, less attention seems to be paid to the identity of this creator God and how his divine creative activity can be understood. Following the logic which Thomas Aquinas deployed so influentially in his *Summa Theologica* and his *Summa Contra Gentiles,* many Christian theologians, at least in the West, defended the existence of God as a logical condition for talking about God's activity in creation and salvation as witnessed in the Bible. The complexity of apologetic challenges, however, rapidly increased after the 16th-century Reformation. Spinoza's pantheism, Newtonian physics, Kant's critique of traditional metaphysics, and Darwinian evolution biology created a most complex constellation of challenges, all of which served to question not only the existence of God, but also the ontological distinction between God and the world and the necessity of his on-going providence.

But even apart from any apologetic strategy there has also been an internal theological inclination to approach dialogue in such a way as to focus on the existence of God in abstraction from his creative activity. This inclination is rooted in the dynamics of Trinitarian theology, which eventually led to separate theological discourses on creation and new creation. As a result the "question of how the 'Spirit of creation' and the 'Spirit of righteousness' are to be understood as the *one* Spirit of God is one of the greatest theological challenges"[1] — as Michael Welker states. It is necessary, therefore, to consider the unity of the *one* Spirit of God, active in creation and granting righ-

---

1. M. Welker, *God the Spirit,* translated by J. F. Hoffmeyer, Minneapolis: Fortress Press, 1994, 158.

teousness in new creation, with a view to preserving the internal consistency of theological thought, but also with respect to the challenges from New Atheism and new evolutionary theories, both of which must be met on the ground of a theological understanding of the very being of God, which in turn is *based* on a consistent account of God's creativity as Spirit. In order to elaborate this point, I will first describe some of the leading theological ideas which shaped the development of Christian pneumatology and eventually fostered a disconnect between Christian talk on creation and on new creation. Second, by looking at the special character of the Spirit's activity as described in biblical texts on creation *and* new creation, I will lay out a way of rethinking the very character of God's creative power as Spirit which has been presented by Wolfhart Pannenberg in his *Systematic Theology.*

1. Theological and Soteriological Issues in Protestant Teaching on Creation and New Creation

Up to the period of Enlightenment the biblical reports on God's creation in Genesis 1 and 2 were taken as answers to the question as to how God had made the world and how his creative activity could be understood. When the traditional Jewish-Christian account of creation was called into question in the 19th century by Charles Darwin's theory of evolution, historical-critical methods of reading biblical literature — themselves a product of the Enlightenment — were further refined, allowing eventually the end of a literal understanding of the biblical reports on the process of creation. As a result, Protestant theology in its doctrinal approaches now focused on the decisive role of the biblical notion of creation through the word of God, and interpreted God's creative activity in creating the world and reconciling his creatures along the lines of Luther's *theologia verbi,* that is, in terms of the performative character of language. Another decisive step was made by Karl Barth in his *Church Dogmatics* when he argued that the whole idea of creation and the perception of creaturely dependence could only be adequately recognized through God's self-witness in Jesus Christ. He thereby took Christology to be the epistemological basis for any doctrinal proposition on creation.[2] Both dogmatic moves, the

---

2. See K. Barth, *Church Dogmatics,* Vol. III, 1, ed. G. W. Bromiley and T. F. Torrance, Edinburgh: T&T Clark, 1958, § 40, 3: "The insight that man owes his existence and form, together with all the reality distinct from God, to God's creation, is achieved only in the recep-

Christological foundation of the doctrine of creation and the focus on the idea of creation through the word of God, however, helped to separate theological reflection on creation from scientific discourse. Moreover, the Christological focus together with the account of creation through word did not encourage but rather impeded reflection on the *distinctive* character of the divine Spirit's activity *as* Spirit. This muting of the Spirit's activity is not only characteristic of post-Enlightenment Protestant theology in general, but can also be traced back to the teachings of the early Church.

Although the notion of God's Spirit is a constitutive part of the Christian message, it was not a major topic in the discussions of early Church theologians. The provocative and challenging Christian message within a Jewish, Hellenistic, and Roman environment was not the idea of God's Spirit at work, but the proclamation of Jesus Christ as the Son of God. Thus, the crucial task of early Christian theology was to defend this christological idea against different objections or interpretations which in some way or other dismissed the role of Jesus Christ as the revealer of God's true will and the savior of humankind. By comparison not much effort was spent on the specific role of the divine Spirit. Only when the first ecumenical synod of Nicea in 325 had declared the Son to be consubstantial *(homoousios)* with the Father was the role of the Spirit in his specific relation to God the Father and the Son discussed more intensely. On the premise of God's essential unity in the three hypostases, the second ecumenical synod at Constantinople (381) explicitly applied the notion of consubstantiality also to the Holy Spirit. In order to defend God's essential unity in a consistent way against the accusation of polytheism or the idea of subordination, it seemed necessary also to claim the indivisibility of God's energy towards the world. This idea was elaborated especially by Athanasius,[3] Ambrose, and Augustine.[4] However, with respect to those biblical references in which certain divine activities are

tion and answer of the divine self-witness, that is, only in faith in Jesus Christ, i.e., in the knowledge of the unity of Creator and creature actualized in Him, and in the life in the present mediated by Him, under the right and in the experience of the goodness of the Creator towards His creature."

3. Cf. Athanasius, *Ad Serapion*, 1, PG 26, 596A. Opposing Origen's doctrine of three different circles of operation on the part of the divine persons, Athanasius claimed the unity of the Trinitarian energy towards the world. See also *The Letters of Saint Athanasius concerning the Holy Spirit,* translated with introduction and notes by C. R. B. Shapland, Eugene, Oregon: Wipf & Stock, 2004. For the development of pneumatology in the Early Church see W.-D. Hauschild and V. H. Drecoll (eds.), *Pneumatologie in der Alten Kirche,* Bern/New York: Lang, 2004.

4. Cf. Augustine, *De Trinitate* 1.4 (7): inseparabiliter operentur. See also 4.21 (30).

ascribed only to the Father or to the Son or to the Holy Spirit, the concept of God's indivisible energy towards the world needed further nuance. In Protestant theology this was achieved through the concept of appropriations, according to which the different actions of God towards the world in creation, redemption, and sanctification were, despite their indivisibility as Trinitarian acts, assigned to one of the Trinitarian persons.[5] Thus the work of creation could be ascribed especially to the Father, while redemption was appropriated to the Son and sanctification to the Holy Spirit.

In an attempt to reconcile Christian metaphysics with biblical language, Protestant theologians combined the principle of indivisible divine actions towards the world with the notion of certain appropriations involving single members of the Trinity. The order of assigning certain operations to the Trinitarian persons was developed according to the order of their internal relations. Thus, the creation of the world was defined as the particular work of the Father in his *agenesia* or fatherhood; the redemption of fallen creatures was ascribed to the Son in his *genesia;* and the work of new creation in sanctification and consumption of the world was ascribed to the creative agency of the Holy Spirit in his *procession* from the Father through the Son. Contrary to its intention, however, the doctrine of appropriations yielded the impression that the Trinitarian persons were three agents each having a special responsibility for one stage in the divine economy, while the others were only "cooperative." Especially in the doctrine of creation the divine agency of the Father was emphasized in a way that the Son and the Holy Spirit appeared to participate in the process of creation only in a passive way[6] — all of which is hardly compatible with

5. Cf., for example, A. Calov, *Systema locorum theologicorum* III, 153ff and 194f. See also J. A. Quenstedt, *Systema,* I, 327: "From the real distinction of persons arises their order, both in subsisting and in operating. Nevertheless, we must distinguish between the order of nature, of time, of dignity, of origin, and of relation. Among the divine persons, there is not an order of nature, because, they are *homousios* [consubstantial]; nor of time, because they are co-eternal; nor of dignity, because they have the same honor. But there is among them an order of origin and relation, . . . it follows that the Father is the first, the Son the second, and the Holy Ghost the third person, and this order, both fixed in nature itself and unchangeable, is clearly shown in the formula of baptism. Matt. 28:19." (Translation taken from H. Schmid, *The Doctrinal Theology of the Evangelical Lutheran Church,* 3rd edition revised, translated by C. A. Hay and H. E. Jacobs, Minneapolis 1961, 150.)

6. According to Wolfhart Pannenberg not only post-Reformation Protestant teaching, but already the scholastic approach of Thomas Aquinas did not "differentiate the specific contribution of the individual divine persons," cf. W. Pannenberg, *Systematic Theology* vol. II, translated by G. W. Bromiley, Grand Rapids, Michigan, 1994, 26.

biblical notions about the creative role of the Spirit (cf. Gen 1 and 2; Ezek 37; Rom 8) and the Son of God as mediator in the process of creation (cf. John 1:1; Col 1:15-20; Heb 1:2). Moreover, one may ask how the unity of God's Spirit can be claimed if his agency appears to be different in creation and new creation. Before we come back to this problem, it is necessary to look more closely at the development of Protestant teaching and the evolving disjunction between its doctrine of creation and pneumatology.

For the 16th-century reformers[7] to be able to implement their reforms of the medieval Church it was necessary to have a systematic account of their new insight into the Gospel, one which could serve as a guide for theological education of church ministers. Towards this end, Philipp Melanchthon introduced the loci-method[8] which was adopted not only in Lutheran theology, but also Reformed and Roman-Catholic approaches. When in the late 16th and early 17th centuries Lutheran theologians increasingly recurred to Aristotelian metaphysics in their analyses of soteriology, which was based upon Christology and set against Roman-Catholic and Reformed objections, it became necessary to clarify the specific task and profile of Christian theology in relation to other university disciplines. In keeping with Luther's and Melanchthon's soteriological focus, Lutheran theologians used a certain analytic method, which Aristotle had defined for practical sciences, so as both to distinguish theology from philosophy and to ensure its status as a practical scholarly discipline. In terms of the analytic method, the traditional theological *loci* had to be organized with a view to explaining which causes and media God had ordered for human beings as they sought to overcome their separation from God as sinners and to gain new community with God. Accordingly, the doctrine of God and his creation were identified as the *finis theologiae.* The human condition in its original integrity and its corruption through sin was seen as the subject of theology, and God's salvation through election, redemption, and sanctification was expounded under the heading of *causae et media salutis.* With this analytic approach Lutheran theology achieved a systematic reconstruction of the Christian faith which — along with Luther's theology — strictly focused on God's grace as revealed in the salvation of his fallen human creatures.[9]

7. For an innovative understanding of the Reformation cf. B. Hamm and M. Welker, *Reformation — Potentiale der Freiheit,* Tübingen: Mohr Siebeck, 2008.

8. Cf. F. Nüssel, *Allein aus Glauben. Zur Entwicklung der Rechtfertigungslehre in der konkordistischen und frühen nachkonkordistischen Theologie (Forschungen zur systematischen und ökumenischen Theologie 95),* Göttingen: Vandenhoeck & Ruprecht, 2000, 31ff; 113ff.

9. One of the achievements consisted in the fact that the Trinitarian and Christological

While Lutheran theologians, in accordance with the principle of *opera ad extra indivisa sunt*,[10] conceived of the salvation of humankind as an indivisible action of the triune God, Trinitarian appropriations served as a structure for distinguishing the causes of salvation. Thus the Father's benevolence in election was defined as the first cause of salvation, the redemptive work of Jesus Christ as the second cause, and the application of God's grace through the Holy Spirit as the third cause. In expounding the third cause of salvation the crucial issue for Protestant pneumatology was to argue for God's unconditioned grace through justification by faith alone.[11] But since the concept of justification on the ground of the literal exegesis of the Pauline texts was understood to refer only to the forensic act in which God offers acquittal from sin and imputation of the righteousness of Christ, it became the special task of pneumatology to systematize all the other biblical terms which describe how the Spirit converts humans and renews them in their faith and in their life. Thus, the process of sanctification in Lutheran dogmatics was differentiated into vocation, illumination, regeneration and conversion, mystical union, and renovation of the human will as exercised in good works. In this pneumatological account, the Spirit's activity was not reduced to evoking new faith and trust in God's promise, but it was understood to *re-create* all human capacities — the human intellect, the emotional receptivity in affects, and the human will — to their full integrity and perfect interaction.[12]

---

dogma which Melanchthon in his first edition of *Loci theologici* in 1521 had excluded as merely speculative could be integrated in such a way that their impact on salvation was easily seen.

10. Protestant theologians like Johann A. Quenstedt addressed this principle as an Augustinian rule, following from his doctrine of the trinity. Cf. C. H. Ratschow, *Lutherische Dogmatik zwischen Reformation und Aufklärung,* Part II, Gütersloher Verlagshaus: Gütersloh 1966, 156, 158.

11. It is important to keep in mind that the pneumatological account cannot be separated from Christology and the doctrine of God's benevolence, because it is nothing but the unconditioned grace of God the Father revealed in the redemptive work of his Son which the Spirit applies to individuals in the process of sanctification.

12. According to N. T. Wright "One of the greatest tragedies of the Schism of A.D. 1054 was that the West was able to develop a view of 'salvation' and the East a view of 'transformation,' each of which needed the other for a balanced completeness." Cf. N. T. Wright, *Justification. God's Plan & Paul's Vision,* Downers Grove: IVP, 2009, 235. With respect to Lutheran teaching in early post-Reformation times, however, one should realize that there is no intention to separate salvation from the idea of transformation, but rather to give a precise account of how salvation causes transformation. The way in which Lutheran theology elaborated pneumatology in the so called *ordo salutis* did not restrict salvation to a forensic

If one inquires after the special character of the Holy Spirit's activity in sanctification, as presented in the Lutheran pneumatology, one may identify it in the unifying power in which the Spirit restores human capacities and recollects humans into communion with God and with fellow creatures. This characteristic power of the Spirit's activity as *distinct* from the activities ascribed to the Father and to the Son, however, was not thematized explicitly in the old Protestant dogmatics. Neither was attention paid to the similarity between the creative power of the Spirit in creation and new creation. Reflection on the distinctive character of the Spirit's activity would probably have been seen as compromising the principle of *opera ad extra indivisa sunt*. But apart from this principle it was also the soteriological focus which kept Lutheran theology from discussing the distinctive activity of the Spirit in creation and new creation as a theological issue in itself.

To understand this better we need to turn to Martin Luther's theology of creation for a moment. His perspective on the idea of creation can be perceived best in his catechisms, especially in his explanation of the first article of the Apostle's Creed in his Small Catechism. Luther explains the first sentence of the Creed, "I believe in God the Father Almighty, Maker of heaven and earth," as follows:

> I believe that God has made me and all creatures; that He has given me my body and soul, eyes, ears, and all my limbs, my reason, and all my senses, and still preserves them; in addition thereto, clothing and shoes, meat and drink, house and homestead, wife and children, fields, cattle, and all my goods; that He provides me richly and daily with all that I need to support this body and life, protects me from all danger, and guards me and preserves me from all evil; and all this out of pure, fatherly, divine goodness and mercy, without any merit or worthiness in me; for all which I owe it to Him to thank, praise, serve, and obey Him. This is most certainly true.[13]

This interpretation shows three characteristics of Luther's approach. First, he explains the notion of creation in terms of the individual experience. Second, it is much more important for Luther to give a detailed interpretation of God's providence than to point to the fact that everything

---

judgment of God. Rather the dogmatic piece on *De gratia Spiritus Sancti applicatrice* was meant to describe the enlivening and transforming power of the Holy Spirit on humans.

13. http://www.bookofconcord.org/smallcatechism.php.

is dependent upon God's existence as the creator. Third, there is no reference to cosmology. Luther in his understanding of creation focused on God's providence in everyday life rather than on cosmological questions. God's creative activity he understood in the light of the *Deus revelatus* offering his mercy to reconcile humans through the incarnation, death, and resurrection of his Son. Luther in fact discussed creation in the light of new creation.

Luther was not the first one to approach the doctrine of creation this way. In fact the central burden of the doctrine of creation, as it was developed in the Jewish-Christian tradition, has always been to explain God's providence which believers experience in his powerful guidance and miraculous sustaining human life. Cosmological questions about the origin of the universe were only treated as a side topic. The concept of *creatio ex nihilo* (cf. 2 Macc 7:18; Rom 4:17; Heb 11:3) was not developed to provide a cosmological theory but to exclude a dualistic worldview. Protestant thinking reinforced this perspective. Accordingly, Protestant accounts of creation emphasized the notion of *creatio ex nihilo* and used the doctrine of creation to describe the presuppositions without which the existence of humans and their need for salvation cannot be understood. When in response to Immanuel Kant's criticism of traditional metaphysics Friedrich Schleiermacher reconstructed Protestant confessional teaching to explain Christian faith as a certain form of religious consciousness, he developed the doctrine of creation in accordance with the Lutheran perspective, that is, as an explication of what is implied in the Christian consciousness of sin and grace.[14] As mentioned before, Karl Barth radicalized this approach by saying that God's creation could not be conceived at all apart from Jesus Christ. This development of the doctrine of creation within Protestant teaching follows an internal rationality in focusing on soteriology and taking Christology as the epistemological principle. The role of the Spirit, however, tends to be reduced to making present God's self-revelation in Jesus Christ to human minds, while the more complex notion of the Spirit's activity as witnessed in the Bible tends to be ignored. This in turn fostered the isolation of theological discourse from other, especially scientific, discourses in the 20th century.

14. Cf. F. Schleiermacher, *The Christian Faith.* Edited by H. R. Mackintosh and J. S. Stewart, London/New York: T&T Clark Ltd, 1999, 142-193.

2. Wolfhart Pannenberg's Account of the Creative Power of the Divine Spirit

One important attempt to overcome the gap between theological and scientific discourse and to renew theological reflection on creation comes by way of Wolfhart Pannenberg's *Systematic Theology,* especially the chapter on the creation of the world.[15] According to Pannenberg, Christian theology has the task of explaining and defending the truth claim of the Christian faith not only within immanent theological reflection but also in discussion with the humanities and the sciences. As he states, Christian theology has "to show how the event of revelation which the Christian faith claims makes it possible to develop an integrated interpretation of God and humanity and the world which we may with good reason regard as true in relation to the knowledge that comes from experience of the world and human life, and also to the knowledge of the philosophical reflection, so that we can assert it to be true vis-à-vis alternative religious and non-religious interpretations. A comparative discussion and appraisal of the opposing truth claims of different interpretations has to presuppose expositions of the views that are to be compared."[16] It is important to note that this understanding of the task of theology in Pannenberg's approach is a consequence of the general concept of God as the all-determining reality which is implied in the Christian image of the Divine.

The major task of the doctrine of creation, according to Pannenberg, is to demonstrate that "the world has its origin in a free act of God"[17] and "does not emanate by necessity from the divine essence or belong by necessity to the deity of God."[18] Thus, Pannenberg, like Karl Barth, rejects Hegel's concept of God as absolute Spirit who needs to create the world in order to realize his deity. Instead he argues for God's self-sufficiency in his internal life and self-communication in the doctrine of God's immanent trinity. Unlike Barth, however, Pannenberg interprets God in his divine autonomy not as an absolute subject, but rather conceives God's freedom as his self-

---

15. Cf. Pannenberg, *Systematic Theology II,* Chapter 7, 1ff.

16. Pannenberg, *Systematic Theology II,* XIV.

17. Pannenberg, *Systematic Theology II,* 1. According to Pannenberg it "is essential for the Christian understanding of God's freedom in his activity as Creator that he did not have to create the world out of some inner necessity of his own nature. If he did, he would be dependent in his very essence on the existence of the world as a tiny aspect of the divine self-actualization" (ibid., 19).

18. Pannenberg, *Systematic Theology II,* 1.

realization in which he determines himself to grant existence to a world and to care for his creatures in their distinctiveness from him.[19] Although "God is independent in himself, yet with the act of creation and in the course of the history of his creatures he makes himself dependent on creaturely conditions."[20] Thus for "God's action no creature is merely a means."[21]

But for creatures to exist in distinction from God, it is necessary to be granted existence over a period of time, because "(w)ithout duration there is no independent existence."[22] Consequently, it can be regarded as an essential implication of God's intention to grant existence to his creatures in distinction from his own existence that the evolution of life including the development of consciousness and self-understanding takes place in a historical process. To understand duration as a necessary condition of creaturely existence, however, presses us to solve the theological problem as to how God in his very simplicity can be conceived of continuously acting towards his creation in the process of time. Pannenberg meets this challenge by arguing that God's actions towards the world are not different in character from God's eternal activity in the relation of Father, Son, and Holy Spirit. Rather, in his activity towards the world God reveals the structure of his internal self-determination and self-communication. Thus, the Trinitarian structure of God's immanent action is repeated in the act of creation. The act of creation, in turn, is understood to refer not only to the first moment in which God created the universe but also to the ongoing process of *creatio continuata*.

Starting from the fact that "the Christian belief in creation relates first to the person of the Father,"[23] Pannenberg goes on to develop the eternal relation between the Father and the Son, according to which the Father generates the Son and loves him. The Father, therefore, is conceived as the *principle of origin* proving his goodness by allowing the Son to be a second *hypostasis* distinctive from him. In correspondence to the Father, the Son's distinctive character consists in his self-distinction from the Father, which is revealed "in the earthly existence of Jesus."[24] As the Son's personality is

---

19. Pannenberg explains this as follows: "God had only one reason to create a world, the reason that is proclaimed in the fact of creation itself, namely, his own divine being and in distinction from him" (*Systematic Theology II*, 20).

20. Pannenberg, *Systematic Theology II*, 7.

21. Ibid.

22. Pannenberg, *Systematic Theology II*, 20.

23. Pannenberg, *Systematic Theology II*, 21.

24. Pannenberg, *Systematic Theology II*, 22.

determined by his eternal self-distinction from the Father, he can be understood as the *principle of otherness*. In elaborating the idea that "the Son is the origin of all that differs from the Father,"[25] Pannenberg interprets what is said in the New Testament about the mediatorship of the Son in creation. This is to say that through internal self-differentiation God may grant existence to the multiplicity of creatures being distinctive from him. The self-distinction of the Son as the "structural model (and in this way the Logos) of the determination of all creaturely being,"[26] however, is not to be understood as ending up in self-abandonment or self-alienation. Rather, "the free self-distinction of the Son from the Father"[27] and his affirmation of the community with the Father is possible only through the Spirit of freedom, which grants that "even as the Son moves out of the unity of deity, he is still united with the Father by the Spirit."[28] Thus, the Spirit is conceived as the *principle of community*.

This way of describing the act of creation as originating from God's immanent Trinity allows for recognizing the special character and the continuity of the *one* Spirit's activity in creation and new creation. Fundamental to his understanding of the Spirit is the biblical testimony in which the Spirit is addressed as "the life-giving principle, to which all creatures owe life, movement, and activity"[29] (cf. Gen 2:7; Ps 104:30; Job 33:4). As Pannenberg shows from biblical testimony, the Spirit is not conceived as an immaterial *nous* opposed to matter, but rather as God's breath which blows like a wind.[30] While this description is metaphorical, it indicates that the biblical notion of the Spirit is not based upon a dualist distinction between mind and matter. The characteristic contribution of the Spirit in creation — in his interaction with the Son as the mediator of creation and the Father as the principle of origin — is to move and enliven creatures in the process of creation. As the principle of movement and life, the Spirit allows for the origin and growing complexity of life and the multiplicity and diversity of creatures. This diversity of creatures and their more and

25. Ibid.
26. Pannenberg, *Systematic Theology II*, 29.
27. Pannenberg, *Systematic Theology II*, 30.
28. Ibid.
29. Pannenberg, *Systematic Theology II*, 76.
30. Cf. Pannenberg, *Systematic Theology II*, 78f. Pannenberg relates the biblical notion of Spirit as a dynamic principle in and through matter to the modern physicist field theory in order to elaborate a theological understanding of the dynamic power of the Spirit which overcomes a dualist perspective, cf. ibid., 79-84.

more complex features, however, could not be sustained and developed further without the synthesizing power of the Spirit which prevents creatures from drifting apart from their source of life. This very character of the Spirit's creative activity can also be recognized in his liberating power by which he frees humans from the power of sin and evokes faith and new life in the fellowship with Jesus Christ. Thus, there is no gap between creation and new creation, since the creative activity of the Spirit is always one in character. In interaction with the Father and the Son, the Spirit dwells in the universe and in every single creature, enlivens it, and as a synthesizing power overcomes corruption and alienation.

3. Conclusion

As I have tried to indicate in this paper, the disconnection between the Christian teaching on creation and new creation and the isolation of theological discourse on creation from modern cosmological reflections have been fostered by competing principles of the internal development of Christian teaching. While the focus on the unity of God's action towards the world in combination with the doctrine of personal appropriations in the doctrine of the Trinity did not allow for a detailed reflection on the creativity of God's Spirit, Protestant interpretations of the doctrine of creation tended to neglect cosmological questions and instead focused on the notion of God's providence in salvation. However, by understanding the special character of the Spirit's activity in terms of a synthesizing creativity allowing for diversity without alienation in creation and new creation as proposed in Pannenberg's *Systematic Theology*, it is possible to overcome the gap between the accounts of creation and new creation and develop a coherent strategy to respond to modern challenges to both theological concepts.

One may, however, wonder how Pannenberg's Trinitarian analysis of God's creative activity as Spirit can meet current challenges from New Atheism[31] and the neurosciences. I can only briefly indicate some possible directions in which the potential of a Trinitarian theology can be employed to respond to these challenges. According to the Christian doctrine

31. For a summary and critique of New Atheism cf. H. Schulz, *Alter Wein in neuen Schläuchen oder der Siegeszug des Trivialen,* in: *Theologische Literaturzeitung,* Evangelische Verlagsanstalt Leipzig, 135/1 (2010), 3-20.

of God, God's very being is constituted by an internal self-relation in which he loves himself and through this love is free to grant existence to creatures distinct from him and to care for them with unconditioned grace. This interpretation of the one God's divinity needs to be taken into account if one discusses the claim in New Atheism that monotheistic religions involve a potential of violence.[32]

From the perspective of neurosciences, however, this idea of a loving and gracious God appears as a product of human social orientation shaped and refined in the process of evolution. As neuroscientist Michael Graziano puts it: "The spirit world, from God on down, is the product of the machinery for social perception."[33] A Trinitarian theology is not equipped to either confirm or contradict such a view. Apart from the fact that this could easily result in a category mistake, it may not even be of theological interest to deny that the idea of God is a product of social orientation. From a theological perspective it is more important to closely observe the special character and structure of social perceptions as they allow for social orientation. Social perceptions involve the interaction of generating, differentiating, and synthesizing perceptions. This dynamic process bears a structural analogy to the character of the creativity which

---

32. For the historical development of this challenge cf. K. Müller, *Streit um Gott. Politik, Poetik und Philosophie im Ringen um das wahre Gottesbild,* Pustet: Regensburg, 2006, introduction.

33. Cf. M. Graziano, *God, Soul, Mind, Brain: A Neuroscientist's Reflections on the Spirit World,* A Leapsci Book, Teaticket, MA, 2010, 49. According to Graziano the "[s]pecial-purpose machinery in the human brain, that evolved over millions of years to make us socially intelligent animals, results in our perception of our own consciousness, and in the perceptual illusion that disembodied minds fill up the space around us" (10). Therefore, "when we perceive intentions, emotions, mind *soul,* in another person, it is the specialized social hardware in the brain that is responsible for constructing those perceptions" (13f). Moreover, "it is the same hardware again, creating perceptions of mind and intent to explain the events around us" (14) and "we perceive our own minds using the same neuronal machinery and essentially the same processes that we use to perceive other minds" (51). While Graziano describes the spirit world as a product of social perception, he does, however, not share the idea of atheistic scientists like Richard Dawkins or Bill Maher "that God is an anachronistic and benighted belief, a silly fable, both ignorant and dangerous" (47). Rather, he argues "that a belief in God is a natural extension of the way the human brain is wired" (47). For a proper understanding of Graziano's account it is important to see how he distinguishes the notion of perception from belief, imagination, and theory. "Perception supplies our reality" (50). Therefore, "calling God a belief is a misnomer. It is more than a belief; it is more than a theory; it is more than imagination; it is a perception. That is precisely why it feels real to people" (47).

the biblical tradition ascribes to God's Spirit. While such an analogy cannot be used as a proof for the existence of a divine spirit in distinction from human minds, it may help to overcome a supernatural account of God's activity towards the world in theological discourses and to develop a deeper understanding of the permeating dynamic of the Spirit in all processes of creation and new creation. Such an attempt to achieve a more consistent theological understanding of God's creative activity may itself be understood as an endeavor of Christian reflection "in the struggle of religions for the true form of deity."[34]

---

34. Cf. Pannenberg, *Systematic Theology II,* 171. It is interesting to note that Graziano from the perspective of a social neuroscientist comes to a similar account of religion in saying "that a religion can be thought of as an organized bundle of convictions, replicating from person to person in competition with other religions" (Graziano, see footnote 33, 162). Thus, "religion is something that changes through time, that the parts of religion that work well tend to spread, and that the parts that work poorly tend to die out" (ibid., 160).

The Human Spirit and the Spirit of God

Michael Welker

General talk of the "spirit" is highly ambiguous. In some languages "spirit" refers to the depth and brilliance of a human mind and is used for the person as a whole (e.g., the great German poet Goethe is said to have been a great "spirit"). "Spirit" can also stand for the power or force which gives orientation to the thinking, behavior, and actions of a group, a society, a culture, and even an epoch ("the spirit of a school," "the spirit of an age"). However, the term "spirit" can have negative connotations, for instance when it refers to pathological phenomena ("He saw spirits and was put in a psychiatric institution"). Given such a broad spectrum of meanings, how are we to gain some clarity in the discussion of the "spirit"?

1. Human Mind and Human Spirit

First, in order to gain a clear perspective on the "human spirit," it will be helpful to examine the amazing mental and cognitive capabilities of human beings, beginning with apparently simple and indisputable "basic" cognitive and mental operations. The seemingly trivial ability to take external events and "internalize" them within us is attributed to the human "mind." But we do not just "store" an abundance of signs, sounds, words, and stories in our minds. We do not just bring them forth again and again, and we do not just reproduce impressions and repeat expressions. We create new constellations and connections in our minds which unfold, deepen, and sharpen both our memories and our imaginations. As soon as we want to address the complexity of this enterprise and as soon as we want to acknowledge a remarkable quality of this storing, selecting, connecting, and creative representing and imagining, we do not only speak of a human "mind," but also of the human "spirit."

In order to grasp this human spirit, we have to acknowledge that even the most trivial internalized "depictions" in our mind are incredibly complex. We internalize an object, many objects, networks of objects, indeed an entire environment, or multiple environments, together with their diverse signals, feelings, and impressions which are all taken up into human memory and imagination and thus "spiritualized." These objects, constellations of objects, environments, realms of impressions existed or still exist in physical reality and as potentials of a mental or "spiritual" depiction within our memory and imagination.

On the one hand our "mental (or spiritual) depiction" can be totally inadequate, fleeting, and tainted with self-deception. It remains, as we tend to say, more or less "far removed from reality." A spiritual or mental impression can begin to torment us, can become traumatic and obsessive. It can hinder normal life, and can have an impact on our mental health. In both these instances, "the spiritual" takes on a negative character. Either such mental impressions can never be a match for the fullness, plasticity, and solidity of reality; or they break free into their own independent, ghostly apparitions.

On the other hand we should not let these boundary cases disguise the solidity, richness, and positive power of the spirit and its spiritual dimensions, nor should we underestimate its blessings. We have the power to concentrate on specific objects, networks of objects, events, situations, histories that we can "internalize," store away, and then later recall and recombine. There is room within our memories and imaginations for entire worlds of images and whole "spiritual films." In addition acoustic and spoken impressions are filed away in all their richness: stored, connected, catalogued, and bound together in a variety of ways with individual snapshots and whole series of images and stories. Scents, sounds, and melodies, not to mention tactile impressions, all enrich this mental, spiritual world. And bound to them all are strong impressions and powerful emotions.

The interplay as well as the selection and limitation of these elements are all vitally important and influence the quality and power of our mental operations. Literature, the fine arts, and music all demonstrate the power of the spirit at different levels. Modern film combines pictorial impressions, music, and language and uses them in ways that can provoke incredible fascination. Abstract symbol systems such as mathematics, formal logic, and analytical thought allow us to discover principles, rules, and correlations of order in the natural and intellectual worlds, enabling us to give sensible order to the wealth of these mental impressions and unleashing within us great powers for "world dominion." Using some of these spiritual powers, we can reconstruct past situations and even entire states of the world, and can reliably predict future events and the correlations between these events. They also enable us to communicate with each other over vast distances, not only relaying information, ideas, and stories but also sharing fairly complex emotions, coordinating memories, and expectations, and creating shared spiritual environments and a common world.

This brief sketch of our mental capabilities might give rise to great enthusiasm for the "powers of the spirit," especially when we consider a constellation that fascinated occidental professional and popular philosophy and was often connected with the term "reason." In Book XII of his *Metaphysics,* Aristotle observes that human persons have the (mental) ability to connect their discovery of the world with a growing knowledge of their selves (and to do so in systematic ways), and the tendency of these two forms of knowledge to mutually amplify and strengthen one another. "Thinking in itself deals with that which is best in itself, and the more it is thinking, the more it deals with that which is best. Spirit (= *nous,* which might be more appropriately translated as reason) thinks itself by participating in that which is thought. Spirit (reason) becomes itself an object of thought by grasping and thinking that which is thought, so that spirit (reason) and that which is thought are identical."[1] Aristotle sees in this not only the spiritual power of thinking and "reason" *(nous),* but also nothing less than the existence of the divine. "For that which is capable of receiving that which is thought and which is, is also spirit, to be sure, but it is in actual activity only when it has (that which is thought). Thus actually active thought, more so than the capacity to think, is the divine element that spirit seems to have."

However, we should be extremely cautious not to glorify the spirit in ideological ways (be it even in the forms of thought and reason). Apart from recognized psychotic phenomena, the many and varied ways in which spiritual communication can be used (consciously and unconsciously) for what is ill and evil must always be taken into account when we examine the phenomena of the spirit. It is not only the helpful and healthy communications, illuminations, and reductionisms but also the emotionalizations and the trivializing and banalizing forms of thought (even under the title of

---

1. Aristotle, *The Works of Aristotle,* vol. 8, Metaphysica, transl. W. D. Ross, Oxford: Clarendon Press, 1928, 1072b, 19-32.

philosophy or theology) which can be transported spiritually, and which can become communicatively and culturally engrained.

On the one hand, monistic, dual, and dualistic forms of thought serve to harness broad cultural concepts and enable the controlled progress of thought and quick and dependable communication. Yet on the other hand, these forms also serve to highly degrade thought and experience, distanced as they are from the fullness of real life and its formative opportunities. When combined with strong emotion, reductionistic thought can blind people in highly dangerous ways and pledge them to harmful ideologies both cognitively and morally. An "evil spirit" then controls the minds and souls and employs the many mental abilities towards the corruption and destruction of our human and created conditions of life. In this light, it would be highly problematic to simply invest that tremendous spiritual world automatically with associations such as "good," "promotive of life," or even "divine."

2. Human Spirit and Divine Spirit

These observations of the deep ambivalence of the power of the spirit challenge us to develop a nuanced understanding of the relationship between God's Spirit and the human spirit. The Apostle Paul perceives the incredible complexity of the human spirit when he marvels at its ability to overcome spatial and temporal distances, to enter into contact not only with other human beings but even with God Himself. However, he also sees the limitations of the complex spirit which intervenes for us before God "with sighs too deep for words" (Rom. 8:26). "For we do not know how we ought to pray; the spirit himself pleads with God for us in groans that words cannot express." By speaking in tongues the spirit seeks in a highly ambiguous way to enter into contact with God (1 Cor. 14:1ff.). Paul comments: "In church I would rather speak five words with reason *(nous)* . . . than ten thousand words in tongues" (1 Cor. 14:19). This indicates clearly that a spirit on its own does not automatically lead to clear insights and clear speech. But even clear speech, apparently firm hearts, and clear consciences can be lied to and deceived, determined, and led astray by a "spirit of the world" (1 Cor 2:12, and often) which closes them off from God. So-called "final concepts of God" may be clear and impressive, yet still spiritually impoverished or empty; and they may systematically distort and deform our relationship to God.

Therefore it is important that we never just simply associate the spiritual world with the divine world, nor simply equate the divine Spirit with the intellectual world. "God is Spirit" — but God is not, as Aristotle and many of his followers seem to suggest, essentially reason and intellect. The creative Spirit of God also touches and shapes the natural world and the natural networks of life. Again, Paul emphasizes this frequently in the area of anthropology when he says that God's Holy Spirit pours God's love into the human hearts (of flesh!) (Rom. 5:5) and that human bodies are supposed to be the "temple of the Holy Spirit" (1 Cor. 6:19). Yet the workings of the Spirit should not be limited to the realm of anthropology and "the increasing complexity of hominin social life over the past two million years."[2]

Neither should this insight lead us, with Spinoza, to equate God and nature *(deus sive natura)*, nor should we derive an abstract theism or even pantheism from the occasional use of the biblical phrase "all things," connected with God's workings. The biblical talk of the restoration and renewal of "the whole" *(panta)* should not be confused with the meaning "anything and everything." The biblical traditions make it very clear that God can "withdraw" His hand and His Spirit, that God can turn His "countenance away" and leave creation to self-jeopardy, self-destruction, decay, and death.[3] Therefore we must ask which specific creativity is to be connected with the Spirit of God. Here we need to take into account the connection between creation and new creation, as well as the way in which the Spirit of God has been christologically shaped.

The setting in motion of the cosmos and the processes of natural evolution are certainly deserving of our wonder and our research efforts. Yet they cannot answer the problem of theodicy — for "life is robbery" (Whitehead), life lives off other life.[4] And the incredible extension of the universe, given the highly probable finitude of all natural life, can hardly dispel the impression of its and of our final futility and senselessness.[5]

---

2. D. Alexander, *The Spirit of God in Evolutionary History*, in this volume; see also the contributions in this book of J. Schloss, *Hovering Over the Waters: Spirit and the Ordering of Creation*, and S. Horujy, *How Exactly Is the Spirit Present in Creation?*

3. Cf. the dialogue and discussion between John Polkinghorne and Michael Welker in *Faith in the Living God. A Dialogue*, London and Philadelphia: SPCK and Fortress, 2001.

4. Michael Welker, *Konzepte von 'Leben' in Nietzsches Werk. Eine Sichtung von Denkansätzen*, in *Leben, Marburger Jahrbuch Theologie IX*, ed. W. Haerle and R. Preul, Marburg: Elwert, 1997, 41-52.

5. Cf. the first chapters of J. Polkinghorne and M. Welker (eds.), *The End of the World and the Ends of God: Science and Theology on Eschatology*, Harrisburg: Trinity, 2000.

What we need here is an examination of the Spirit of God, an examination which takes into account the forces of new creation revealed in the resurrection of Jesus Christ and in the Pentecostal outpouring of the Spirit. Yet these forces of salvation and exaltation must not be isolated in an end-time eschatology. They are also formatively at work now, in this creation. For this reason, the discourse between theology and the natural sciences, on topics dealing with the real, natural, and social world, are not only advisable but utterly indispensable.

Thus genuinely christological and pneumatological perspectives on the workings of the Spirit must return and refer back to the forces of creation. For the biblical witnesses, creation right from "the beginning" aims at the sabbath, the cult, the temple, and the mutual communication between God and humanity; and likewise today we need a differentiated understanding of the continuity and discontinuity of "creation and new creation." The great significance of the spirit, even with regard to the astonishing individual and cultural abilities discussed above, needs to be reevaluated in this context — and also subjected to a "discernment of the spirits." For by no means do all natural and all mental or spiritual powers correspond to the intentions of God the creator. We need to examine whether their impressive achievements can indeed be put in relation to the Spirit of God — or whether they finally just disguise and strengthen those forces which render earthly life increasingly more banal, and then finally destroy it.[6]

3. The Spirit in New Creation

It is most important not to identify "new creation" exclusively with end-time theophany. Rather, the creative God, the resurrected and elevated Christ, and the workings of the Holy Spirit bring the powers of "new creation" into creaturely and human life on earth, into nature and history. The coming reign of God or the reign of Christ, for which Christianity prays in the "Lord's prayer," connects "present eschatology" and "future eschatology" and constitutes the "new creation" in the midst of the "old creation." A transformation and renewal of creation takes place which will be fulfilled in the end-time theophany but is not restricted to it.[7]

---

6. This concern governs Vladimir Shmaliy's contribution in this volume.

7. Cf. the contributions in T. Peters, R. Russell, and M. Welker (eds.), *Resurrection: Theological and Scientific Assessments,* Grand Rapids: Eerdmans, 2002.

The promise and the event of the "pouring of the Spirit" offers a powerful witness to the work of the Holy Spirit in new creation. The announcements of the Messiah on which the Spirit of God will "rest" (cf. esp. Isaiah 11, 42, and 61) say that the Messiah will bring "justice, mercy and the cognition of God" to Israel and to the gentiles.[8] The New Testament sees these promises fulfilled in the coming of Jesus Christ. "Justice, mercy, and faith" are the "weighty matters of the law" (Matt. 23:23). Thus the Messiah will bring the "fulfillment of the law." He will, however, bring it by "baptizing with the Spirit," by involving His witnesses as the "members of His body" into His post-Easterly, resurrected life. James Dunn has noticed that the New Testament coined a fresh image that strengthened the hope for a "richer experience of God's vitalizing presence and activity" on earth. Jesus, "who had been inspired by the Spirit, had now become the dispenser of the Spirit."[9]

The pouring out of the Spirit as an act of "new creation" is in many respects revolutionary. It transcends the boundaries and limits of an ethnic religiosity. It also questions the patriarchal, ageistic, and class fostering structures by stressing with Old and New Testament voices that God's Spirit will be and has been poured out on "males and females, old and young, masters and slaves" (cf. Joel 2:17f and Acts 2:17f).[10] The edification of the "body of Christ" thus transforms sexist, ageist, and social conflicts and tensions. This does not mean that the Holy Spirit brings an abstract unification, turning all members of the body of Christ into standardized "subjects" in the sense of some popular modern philosophies. John Polkinghorne has stressed the "context-sensitivity" of the working of the Holy Spirit. For this reason the Spirit is rightly attributed a "personality,"[11] although the Holy Spirit does not exhibit structures of self-referential personhood which are basically shaped by thought and reason.[12] The Holy Spirit "will not speak on his own authority" (John 16:13; cf. Rom. 8).

---

8. Cf. M. Welker, *God the Spirit,* Philadelphia: Fortress, 1994, part 3.

9. J. Dunn, *Towards the Spirit of Christ: The Emergence of the Distinctive Features of Christian Pneumatology,* in M. Welker (ed.), *The Work of the Spirit: Pneumatology and Pentecostalism,* Grand Rapids: Eerdmans, 2006, 3-26; see also the contributions of Frank Macchia in that book and in this volume.

10. M. Welker, *God the Spirit,* part 5; see also the contribution of Jürgen Moltmann in this volume.

11. J. Polkinghorne, *The Hidden Spirit and the Cosmos,* in M. Welker (ed.), *The Work of the Spirit,* 169-182.

12. I have shown this in *God the Spirit,* part 6.

Enormous dynamics come with the work of the Holy Spirit, a fact which makes it very clear that the new creation is not a black picture of a death-like "eternal rest," but an "eternal life" which is already reflected and expressed in the true worship of the church, in its celebration of the sacraments, and in its proclamation and teaching, but also in the diaconical and prophetic existence which bear witness to the resurrected and elevated Christ in the power of the Holy Spirit. Thus we see the differentiated spiritual presence of God more clearly, despite its immense power and richness, when we consider its Christo-morphic shape of the elevated Christ in continuity and discontinuity with the incarnation, the cross, and the resurrection of Christ. The spiritual presence of Christ and the triune God brings the creative transformation of the whole creation into the new creation, the elevation, purification, and glorification of creation.

First, in the light of the pre-Easter life of Christ, a *theological humanism*[13] is generated. The powers of love and forgiveness radiate oriented on the caring, sustaining, and rescuing God whom Christians see revealed in the brotherly *kingship of Christ.* This spiritual reign is concerned with the care for very basic human needs, such as nourishment, healing, and fellowship. It is intensely correlated with the familial and educational systems, with the establishment of health care and basic human social and diaconical routines, with the rule of a just law and, in our time, of human rights. These powers of the new creation, already at work in the middle of the old creation, are not confined to human societies and cultures. They have an impact, visibly or in latent and emergent ways, on the rest of creation.[14]

The second dimension brings the revealing and judging aspects of the presence of the divine, which are attributed to the *prophetic office of Christ* and which should be correlated with the complex understanding of the dimension of the cross. In this respect, not only the co-suffering and kenotic presence of God, but also the disclosure at the cross of the principalities and powers which dominate even religion, politics, morals, and public opinion are crucial. Here the real and the symbol-political conflicts, the critique and self-critique of religion, the critique of academic, moral, legal, and political developments which are not compatible with the search for truth, justice, and mercy, and the striving for freedom and peace, become

---

13. Cf. D. R. Klemm and W. Schweiker, *Religion and the Human Future: An Essay on Theological Humanism,* Chichester: Blackwell Publ., 2008.

14. See the contributions of John Polkinghorne and Jürgen Moltmann in this volume.

important. And here again, we see a broad impact on the whole of creation which has suffered and still suffers from all sorts of chauvinism, colonialism, racism, and ecological brutalism. In the middle and against the groaning of creation under the powers of sin and death, the Spirit of new creation is constantly working towards "new heavens and a new earth in which righteousness dwells" (2 Peter 3:13).

Finally, we have to envision the sanctifying and ennobling presence of the divine Spirit, which Christian faith correlates with the priestly office of Christ and with the powers revealed in the resurrection. As Francis Fiorenza has shown,[15] the resurrected Christ brings the basic spiritual forms of the constitution of the life of the church, such as the breaking of the bread, the illumination and opening of the Scriptures, the greeting of peace, the sending of the disciples, etc. — basic forms which Christians connect with the constitution of the body of Christ and its service in the world. All these spiritual powers of the new creation — the diaconical, prophetic, and pastoral forms — reach far beyond human societies, cultures, and the realms of the church. The reign of the triune God and thus the reign of Christ want to gain shape and clarity in the life of the church, but they are not confined to it.[16]

All three dimensions of the spiritual presence of the divine which Christians see revealed in the life and lordship of Jesus Christ show various interdependences and a multitude of specific radiations into the different spheres of our cultures, our systems of memories and imaginations. They work for the transformation of the human spirits, souls, and minds, the fleshly hearts and the bodies — and through it on a constant transformation of all dimensions of spiritual and natural creation. This orientation will help us to replace all sorts of vague visions, mere wishes, soft pleas, and illusions by a biblically oriented and realistic eschatology to which both theology and science have to contribute.

---

15. F. Fiorenza, *The Resurrection of Jesus and Roman Catholic Fundamental Theology*, in S. T. Davis, D. Kendall, and G. O'Collins (eds.), *The Resurrection: An Interdisciplinary Symposium on the Resurrection of Jesus*, Oxford: Oxford University Press, 1997, 213-248, 238ff.

16. Cf. the "General Eschatology," which deals with the "transition of the contemporary shape of the world to the renewed one," developed by D. Staniloae, *Orthodoxe Dogmatik III*, Düsseldorf and Gütersloh: Benzinger and Gütersloher, 1995, 318ff., with strong references not only to the church fathers but also to Sergej Bulgakow, Nicolai Lossky, and Paul Florensky.

'Keep Thy Mind in Hell and Despair Not': Implications for Psychosocial Work with Survivors of Political Violence

Renos K. Papadopoulos

This is not a theological essay. I am not a theologian but a social scientist and academic who is also involved in field projects offering psycho-social assistance to refugees and other survivors of political violence but also traumatised victims of natural disasters. In this paper, I will attempt to develop some reflections about aspects of my work from an Orthodox Christian perspective which, to my understanding, address the theme of our symposium, the Spirit in Creation.

1. New Creation and Spirit in Social Sciences

At the outset, it seems appropriate to ponder on what could be understood by the Spirit and its role in the movement from Creation to New Creation in the context of social sciences. My esteemed colleagues in this volume address the same question mainly from the perspectives of theology and natural sciences where there is a considerable body of literature dealing with these connections. However, when we move to the human and social sciences it is rather difficult to find any established tradition within which to formulate further observations.

However, by making use of part of Welker's contribution, it will be argued that it is possible to create a working framework within which to locate meaningfully an attempt to relate this theme within the context of social sciences.

Welker emphasises that the term 'New Creation' should not be restricted to its eschatological meaning. He argues that 'It is most important not to identify "new creation" exclusively with end-time theophany'

143

(p. 139) and emphasises that the transformative power of the Spirit is 'also formatively at work now, in this creation' (p. 139). According to him, it is the Holy Spirit that could be accepted as responsible for the 'transformation and renewal of creation' (p. 139) now, 'in the midst of the "old creation"' (p. 139).

He develops this understanding on the basis of a Christological dimension of the Spirit as it manifests itself in what he calls 'diaconical, prophetic, and pastoral forms' (p. 142). The diaconical 'is concerned with the care for very basic human needs, such as nourishment, healing, and fellowship. It is intensely correlated with the familial and educational systems, with the establishment of health care and basic human social and diaconical routines, with the rule of a just law and, in our time, of human rights' (p. 141); the prophetic relates to the 'complex understanding of the dimension of the cross' (p. 141) according to which the 'real and the symbol-political conflicts' that 'the whole of creation . . . has suffered and still suffers' become transformed through the 'groaning of creation under the powers of sin and death' into 'the Spirit of new creation' (pp. 141-42) that relates to 'the search for truth, justice and mercy, and the striving for freedom and peace' (p. 141). Finally, the last spiritual power of the new creation, for him, is the pastoral one that relates to the 'basic forms which Christians connect with the constitution of the body of Christ and its service in the world' (p. 142).

Making use of Welker's approach, it would be possible to argue that in social sciences the Spirit in New Creation could be related to the power that enables transformation even now, in this creation, not only in an eschatological context, at all the spheres of social life, indeed, the power of 'a constant transformation' of 'the human spirits, souls and minds' (p. 142). In other words, New Creation could be understood as a renewed form of the existing creation in so far as it reflects and indeed incorporates and embodies elements of the eschatological celebration of a world in truth and in harmony with its creator, imbued by the very spirit of creation.

Moving on to the three specific forms of the spirit that may transform the creation into a renewed creation, the 'diaconical' one could be related to any service endeavours that are directed towards the attending of needs of our fellow human beings that are undertaken in the spirit of selfless love and care promoting dignity and respect, without violating any aspect of the divine nature of creation but, in fact, celebrating it; the 'prophetic' could be related to the power of transformation that enables an impossibly bleak situation devoid of hope and realistic resolution to be turned into an unexpected epiphany, indeed, the transformative power of the cross that enables Christ to 'overcome death by death.' It seems that the characterisation of 'prophetic' here refers to the resurrection and eschatological apocatastasis. Finally, the equivalent of 'pastoral form' in social sciences could relate to the spiritual and inspirational dimension of an organised body of committed service in the world.

Having established this tentative and working framework, let us now move on to the subject matter of my own speciality in order, later, to relate it back to the Spirit in Creation and New Creation. However, before proceeding, an important methodological comment is warranted.

The words 'Spirit' and 'New Creation' are theological terms and more specifically belong to the Christian theological tradition. Within that context they refer to the actual Holy Spirit and the idea that this universe is God's creation which He did not abandon; rather, He still attends to it and constantly wishes to renew it with the ultimate eschatological plan to transform it into its original true nature devoid of evil, corruption, and death. Using the same terms in the context of Social Sciences, they may have two independent or interrelated meanings.

The first is metaphorical, understanding them as referring to transformation in the realm of human societies where we observe that renewals of different types, shapes, and forms do take place. Undeniably, we may appreciate that there is a discernible degree of development in the history of human awareness with regard to what promotes and what impedes human dignity (e.g. identification of different forms of abuse and their condemnation, abolition of the death penalty, denunciation of torture). Accordingly, the Spirit here would refer to the power of positive transformation in general and New Creation to any forms of improved human societies.

The second is in fact literal, i.e. Christian. According to this, all the discernable changes are accepted as evidence of the work of the Holy Spirit that enables the gradual maintenance and renewal of this creation aiming to lead humanity to the ultimate New Creation that will be realised with the triumphal second coming of Christ. According to this literal meaning, the observable changes would be analogous to the changes in human evolution and in natural sciences as they are discussed in the other chapters in this volume.

These two meanings can be separated but also can be appreciated as complementary.

Renos K. Papadopoulos

2. Trauma and Psychosocial Interventions

Often our world is overwhelmed with images of conflict and disaster and the resulting human suffering. In parallel, there has been a growing propagation of psychological theories attempting to explain these phenomena. Despite the differences in the theories as well as the diversity and complexity of the contexts and circumstances of these events, there is a prevailing belief that tends to be oversimplified and which holds that almost everybody affected by these events is 'traumatised.' The word 'trauma' has entered the popular vocabulary of our everyday lives and is used fairly indiscriminately. There is a widespread tendency to call 'traumatic' virtually any experience of discomfort, however trivial.

Yet, there is a central paradox connected with the word 'trauma.' Despite its oversimplification, this term can have a considerably powerful effect on individuals and groups, on journalists and politicians, mobilising them to act in ways that they would not have acted had this term not been used.

It seems that the presentation of collective phenomena of human suffering in mass media tends to activate what we could refer to as a 'societal discourse on trauma'; by this we could understand the cluster of all the society's ideas, images, feelings, perceptions, thoughts, stories, reactions connected with 'trauma.' All these elements form a whole that, despite its loose structure and vague content, nevertheless has a strong impact on society. These 'traumatic' events generate a powerful sense of engagement and urgency as well as a corresponding sense of helplessness. Everybody wants to 'do something about it,' anything, to alleviate or even extinguish human suffering that is depicted (and experienced) as being unbearable. In this emotionally charged climate, the 'societal discourse on trauma' appears to fulfil an important function in society insofar as it offers (a) a seemingly intelligible grasp of the (otherwise often) incomprehensible calamity, (b) some sense of care and concern thus counteracting helplessness, and (c) some sense of order in so far as it identifies roles and tasks, e.g. by medicalising human suffering it assigns to the health professionals the role of attending to the 'traumatised' people.

The 'societal discourse of trauma' galvanises energy and initiates relief activities of various kinds. Needless to say, not all of this action is effective or even appropriate; on the contrary, often such action tends to be ineffective, at best, or even detrimental, at worst. However, it enables people to feel that they have 'addressed' the issue, done their best, and they can now move on with their lives.

Some of the consequences of the 'societal discourse on trauma' include the development of the following: a 'trauma industry' that is mobilised whenever such phenomena occur, intending to address the plight of the 'traumatised' people; distinct identities of those who are considered to be 'traumatised victims' and those who are acting as 'caring rescuers'; the tendency to form sharply polarised and oversimplified perceptions and judgements at all levels, in relation, for example, as to who is the perpetrator and who the victim, what led to the tragedy and who is to blame for it, what is the best way to help those who suffered, how to resolve the conflict, etc.

Some of the more problematic implications of the 'societal discourse on trauma' include the following: the tendency to enwrap those whom we want to help within the identity of the victim, victimising the survivors in order to politically attack the perpetrators, psychologising the political dimensions, pathologising and medicalising human suffering.

According to the classic formulation of the 'trauma industry,' the problem was defined in terms of the 'traumatised victims' and the solution proposed was to treat them medically or psychiatrically. An improvement of that formulation was offered by the emergence of what is referred to as a 'psychosocial' approach that emphasises the importance of developing creative combinations of interventions that address not only the psychological but also the various actual social dimensions of the suffering and deprivation experienced by those affected by the adversity. A wide range of factors and areas affecting the adversity survivors is identified addressing the basic and gradually more advanced human needs, e.g. need for safety, shelter, food, water, sanitation, then basic health care and education, then basic family spaces and relationships, community and vocational involvement, etc. However, both approaches seem to share many underlying assumptions in that they focus mainly on the 'traumatised victims,' construed as people being helpless individuals who passively receive assistance from others.

3. The 'Trauma Grid'

Appreciating the importance of avoiding the predominant oversimplification that is generated by the 'societal discourse on trauma,' the 'Trauma Grid' (Papadopoulos, 2004, 2006, 2007) was developed in order to identify the wide range of responses to adversity and increase the complexity of comprehending these phenomena.

To begin with, this grid proposes that the responses are divided into three groups, i.e. negative, positive, and neutral. Moreover, it subdivides the negative responses into three degrees of severity:

1. *Psychiatric Disorders (PD):* this is the most severe form of the negative consequences of exposure to adversity and it certainly requires specialist professional treatment. The most common type of this effect is the Post Traumatic Stress Disorder (PTSD) and most of the literature on refugees and other survivors of political violence who experience trauma tends to be focused on this disorder. However, there are also other responses to adversity that fall within the range of psychiatric, disorders, such as psychotic or depressive reactions. However, undeniably, since its inception in 1980, PTSD has been the most common psychiatric disorder that has been attributed to responses to these types of adversity.

2. *Distressful Psychological Reactions (DPR):* this category includes the various combinations of psychological symptoms (e.g. persistent flashbacks of the initial traumatising events, startling response, disturbances of sleep and or eating, etc.) that do not amount to a full diagnosis of PTSD or any other psychiatric disorders.

3. *Ordinary Human Suffering (OHS):* this is the most common response to tragedies in life. This category includes all the responses that people usually have to human misfortune: sadness, despair, anger, as well as hope and trust that time would heal their wounds. Often, people have various systems of meaning that render meaningful and intelligible their suffering, thus offering them not only sufficient support during their difficult times but also hope for the future. Such systems include political, religious, ideological, etc. For example, Mandela appreciated that his extensive term of 27 years' incarceration (most of it in solitary confinement) was not an unexpected consequence of his lifelong commitment to political struggle for the abolition of racial discrimination in his country, South Africa; consequently, Mandela is often seen as an inspirational example of a person who dedicated his life to a just cause, rather than a person who was traumatised by his adverse conditions of lengthy imprisonment. Undeniably, his own writings and very life testify to the fact that indeed he saw himself as a freedom fighter rather than as a traumatised prisoner.

In addition to the negative effects, there are also positive responses to and effects of being exposed to adversity:

Undoubtedly, there are refugees and other survivors of political violence who not only survive the inhuman and cruel conditions they had endured with a significant degree of intactness but, moreover, they become strengthened by their exposure to adversity. It is for this reason that this response has been termed 'Adversity-Activated Development' (AAD) (Papadopoulos, 2004, 2006, 2007). AAD refers to the positive developments that are a direct result of being exposed to adversity, to the development that was activated specifically by the adversity. For example, having survived life-threatening situations one may develop a new zest for life, compassion for the suffering of others, a deep religious attitude, etc. The human capacity to transform adversity into positive development is a well-known phenomenon that exists in all cultures and religions.

Finally, the 'neutral' responses refer to the various positive personality qualities, functions, characteristics, and abilities that were not affected either positively or negatively by the person's exposure to adversity. They are called 'neutral' not because they are not positive in their essence but because they were not affected at all by the experienced adversity. This means that these existing strengths are *resilient* to the impact from adversity and continue to exist as they did prior to the person's exposure to adversity. This is the real meaning of resilience — the ability not to be affected by a negative impact and to retain existing positive qualities.

It is important to distinguish between AAD and *resilience* (which is not done by the existing literature): AAD refers to new and positive qualities that were developed as a result of being exposed to adversity whereas *resilience* refers to existing positive characteristics that survived the impact from adversity. Resilient are the qualities that were retained despite the adversity whereas AAD are the positive qualities that were developed because of the adversity.

The grid enables the identification of a wide variety of responses to adversity not only by an individual but also by families, communities, and societies/cultures, at large. In this way, it avoids crude generalisations and aims to achieve maximum differentiation. Human beings are complex and may exhibit simultaneously a variety of different responses; e.g. in some respects, an individual may be traumatised but at the same time certain positive functions and characteristics may have survived the trauma and they may still be active in her/him; also, at the same time, the same person may have acquired new positive qualities as a direct conse-

Levels	Negative responses			'Neutral' responses	Positive responses
	Injury, Wound			Resilience	AAD
	PD, PTSD	DPR	OHS		
Individual					
Family					
Community					
Society/ Culture					

AAD = Adversity-Activated Development   PD = Psychiatric Disorder
DPR = Distressful Psychological Reactions   PTSD = Post-Traumatic Stress Disorder
OHS = Ordinary Human Suffering

quent of his/her traumatic experience and it is important that both adversity survivors as well as staff working with them are aware of this differentiated complexity.

It is often thought that there is a temporal progression from negative to positive responses to trauma, from the left to the right boxes of the grid. This is not untrue. However, what is more important is to appreciate that all these responses also exist simultaneously. This means that the same person at the same time exhibits a wide variety of responses to adversity, including some positive, some negative, some neutral. It is crude to consider a person either as being 'traumatised' or being 'resilient.' It is important to develop a more differentiated perception of the complexity of each person's specific responses to adversity.

The theoretical background of the grid could be traced to the ideas of Carl Gustav Jung (1878-1961) who advocated that the therapist should not attempt just to eliminate the presenting psychological symptoms but should endeavour to explore their meaning. He maintained that the symptoms should be respected because they are expressions of the psyche's effort to heal itself, emphasising that once we appreciate that suffering can be meaningful, it is very likely that it will promote the required psychological development and transformation. Jung urged that we should not be overwhelmed by the negative effects of suffering but also see the opportunities they open up for us to develop further. In short, for Jung, suffering is inevitable and meaningful and it can facilitate transformation.

4. 'Keep Thy Mind in Hell and Despair Not'

Experiences from the application of the trauma grid in clinical and field work with refugees and other survivors of political violence show that the grid can be most helpful in facilitating workers to maintain the delicate balance between two seemingly contradictory positions: on the one hand, to connect deeply with the painful experiences of the adversity survivors whilst, on the other hand and at the same time, appreciating the reality of the positive effects that adversity activates in the same persons.

Reflecting on these experiences, the saying *'keep thy mind in hell but despair not'* can provide a meaningful framework that can not only render intelligible these paradoxically oppositional directions but also enrich our understanding of these complex and painful processes.

To begin with, it is essential to make an important clarification. *'Keep thy mind in hell but despair not'* is located within a very specific spiritual context and tradition. As such, it refers to a state of a high spiritual functioning that is the outcome of a long and arduous regime of spiritual practices within the Orthodox Christian ascetic tradition; it refers to a process that cannot be grasped easily, let alone practiced. Therefore, this dictum is used in this paper not in its natural context but in approximation, endeavouring to explore its theme and message in other contexts, mainly psychological. In other words, it needs to be clarified that the discussion below represents an attempted adaptation of this saying in relation to psychosocial work with adversity survivors.

'Keep thy mind in hell but despair not' is not just a simple saying but a full formulation of a highly intricate stance in relation to many fundamental themes in life. In short, this saying urges one not to reject or minimise the seriousness and importance of the experiences of 'hell' whilst, at the same time, not to 'despair' and, therefore, open up to the more positive effects of such an exposure.

The saying is by a Russian monk called Silouan (1866-1938) who spent forty-five years on Mount Athos and was canonised by the Christian Orthodox Ecumenical Patriarchate in 1987 (S. Sakharov, 1991). This virtually uneducated monk, whose birth name was Simeon Ivanovich Antonov, grew to become a renowned ascetic and spiritual master whom Thomas Merton characterised as 'the most authentic monk of the twentieth century.'

In general terms, in Christian theology, 'hell' would be understood as the absence of God and as the locus where there is an absence of the healing power of the Holy Spirit. More precisely, 'hell' would be the location persons occupy (consciously or unconsciously) where they find it impossible to access God and the healing Spirit.

In a comparable way, from a psychological point of view, hell could be understood as the location persons occupy (consciously or unconsciously) where they are overwhelmed with pain, despair, and unbearable suffering, where they experience pain and suffering as meaningless, and where they find it impossible to access:

(a) any outside agency (person or any other entity, e.g. community, organisation, ideology, etc.) that could contain their suffering, give it meaning, provide relief, and even end it

(b) any capacity in themselves that possibly could give meaning, relief, or end their pain and suffering.

An important characteristic of the 'hell' experience is that the person does not perceive the unbearable situation as being temporary, time-limited, or with any improvement in sight. The sense that the hell state is unending gives it an even more insufferable quality.

The dictum specifies that despair should not overwhelm us. However, whereas the main emphasis in Orthodox ascetic practices is on the heart and not the mind, it is in the mind that we are urged to keep hell and not in the heart. The distinction is crucial. Archimandrite Zacharias Zacharou clarifies that 'when man receives illumination and sanctification, then his whole being becomes a heart. The heart is synonymous with the soul, with the spirit; it is a spiritual place where man finds his unity, where his mind is enthroned when it has been healed of the passions' (2007, p. 27).

'*Keep thy mind in hell*' means that one remains mindful that one is living in a state of hell. The '*despair not*' part of the saying refers to the effort to keep the heart away from hell so that hope will still be possible. Heart, being the spiritual centre of the being, should always be turning to and remain connected with God.

The saying implies two simultaneous states, i.e. awareness of being in hell as well as firmness in the belief that there is hope, two simultaneous feelings, i.e. unbearable pain for being lodged in hell but also hope and not despair, trusting that deliverance is possible. The mind is connected with the awareness of the present fallen state and the heart is connected with the potential glorified and sanctified state of new creation beyond evil and suffering and death. This stereoscopic perspective grasps both realities and dimensions of the human existence synchronically.

From a psychological perspective, the *'keep thy mind in hell but despair not'* dictum would provide a person with the stamina to endure such hell states, render them meaningful, enable transformation, and open up the possibility to access healing from outside and from within.

Psychologically speaking, we may differentiate between two types of hell: the internal and external which, of course, are closely interlinked.

External hell would refer to any set of external conditions and circumstances that induce a person to locate him/herself in a hell position. These would include any types of adversity ranging from being subjected to physical violence, intimidation, and injustice, being deprived of material possessions, basic home comforts, ordinary work routines, to experiencing a wide variety of losses (e.g. persons and family, material, community, psychological, professional, cultural, linguistic, etc.).

Internal hell would refer to any set of internal states and conditions that induce a person to locate him/herself in a hell position. These would include any types of psychological encapsulation, alienation where a person is not able to access any healing either from self or from others or from any other dimension. In such states, a person, as a closed system, suffers from psychological entropy where no new information is able to enter or be exchanged with anything/anybody outside him/herself. Examples of these would be fear, self-pity, consuming anger, envy, suspicion, hatred, pride, etc., as well as asphyxiating over-identification with certain identities, e.g. as a victim, as a saviour, as a hero, etc.

Understandably, these two types of hell (internal and external) are closely interconnected and the one can trigger off or strengthen the other. For example, a brutalised and severely deprived refugee who sustained a lot of external losses may develop such mistrust that it may, in turn, prevent him/her from opening up, relating to a humanitarian worker, and being able to receive external (material) and psychological relief.

From a psychological point of view, *'keep thy mind in hell but despair not'* refers to a process by which a person confronts directly the limits of his/her existing state and, insofar as it suggests 'hope against hope,' it forces one to transcend oneself and access deeper realms of the personality. In Jungian terms, this transcendence would be the movement from the personal conscious ego to the deeper Self which is connected both with inner wisdom and with wider collective realms. This process, in effect, represents the key mechanism of psychological healing and transformation.

Again, it is important to reemphasise that these considerations are only hints of distant approximations of the real meaning and actual practice of *'keep thy mind in hell but despair not.'* Obviously, Saint Silouan did not refer to this saying in the contexts this paper addresses; instead, here the theme of this saying is transposed in the context of psychosocial realms of working with adversity survivors.

5. 'Hell' in Work with Refugees and Other Survivors of Political Violence

The image and experience of hell is not uncommon in working with this group of people. Hell may be experienced by the survivors themselves in relation to many possible contexts, e.g. the original conditions that created the conflict, the conditions of living in displacement, the treatment by the humanitarian agencies, the prospects for the future, etc. The humanitarian workers may also experience hell in relation to many related contexts, e.g. the brutalities that are connected with the initial conflict, the inhuman living conditions of both survivors and themselves, the awkward relationships with other agencies, the difficult relationships with the survivors they attend to, the lack of resources, the bleak prospects for the future, etc.

It is very easy for both survivors and helpers to enter into the overconsuming despair of hell. Often the unspeakable evil nature of human brutality is so incomprehensible that only the image of hell can capture it in some way. The same can be said about the horrendously miserable and cruel conditions that human beings are forced to live in after they are rescued from the initial humanitarian disaster. The list of such tangible places, conditions, and experiences of hell in such situations is endless.

Saint Silouan's dictum (always as it could be transposed outside its original context) then encourages us not only not to run away from the excruciatingness of these hell situations but also to trust that this very persistent focus on the awfulness of the situation will activate a certain process of transcendence that will bring about a radical transformation, a paradigmatic shift, resulting in a new epistemology that will enable access to healing from sources and in ways that our previous state of being could not even have registered before.

More specifically, in the context of this work, we could ask the following two questions:

What is the sense of *'keeping thy mind in hell'?* By facing the acts of inhumanity we deepen our understanding of the complexity of human nature and of our own individual nature. By attempting to comprehend the meaning of such acts of human depravity, of such living conditions of in-human deprivation, etc., we have the opportunity to put into perspective our own personal, family, and community priorities, review our lives, ap-preciate that conscious and committed decisions are required of us if we wish to lead a full and responsible life, we realise that we need to take a stand in life and not live an unquestioning life according to vague and un-consciously adopted formulas, we become aware that, indeed, there is a great deal of evil in this world and we do have an option as to whether we respond to evil by evil or we endeavour to retain our values, at whatever cost.

What is the sense of *'despair not'*? By enduring hell in this way, we trust that something beyond our conscious and insular system will break through and enrich our perspectives. We are reminded that healing and enhancing opportunities are available to us, if we would only alter our per-spectives and allow them to become visible to us. We can appreciate that inner and outer resources can be accessed. We are enabled to discern that in circumstances where we are overwhelmed by experiences of distilled evil there we can also uncover instances of distilled good, e.g. acts of self-sacrifice, of magnanimity, of unconditional love and care.

In particular, in the context of the trauma grid, *'despair not'* enables us to appreciate that in addition to (and not instead of) the negative conse-quences, there are also existing positive qualities that survive adversity (re-silience) as well as new positive characteristics that are activated as a result of being exposed to adversity (AAD).

Understood in this way, this dictum can provide a most eloquent con-text for appreciating the phenomena of AAD that demonstrate that the very experience of adversity activates development that would not have occurred otherwise.

Moreover, Archimandrite Sophrony Sakharov emphasised the specific *'on the verge'* quality of this saying. He wrote that Saint Silouan used to say, 'that many ascetics when they approached that state [of hell] — which is vital if one would be cleansed of the passions — would fall into despair and be unable to continue. But the one who knows "how greatly the Lord loveth us" escapes the pernicious effect of total despair and knows how to stand prudently on the verge so that the hellish fire burns away his very passion and does not fall victim to despair' (1991, p. 211). This 'on the verge' characteristic relates to the simultaneous awareness of the realities and possibilities of two opposites — hell and hope for salvation, a state of utter denial of God and a state of complete trust in God's love and hope for it.

Polkinghorne (in this volume) identified a comparable state to 'on the verge of hell' which he called 'at the edge of chaos' and considered it as being characteristic of the conditions of the activity of the Spirit. Firstly, he observed that 'There is, it seems, a kenotic self-effacement present in the manifestations of the Spirit.' He arrives at this through Lossky's own comments on the Orthodox iconography of the Spirit in the Holy Trinity where the Son is depicted as the image of the Father and the Spirit as the image of the Son but the Spirit has no image of itself and 'remains unmanifested' (p. 3). Polkinghorne further observes that in the creation, 'agency, whether human or divine, operates in regimes characterised by the cloudiness of intrinsic unpredictability, an insight that is in accord with the theological insight of the hidden character of much of the work of the Spirit' (p. 9). This suggests that the Spirit, as in the Silouan dictum, is active in a hidden way, always *in potentio*.

Then, Polkinghorne argues that 'Science has discovered that the regimes in which truly novel possibilities are realised are always to be found at "the edge of chaos," that is to say in situations in which order and openness, regularity and contingency, necessity and chance, interlace each other. If things are too orderly, they are too rigid for more than the possibility of the rearrangement of already existing elements. If things are too haphazard, any novelty that emerged would fall apart too quickly to be able to persist' (p. 9).

This observation seems to be fitting well with the *'keep thy mind in hell but despair not'* dictum, which could be characterised as state at the 'edge of chaos' *par excellence.* If a person were to be too orderly and dominated by his/her mind, the person would be too rigid and no possibility of rearrangement would exist. Logically, one would accept that one is in hell and there is no way out and one would drown in one's own sterile logicality devoid of any hope. If on the other hand, a person was to be floating on the effervescence of hope, ignorant of or under-estimating the reality of the existing situation of hell, one would equally be unable to hold the reality of hope. It is the state of being on the 'verge of hell,' at the 'edge of chaos' that enables the Spirit to bring about the renewing transformation.

Finally, connecting this perspective on hell with the *'Spirit of Creation and New Creation,'* it is important to note that *'despair not'* refers to the possibility of New Creation, the possibility that the Spirit in this world enables the development of renewal and healing the brokenness of this Creation.

At an individual level, *'keep thy mind in hell but despair not'* emphasises the need that a person sheds his/her existing sense of him/herself and opens up to the Spirit to renew his/her personality.

Sakharov (2003) identifies two significant interrelated elements of this formula: the 'self-kenosis' and the love of the neighbour. The 'self-kenosis' refers to the emptying of oneself in order to be filled by the love for the other and by God. Then, identifying communication, connection, and re-lating as key dimensions of the Holy Spirit, he uses 1 Corinthians (12:1-14) to argue that the gifts of the Holy Spirit 'are given that we serve others'; 'that is how the Holy Spirit teaches us love, to restore our broken relation-ship and attune them to the spirit of humility and service.'

These reflections relate very strongly to work with the refugees and other survivors of political violence. As Sakharov puts it, 'where there is the Holy Spirit there is a ministry to the other.'

These reflections can also be closely interconnected with Welker's three forms of the manifestations of the Spirit, the 'diaconical, prophetic and pastoral forms.'

REFERENCES

Papadopoulos, R. K. (2004), Trauma in a systemic perspective: Theoretical, organizational and clinical dimensions. Paper presented at the 14th Congress of the International Family Therapy Association, Istanbul.

Papadopoulos, R. K. (2006), Terrorism and panic. *Psychotherapy and politics international,* 4 (2), 90-100.

Papadopoulos, R. K. (2007), Refugees, trauma and adversity-activated development. *European Journal of Psychotherapy and Counselling,* 9 (3), September, 301-312.

Polkinghorne, J., The Hidden Work of Spirit in Creation (in this volume).

Sakharov, N. (2003), St Silouan the Athonite and Archimandrite Sophrony. Lecture given at Cambridge University.

Sakharov, S. (1991), *Saint Silouan the Athonite.* Tolleshunt Knights by Mal-don: Stavropegic Monastery of St John the Baptist, Essex.

Welker, M., The Human Spirit and the Spirit of God (in this volume).

Zacharou, Z. (2007), *The Hidden Man of the Heart.* Tolleshunt Knights by Maldon: Stavropegic Monastery of St John the Baptist, Essex.

IV. THE SPIRIT IN NEW CREATION

Pneumatology and the New Creation in the Macarian Writings: An Ecumenical Legacy

Marcus Plested

The year 2009 saw the 1200th anniversary of the Council of Aachen, the first council to proclaim profession of the double procession of the Spirit as a necessary article of orthodox faith. It was also, by some reckonings, the millenary of Rome's formal adoption of the *filioque*. Many centuries on and the *filioque* issue remains, however recast, both contentious and complex. One point that impressed itself on me in this anniversary year was that a specifically pneumatological approach, based on the experiential theology of the great Christian mystics, might yet yield further insights into the nature and workings of the Paraclete, thereby enlivening an often rather tired debate.[1]

One such mystic, arguably the greatest *pneumatophore* of them all, is Macarius (fl. c. AD 370-390), also known as Pseudo-Macarius or Macarius-Symeon). No one before or after him has spoken with such subtlety and range, precision and poetry, of the power and operation of the Holy Spirit.[2] As a preeminent 'flute' of the Spirit, to use one of his many metaphors, Macarius is certainly an apt choice for our symposium.[3] But he also serves as a kind of test case for the patristic witness in general, forcing us to question the extent to which the ongoing value of that testimony is affected (if at all) by the advances in knowledge of the natural world brought

---

1. As Sergius Bulgakov sagely remarks, 'It is remarkable that this *filioque* debate killed all interest in the theology of the Holy Spirit.' ET: *The Comforter* (tr. B. Jakim: Grand Rapids MI 2004), 130.

2. Incidentally, he does so with virtually no trace of the reticence that Andrew Louth has, elsewhere in this volume, distinguished in other figures of the Byzantine tradition.

3. The 'flute of the Spirit' image can be found in Homily II 47, 14 and III 15.4. See below, n. 9, for conventions of citation.

to us by modern science. We must, for example, ask whether the patristic vision of creation is compromised by the revelation that the world is so many billions of years old, or whether the mass extinctions of the remote past and the overwhelming probability of some form of human evolution undermine patristic anthropology.

'Macarius' is the name given to the anonymous Syro-Mesopotamian author of a monumental collection of treatises, letters, questions and responses, and homilies. While he is widely recognised as a preeminent voice within the realm of 'spirituality,' the deeply theological character of his work is too rarely emphasised.[4] His whole enterprise is deeply and explicitly Trinitarian in character, demonstrably linked to the theological achievement of the Cappadocian Fathers. His confession of the triune God is of quite astonishing clarity while his Christology in some key respects anticipates the Chalcedonian settlement.[5]

What makes him perhaps most intriguing for our purposes is his status as a bridge-figure between Greek and Syriac thought-worlds. Although writing in Greek, Macarius is manifestly closely connected with the world of Ephrem the Syrian, hailed as the 'Harp of the Spirit.' He speaks (or sings) the same metaphorical language, displays the same symbolic apprehension of the cosmos, and hymns the Spirit in very similar terms.[6] But Macarius, unlike Ephrem, was able to translate much of the poetic and pneumatic tradition of the Syriac Orient into the language and thought-forms of the Greek East. This double inheritance gives his writing much of its potency and goes some way to explaining his extraordinary and timeless appeal to Christians of both East and West.[7]

Macarius' vision of the divine mystery is simultaneously Christocentric and pneumatocentric. The necessary focus on the Spirit in this short offering should not be taken to betoken any imbalance in this re-

---

4. A tide of interest, notably in Germany, the Netherlands, and Finland, made for some superb work on Macarius in 1960s and 1970s but this tide has, alas, ebbed in recent years.

5. A broader treatment of Macarius (including supporting material for the general claims made here) is to be found in my *The Macarian Legacy*, Oxford 2004.

6. It is no coincidence that substantial chunks of the Greek Ephrem are, in fact, Macarius. See W. Strothmann, *Schriften des Makarios/Symeon unter dem Namen des Ephraem*, Göttinger Orientforschungen, I, Reihe Syriaca, 22; Wiesbaden 1981.

7. Speaking only of the West, we may mention as legatees the Spiritual Franciscans, the Jesuits, the Wesleys, and contemporary Pentecostalism. Macarius also has the distinction of having been condemned four times by the Spanish Inquisition. Doubtless he had not expected this.

spect. I have made some bold claims about the stature of Macarius as a preeminent theologian of the Holy Spirit (and, as we shall see, of the new creation). I trust what follows will show such claims to be more than simply the product of freely admitted partiality.

First, some basic affirmations. The divine status of the Spirit is in no doubt for Macarius (unlike many of his contemporaries). The Spirit is 'uncreated,' for only the divine can deify created beings — also precisely the central plank of Gregory the Theologian's defence of the divinity of the Spirit (I 50.1.7-8).[8] Elsewhere he is even more precise, speaking of

> The divine and holy declaration that has rightly been laid down concerning the exact and pious opinion and faith: one revered divinity of the consubstantial Trinity, one will, one glory and one worship of the one trihypostatic divinity. This is in accordance with our pious affirmation of the good confession before many witnesses in the mystery of holy baptism. (EM 1.3)[9]

But Macarius is vexed by doctrinal questions only in so far as they illumine our understanding and experience of salvation. The whole purpose of the incarnation was that man might be wrenched from the grip of evil and participate in the gift of the Holy Spirit (I 22.2.1). This gift of the Spirit is a gift beyond simple restoration of the prelapsarian state: the Incarnation 'has restored to mankind the original nature of Adam and in addition bestowed upon it the heavenly inheritance of the Holy Spirit' (I 61.1.1).

Participation in the Holy Spirit is described with a stunning range of images and metaphors. This poetic repertoire, a constant hymning of the

---

8. Note on references: I = *Makarios/Symeon: Reden und Briefe,* ed. H. Berthold (Berlin 1973). II = *Die 50 Geistliche Homilien des Makarios,* ed. H. Dörries, E. Klostermann, and M. Kroeger (Berlin 1964); II 51-57= *Macarii Anecdota: Seven Unpublished Homilies of Macarius,* ed. G. L. Marriott (Cambridge MA 1918). III= *Pseudo-Macaire: Oeuvres spirituelles I: Homélies propres à la Collection III,* ed. and tr. V. Desprez (Paris 1980); EM= *Makarios-Symeon: Epistola Magna,* ed. R. Staats (Göttingen 1984).

9. The declaration mentioned is commonly held by Macarian scholars to refer to the Council of 381. The language goes some way beyond that of the Creed and conciliar letter of 381 and is, in fact, rather closer to that adopted by Gregory the Theologian. Note also the argument from baptism — used to such effect by Basil. Gregory of Nyssa had praised certain Spirit-filled Mesopotamians at time of the said council, of whom Macarius may very possibly be one. One might also add that this passage alone confutes de Régnon's claim that the East proceeds from the threeness of the persons to adduce the oneness of the divinity whereas the West proceeds in the opposite direction.

wonders and beauties of creation, is very much Macarius' calling-card. The Holy Spirit is spoken of as, for example, dew, wine, rain, seed, sea, spring, food, fire, and air — and indeed as farmer and bridegroom. But one must note that 'he' is not always the correct pronoun since one of the key features of Macarius' pneumatology, and an unmistakable sign of his Syriac connections, is his interest in the theme of the motherhood of the Spirit. Souls still in this world should call upon the 'heavenly mother,' the Holy Spirit, in order that she might

> Come to the souls that seek her and take them in her arms of life, warm them with the spiritual and heavenly food of the delicious, desirable, holy, rational and pure milk so that day by day they might grow in spiritual maturity and increase in knowledge and perception of the heavenly Father. (III 27.4.2)[10]

All this abundant imagery and metaphor is necessary: 'All these things I have recounted using visible things [. . .] since it is impossible to express or to expound spiritual realities otherwise' (III 16.3.1). But the analogies are real: 'the world of phenomena is a type and icon and pattern of the invisible and eternal world of the divinity' (I 28.1.7); 'all visible things are shadows of invisible things' (I 23.1.3); 'the root of every sensible thing is the noetic' (I 41.3); and 'the inexpressible wisdom of God is manifest through the mysteries and types of visible phenomena' (I 50.1.3). None of this is natural theology as such. As we shall see, the ability to discern God's being and power is essentially a gift of grace.

Macarius dispenses with imagery and metaphor in some of his more direct pneumatological affirmations. When he speaks of the experience of the Spirit as light, this is no analogy. The perfect mystery of Christianity, declaimed by the Apostle Paul, is the experience through divine operation of 'the illumination of the heavenly light of the Spirit.' 'This is not,' he clarifies, 'a revelation of knowledge and concepts but the eternal illumination of the hypostatic light' (I 58.1.1, 2.1). This affirmation was to be of untold value to the Byzantine Hesychasts in their defence of the uncreated character of the light witnessed in prayer.

---

10. More maternal imagery can be found in III 22.3.3-4 — reposing on the breast of the Spirit one acquires a divine mind. Macarius will, however, also speak of the Spirit as 'bridegroom' (III 20.1.2), as if he is underscoring the inadequacy of human gender categories when speaking of God. He will also, with good evangelical precedent, use maternal imagery of Christ.

The constant inner experience of the luminous Spirit has an ontological character. Divine grace is permanently rooted in us 'like a substance' (ὡς μία οὐσία) (II 8.2). The experience and revelation of that grace comes about through *synergeia* with the Holy Spirit. Human participation in this work of cooperation consists in ascetic effort and prayer within the context of the sacramental life of the Church. The Holy Spirit acts in and through the Church and her sacraments. The Spirit 'presides over and participates in the whole liturgy of the holy Church of God' (I 52.2.3). In baptism we receive the effacement of sins and the 'beginning of the life of the Spirit' (I 43.6). Baptism is a pledge, a talent that must be worked with (III 28.3.3), in order that the 'life' of the Spirit might be experienced as manifest within us.

This life of the Spirit is no mere figure but a veritable new creation. The process is frequently spoken of as one of mingling or mixing.[11] Indeed the Spirit so unites him/herself to our natures as to become a *second* or *other* soul within the human person. This 'other soul' *is* the 'divine and heavenly Spirit hearing, crying, praying, knowing, and doing the will of God' in us. This is an explicit outworking from Romans 8:26 (I 63.1.1-4). He also puts the reverse proposition: 'Without that soul which is the Spirit our soul is dead and useless' (II 30.5). But with this soul, the very life of the Spirit within us, we become double, both created and uncreated (III 10.3.4).[12] This is truly a new creation, forming 'a new mind and a new soul, new eyes, new ears, new human beings' (II 44.2).[13]

> When the soul attains spiritual perfection, totally purged of all the passions and perfectly united to and mingled with the Spirit, the Paraclete, in ineffable communion, then the soul is itself vouchsafed to become spirit, being commingled with the Spirit. It then becomes all light, all

11. Again, mixing language is a prominent feature of the Syriac Christian tradition. It is also a marked feature of Cappadocian Christology. Note that in what follows, in accordance with Stoic notions of mixture (specifically *krasis di olon*), Macarius' mixing language allows him to express the intimate and utter union of God and the soul without compromising their ontological discontinuity.

12. The 'second soul' theme is also found in Aphrahat the Persian sage. A similar intuition is present in Irenaeus' identification of body, soul, and [Holy] Spirit as constituent of the perfect human being (*AH* 5.9.1). We may also recall Plotinus' 'more godlike soul' (*Enneads* 6.7.5). The theme of the second soul is found among the condemned propositions alleged of the Messalians — without explanation of its objectionable character.

13. Thus the spiritual senses are, for Macarius, properly understood as the Spiritual senses.

spirit, all joy, all repose, all gladness, all love, all compassion, all goodness and kindness. It is as though it had been swallowed up in the virtues of the Holy Spirit as a stone in the depths of the sea is surrounded
by water. Such people are totally mingled with and embraced by the
Spirit, united to the grace of Christ, and assimilated to Christ. (I 13.2.4)

This mystical experience is in no way hermetic. Such union with the Spirit
necessarily opens up into compassion for all humanity: 'burning with the
love of the Spirit for all mankind, they take to themselves the sorrow and
grief of the whole Adam' (I 13.2.2).

It is vital to underline that this mixing or union does not imply any
sort of confusion of natures, as the distinction between the stone and water unambiguously illustrates. Macarius is consistently and consciously
concerned to maintain the ontological discontinuity between God and his
creation:

He is God, the soul is not God. He is Lord, it a servant. He is Creator, it a
creature. He is maker, it a thing made. There is nothing in common between his nature and that of the soul. But through his infinite, ineffable
and inconceivable love and compassion, he has been pleased to dwell in
this thing of his making, this intellectual creation, this precious and es-
pecial work. (II 49.4)

The ontological gap always endures, even in the resurrection:

All the members become translucent, all are plunged into light and fire,
and transformed; they are not, as some say, destroyed, they do not become fire, their own nature ceasing to subsist. For Peter remains Peter,
and Paul remains Paul, and Philip remains Philip. Each retains his own
nature and hypostasis, filled by the Spirit. (II 15.10)

The renewed human being comes to ever greater knowledge of the whole
visible and invisible cosmos. God 'widens and extends the thoughts of the
intellect to [encompass] the breadth and length and depth and height of
the whole visible and invisible creation' (III 26.7.2). This creation, as indi-
cated above, is in a very real sense God's self-manifestation, brought out of
nonbeing in his infinite wisdom (II 14.11). Those who can see it will realize
that God is present in all things — even in the embryos of living creatures
(II 12.10). This omnipresence is most obviously founded upon the incarnation: 'He is the one who is beyond all and the one who has become all in all

things.' (II 52.7). But the incarnation expresses a deeper coinherence of God and his creation.

> The master of all things, the God who loves humankind, is everywhere and in all created things. And all created things, the heavenly, the earthly, and the infernal, are in God. (I 35.1)

God is in all things and all things are in God. But it is only the operation of the Spirit that will enable us to see this truth. Having said that, we must be absolutely clear that this doctrine of omnipresence in no way applies any form of pantheism. God may be in all things, for Macarius, but all things are, emphatically, not God: the propositions are not reversible. Macarius displays here an acute theological adroitness maintaining the distinction between God and creation while refusing any separation. In this respect he goes some way to achieving a differentiation of God and the world that nonetheless allows for the paradox of divine transcendence *and* immanence. In so doing, he offers a paradigm for the relation between God and the world considerably more satisfactory than the catastrophic transcendence-immanence dichotomy so compellingly critiqued by Jürgen Moltmann elsewhere in this volume.

Having dispensed with the charge of pantheism, a further question arises out of this doctrine of omnipresence: has Macarius sufficiently allowed for the futility and disorder of creation? What place could death, decay, flesh-eating wasps, and the like have in his vision of creation? Is this vision not far too idealistic? Where is the troubled and fluctuating world we inhabit? Modern science has painted a picture of the natural world which is certainly wondrous in parts but also deeply disconcerting. What might Macarius make of this unsettling picture?

The beginnings of a response may be found in his frank affirmation that this world is imperfect. His affirmation, cited above, that this world is 'a type and icon and pattern' of the heavenly kingdom does not mean that the two are in any way identical: 'There is an imperfect world and a perfect world. The imperfect and transitory world contains many forms like those of the perfect eternal world' (III 4.1.1). In this imperfect world, things are certainly not as they should be and this disjunction is strictly the result of the Fall. The Fall, for Macarius, is a cosmic event: the whole creation falls with Adam. Through Adam's subjection unto death, mortality has entered the whole created order — just as when a king is captured and exiled, so too are his followers and servants (II 11.5).

Because the Fall has encompassed the whole created order, it follows that Macarius can use images and metaphors from this world as signs of the dire state of post-lapsarian humanity — and not solely as intimations of eternity. For example, the leaven of the passions has become a cancer within all of us (II 24.2). We have sunk to the level of the irrational animals (II 25.3), behaving like the wildest and most bestial of them (III 8.3, 5). Indeed the irrational animals are in some senses more rational than we for they seek out their own kind whereas we consort with the powers of darkness. In so doing, we make ourselves prey for the enemy who will devour us 'as a bird is eaten up by an eagle, a sheep by a wolf, or like a child who unknowingly stretches out its hand to a snake and is killed by the bite. All these instances are parables of spiritual activity' (II 25.6). In this last observation the death and killing that characterise the natural world are read as signs of the power of evil and as consequences of the Fall.

We must at this juncture note that while he is acutely aware of the power of evil, Macarius is crystal clear that evil has no real existence: 'Those who say that evil is a subsistent reality know nothing' (II 16.1). He continues, 'To God there is no such thing as subsistent evil. . . . But to us, evil is [a reality], because it dwells and acts in the heart suggesting evil and defiling thoughts and not allowing [us] to pray purely but rather imprisoning the intellect in this world' (II 16.5-6). This obscuring power of evil is imaged as fog and smoke while the fragile state of the human condition is likened to a spider's web (III 21.3.3). The struggle against the passions finds its analogy in the backbreaking effort required to bring forth fruit from the soil. The heart, like the land in this fallen cosmos, is full of 'tares and thorns and thistles' (I 22.2.2) and needs much labour and sweat of the brow before the good seed can take root. One of Macarius' favourite images is that of 'working the earth of the heart' (I 54.3.2). This is in no way a bucolic image — as anyone who has seriously engaged in agriculture will attest. Such examples might be multiplied much further, but should suffice to make the point that Macarius has no illusions about the perfection of the natural cosmos for all that he upholds its essential goodness.

Macarius shows himself no mean student of natural world. He comments on the communication effected among certain animals, the nesting habits of certain birds, and the digestive peculiarities of the camel. All bear witness to an acute faculty of observation. He exhibits a sure grasp of animal anatomy, detailing the various internal cavities (III 7.1.1), and draws on the process of decay in meat for an almost unbearably graphic analogy for the fallen human condition (II 1.5). And all this is not solely the product of adventitious learning: he also appears well-versed with Aelian's *De natura animalarium* (II 14.7). Like the Cappadocian Fathers with whom he was closely associated, Macarius is certainly willing to draw upon the science of his day to explicate and illustrate spiritual realities.

In fine, Macarius offers us a quite unique vision of the Spirit in creation and the new creation. The acquisition of the Spirit entails an intimate and almost organic union whereby the Spirit quite literally abides in us, becoming another soul within us and integrating us into the life of the Trinity. This mutual indwelling is effected within the context of a broader doctrine of the co-inherence of Creator and creation, one in which their ontological discontinuity is never compromised. Divine Spirit and human spirit become one in this unitive action while remaining forever distinct.

The whole creation is, for Macarius, a source of abiding wonder and anagogical power, leading us ever farther up into the mysteries of God. Nature in all its beauty and inexhaustible complexity patterns divine reality and manifests the very nature of God. But nature also, in its fallen state, patterns the power of evil in this world and the severity of the struggle against the opposing powers. His vision may be of an 'enchanted' cosmos but this in no way makes it a facile idyll.

I can see little in Macarius that is seriously compromised by recent scientific advances. Macarius displays an openness to the natural science of his day which, *mutatis mutandis,* might in principle be extended to much of what has been unearthed or deduced in our own time. Like all the Fathers, he sets no store by a straightforwardly historical reading of the Genesis narrative and might plausibly find room for any account that did full justice to God's creative power and wisdom. His sense of the implanted wisdom of God in creation could certainly tally with some presentations of the workings of DNA or John Polkinghorne's powerful suggestion elsewhere in this volume as to the 'information' inherent on the quantam level. Even evidence for human evolution might be encompassed within his overarching vision of the consequences of the Fall and the animal-like or even sub-animal existence to which it gave rise.

Of course there remains a basic difficulty in his account of the Fall and of its consequences. From a linear scientific perspective, it is a nonsense to suggest that the disorder and imperfection of the creation might result from a specifically human catastrophe at a certain point in time. Clearly, animals were killing one another and suffering from arthritis long before the appearance of humans in the fossil record. But need realities such as the Fall be considered solely in linear terms? Might we not think of the Fall rather like a crack in the ice, spreading in all directions (and dimensions) from its centre? As Christians, we praise and confess the Lamb 'slain from the foundation of the world' (Rev. 13:8). Might not the very fabric of creation be patterned on and adapted to the drama of Fall and Redemption in a non-linear and non-historical fashion? If we follow Revelation in accepting the slaying of the Lamb in an extra-historical sense, as somehow part of the very make-up of reality, must not the same be said of the Fall? Does not Macarius have a case?

But here we trespass into realms that exceed both scientific and theological conjecture. By way of conclusion, we may assert that Macarius stands as a particularly fine example of the ongoing force and value of the patristic witness in the context of the contemporary dialogue between science and religion. Viewing creation *sub specie aeternitatis* need not preclude (and will even enhance) our understanding and treatment of the world which we inhabit. Similarly, those whose business it is to probe the very building blocks of the cosmos might do well to give ear to the teachings of mystics such as Macarius.

The Holy Spirit in Creation and Re-Creation: The Byzantine Fathers

Andrew Louth

There is a certain reticence, a kind of elusiveness, in the doctrine of the Holy Spirit among the Byzantine Fathers, and the Greek Fathers generally. It is important not to ignore or overcome this elusiveness, if we are to understand correctly how the Holy Spirit is understood in the Byzantine and Orthodox tradition. This reticence manifests itself in various ways. At the beginning of his fifth Theological Oration, St Gregory the Theologian admits that 'there is something especially difficult in the doctrine of the Spirit,'[1] and later in that sermon develops a notion of gradual disclosure to account for the fact that the divinity of the Holy Spirit is not attested as clearly as some would like in the Scriptures. 'The old covenant — he says — made clear proclamation of the Father, a less definite one of the Son. The new covenant made the Son manifest and gave us a glimpse of the Spirit's Godhead. At the present time, the Spirit resides amongst us, giving us a clearer manifestation of himself than before.'[2] This is often treated as if it were some kind of adumbration of a theory of doctrinal development. I am not concerned with that now (though I rather doubt it), but with what Gregory says about the Spirit. The Spirit, he suggests, has been made manifest now, within the Church, by his being present 'amongst us.' Gregory clearly has in mind the notion, present in the Fourth Gospel and in Acts, that the Holy Spirit was given after, and as a result of, the incarnate ministry of Christ: as the Gospel puts it, speaking of an event in the minis-

---

1. Gregory of Nazianzus, *Oratio* 31.2 (in Grégoire de Nazianze, *Discours 27-31*, ed. Paul Gallay, Sources Chrétiennes 250, Paris: Cerf, 1978, 276; translation in St Gregory of Nazianzus, *On God and Christ,* Crestwood NY: St Vladimir's Seminary Press, 2002, 117).

2. Idem, *Or.* 32.26 (*Discours 27-31*, 326; *On God and Christ,* 137).

try of the Lord, 'the Spirit was not yet given, for Jesus was not yet glorified' (John 7:39). It is only with the giving of the Spirit — at Pentecost, according to Acts, but at any rate after the completion of the Paschal mystery of Christ's death and resurrection — that the Spirit is present among the disciples of the Lord, 'giving us a clearer manifestation of himself than before.' But it is the manifestation of a *presence amongst us;* it is not something objective over against us. Gregory's friend, St Basil the Great, had seen this, when in his Treatise on the Holy Spirit he appealed to an unwritten tradition as authority for his teaching on the Spirit: an *unwritten* tradition, not in the sense of an esoteric, whispered tradition, but rather a tradition that is experienced in the life of the Christian within the Church — all the examples he gives are liturgical actions: the sign of the cross, facing East to pray, the prayer of the epiclesis, and so on.[3] What Basil is doing is appealing to an experience of the Spirit in the prayer and worship of the Church. It is something we understand by participating in, rather than by articulating. Basil speaks of the way in which these liturgical acts express more than we understand, and compares them to the obscurity of the Scriptures which again presents us with a 'form of silence' rather than clearly articulated and formulated doctrine. The realm of the Spirit is a mystery, *mysterion,* not a difficulty that we can solve, but a realm in which we experience more than we know.

It is, I would say, important not to erase this sense of the difficulty, the intangibility of the Holy Spirit. If we do we shall find ourselves losing contact with the experience of the Holy Spirit himself and replacing it with merely human ideas.

Another aspect of this mysterious quality of the Holy Spirit is that, for the Fathers as for the New Testament, the Spirit is not separated from Christ. Indeed, one might say that part of the problem of grasping the significance of the Spirit is that he doesn't appear on his own, but always in connexion with Christ. In the Last Discourses in the Fourth Gospel, the Lord says of the 'Spirit of truth, [who] will guide you into all truth': 'He shall glorify me: for he shall receive of mine, and shall show it to you' (John 16:13f.). This does not subordinate the Spirit to the Son — as the Western doctrine of the *Filioque* perhaps threatens to do — but means that the activity of the Holy Spirit is to be seen in relation to the activity of the Son. As Vladimir Lossky put it, 'The Church is *body* in so far as Christ is her

3. Basil the Great, *On the Holy Spirit* 27.66 (in Basile de Césarée, *Sur le Saint-Esprit,* ed. Benoît Pruche OP, Sources Chrétiennes 17bis, Paris: Cerf, 1968, 478-86).

head; she is *fullness* in so far as the Holy Spirit quickens her and fills her with divinity, for the Godhead dwells within her bodily as it dwelt in the deified humanity of Christ. We may say with Irenaeus: "where the Church is, there is the Spirit; where the Spirit is, there is the Church."[4]

This might not seem a very helpful starting-point for addressing the concern of this conference: the Holy Spirit in creation and re-creation, that is, the role of the Holy Spirit in the created universe, and how the doctrine of the Holy Spirit may inform a scientific understanding of the universe, and help us to understand not just the origins of the cosmos, but in some way how the cosmos is developing, where it is going, under the providence of God. How we may cooperate with the Spirit of God so that the cosmos comes to fulfil God's purposes more and more closely, rather than succumb, as it seems planet earth might, to the greed and rapacity of man, now, with technology, given a truly awesome capacity to damage man and his environment. Indeed, one might wonder what recourse to the Church Fathers might offer reflection on such a topic, for the Fathers' conception of the cosmos is so utterly different from ours. Their conception was, mostly, a view they shared with their educated contemporaries, what we dub now the Ptolemaic system of the universe; a few Christian thinkers adopted an even less 'scientific' view of the cosmos, with a flat earth situated beneath the canopy of heaven, based on an unsophisticated reading of the Genesis narrative (the sixth-century Cosmas Indicopleutes is the most well-known representative of such a position),[5] though such a view seems to have been rare (John of Damascus, in his discussion of the cosmos in his *Exposition of the Orthodox Faith*, registers various such views — 'Others say . . .' — but seems to represent the Ptolemaic system as the generally accepted view).[6] According to such a view, the earth was a spherical body at the centre of the cosmos, surrounded by seven planetary spheres, beyond which was the outer sphere of the fixed stars. The cosmos was of no great age — five-and-a-half, or six-and-a-half thousand years — during which time the cosmos had remained pretty much constant; human kind had appeared last on the scene, but the process of creation had been a matter of days, however

4. V. Lossky, *The Mystical Theology of the Eastern Church,* London: James Clarke & Co., Ltd., 1957, 157 (the quotation from Irenaeus is from *Adv. Haer.* III.24.1).

5. Cosmas Indicopleustès, *Topographie chrétienne,* ed. W. Wolska-Conus, Sources Chrétiennes 141, 159, 197, Paris: Cerf, 1968-73.

6. John Damascene, *expos.* 20-4 (in B. Kotter, ed., *Die Schriften des Johannes von Damaskos,* II, Berlin: Walter de Gruyter, 1973, 50-70).

those days had been conceived (it was generally accepted that they were not the same as the twenty-four-hour periods that is the human experience of days). There was no sense of evolution; no difficulty in adopting an anthropocentric view of the cosmos, for human beings occupied the central position of a geocentric cosmos, rather than being the inhabitants of a planet orbiting a moderate-sized star, itself a member of one of many galaxies. What then can be the point of looking to the Fathers of the early Church for inspiration, when we consider the place of the Holy Spirit in a universe that we know to be vast both in space and in time?

There are several aspects to any attempt to respond to such a question. First, whatever form of the Christian faith we hold, it has been shaped by centuries of reflection, and the fundamental contours of any form of traditional Christian belief owe a great deal to the thought of the Fathers. Ignorance is not likely to be helpful in understanding how our faith relates to the world revealed by the sciences. Indeed ignorance is likely to foster false and unhelpful ideas of what 'traditional Christianity' amounted to: many people seem quite unaware of the fact that most of the Fathers took the results of the science of their day for granted, only calling in question principles that seemed incompatible with fundamental beliefs — any fundamental dualism between good and evil, material and spiritual, which were seen to be incompatible with Christian belief in the creation of the cosmos out of nothing by a good God; any notion of causality that entailed a sense of determinism that robbed human beings of responsibility for their actions. Such unawareness lies behind ideas that Christian belief in creation is fundamentally opposed to the theory of evolution, for instance. Secondly, the anthropocentrism of patristic conceptions of the cosmos reflect an important truth, namely, that it seems to have been given to humankind to *interpret* the world in which we live; scientific ideas are *human* ideas, and no dislodging of humankind from physical centrality in the universe affects that fundamental perception. Consequently, while patristic ideas of the human as microcosm and bond of the cosmos certainly need rethinking in the light of modern science, it does not seem to me to be obvious that they need to be abandoned. Thirdly, it is generally recognized that one feature of patristic — and especially Greek patristic thought — is that it embraces a cosmic view of the human and his role in the universe. This seems to me something that it would be folly to ignore, as we seek to work out our own understanding of the role of the Holy Spirit in creation and re-creation.

However, if we are to draw on the resources of the Christian tradition, especially as it has been preserved in its fullness in the Orthodox tradition, we shall find that we have to attend to the way in which they conceived it, and not feel frustrated that their approach seems different from our own. Precisely because the patristic view of the relation between God and the cosmos presupposes a different view of the cosmos from the one (or those) suggested by modern science, it is bound to seem strange, and indeed a sense of strangeness is to be expected, if we are genuinely to encounter and learn from the thought of the Fathers. So there is no way of avoiding my initial perception that we have to seek to understand the role of the Spirit by attending to the doctrine of the Church, as we find it in the Fathers, and their sense of what is involved in living out of the life of the Spirit in the Christian life. There is no doctrine of the Spirit that can be detached and applied in what would be a somewhat arbitrary way.

Lossky quoted Irenaeus, the second-century Greek theologian who became bishop of Lyon. We might perhaps stay with him for our next step. Irenaeus, as is well known, speaks of the Son and the Spirit as the two hands of God the Father: the two hands with which God fashioned humankind. One idea expressed by this image is that God's creation of man is something intimate: he does not just bring him into being, but he tenderly fashions him, with his own hands, as it were. But what are the two hands doing? They are working together, and if we read carefully there is the idea suggested that while the Word, the Son, gives being to humankind, it is Wisdom, the Spirit, that gives form and perfection. The Son, who is the image of the Father, is one after whom humankind is created so as to be according to the image of God, *kat' eikona tou Theou,* while it is to the Spirit that he owes the perfecting in the likeness of God, *homoiosis Theou.* This brings out another aspect of the Spirit, for the likeness of God is our destiny, where we are heading, so the Spirit is concerned with the eschatological perfection of humankind.

These seem to me to be the leading ideas behind the understanding of the role of the Spirit in Byzantine theology, in particular the theology of St Maximos the Confessor and St John Damascene: intimacy, being to perfection, eschatology — and also a direct link with creation and re-creation; it is the Spirit involved in creation who accomplishes re-creation, understood both as restoration of the state lost in the Fall, but beyond that, the fulfilment, the accomplishment of what God intended in his original creation. There is a passage in St John Damascene that gives expression to all this. He is speaking of the Eucharistic presence, brought about by the epiclesis, the invocation, of the Holy Spirit.

And by invocation the overshadowing power of the Holy Spirit becomes rain to this new tillage; for just as everything that he does, God does through the activity of the Holy Spirit, so now too the activity of the Spirit works things beyond nature, which cannot be accepted, save by faith. 'How will this happen to me,' said the holy Virgin, 'since I have not knowledge of a man?' And the archangel Gabriel replied, 'The Holy Spirit will come upon you and the power of the Most High will over-shadow you.' And now you ask, How does this bread become the body of Christ, and this wine and water the blood of Christ? And I say to you, The Holy Spirit is present and works these things that are beyond reason and understanding.[7]

But the real contribution of Byzantine theology to our understanding of the place of the Holy Spirit in creation and re-creation is to be found in Maximos, and this for two reasons. First of all, Maximos developed a pro-found sense of the presence of God in the created order through what he called the *logoi* of creation. Just as the cosmos is created by the *Logos*, the Word, of God, so the everything created has its being and purpose in its *lo-gos;* all these *logoi* are summed up in the one *Logos* of God, so that, as Maximos is fond of repeating, 'the one *Logos* is the many *logoi*, and the many *logoi* are the one *Logos*.'[8] But secondly, Maximos, in the introductory chapters especially of his work, the *Mystagogia*,[9] worked out a developed understanding of the way in which man, the human person, the Church, and the cosmos all mutually reflect one another, so that the Church can be seen as an image of the cosmos (*myst.* 2), man an image of the church and *vice versa* (*myst.* 4), man an image of the cosmos, and *vice versa* (*myst.* 7), and each of them an image of God (for the Church, see *myst.* 1). He also works out at some length the way in which the church is reflected in the soul of man, so that the spiritual life maps on to the liturgical worship of the Church (*myst.* 5). The effect of all this, which is only adumbrated in the *Mystagogia*, but which can be traced out in more detail in some of his other works, is that the Church and the human person are seen as having a cosmic dimension, and the cosmos itself as having an ecclesial and spiri-tual dimension.

7. John Damascene, *expos.* 86. 60-83 (Kotter, 193-94).
8. Especially in *Ambiguum* 7 (PG 91.1068D-1101C; English translation in St Maximus the Confessor, *On the Cosmic Mystery of Christ*, Crestwood NY: St Vladimir's Seminary Press, 2003, 45-74).
9. *I Mystagogia tou Agiou Maximou tou Omologitou*, ed. Ch. Sotiropoulos, Athens: 1993.

In his justly famed monograph on St Maximos, Lars Thunberg remarks, '[c]onsequently, contemplation of the λόγοι in creation (θεωρία φυσική) belongs to the work of the Spirit in man's sanctification and deification.'[10] This is, as we would expect by now, mostly implicit in Maximos' writings, rather than explicit. There are places, however, where this is made explicit. For instance, in the *Second Century on Theology and the Economy:*

> He who devoutly strives to attain philosophy and is on his guard against the invisible powers should pray that both natural discrimination — whose light is but limited — and the illuminating grace of the Spirit abide with him. The first by means of practice trains the flesh in virtue, the second illuminates the intellect so that it chooses above all else companionship with wisdom; and through wisdom it destroys the strongholds of evil and pulls down "every proud obstacle to the knowledge of God" (2 Cor. 10:5). Jesus, [son] of Nave, exemplifies this both when he prays for the sun to stand still upon Gibeon, that is, for the light of the knowledge of God to remain unsetting as it shines for him over the mountain of spiritual contemplation; and when he asks for the moon to stand still in the valley, that is, for the natural discrimination which watches over the weak flesh to remain changelessly wedded to virtue (cf. Jos. 10:12-13).[11]

It is through the Spirit, then, that we attain to natural contemplation and behold the *logoi* of creation. Dionysios the Areopagite equated the *logoi* with predeterminations and divine wills,[12] and Maximos followed him in this.[13] This makes explicit that the *logoi* are not just Plato's Forms, seen as the thoughts of God, but are more concerned with expressing God's will and intention for each of his creatures. This consequently lends to the notion of the *logos* an eschatological dimension: the *logos* expresses God's ultimate intention for each creature as it is worked out in the course of time. And here the Spirit comes into its own, for the last times are brought closer through the invocation, epiclesis, of the Spirit. The goal of creation, the

10. L. Thunberg, *Microcosm and Mediator. The Theological Anthropology of Maximus the Confessor,* 2nd ed., Chicago and La Salle, IL: Open Court, 1995, 78.

11. Maximos, *Centuries on Theology and the Economy* II.33 (PG 90.1139CD; trans., modified, from *The Philokalia. The Complete Text,* trans. by G. E. H. Palmer et al., London: Faber & Faber, 1981, 145-46).

12. Dionysios, *Divine Names* 5.8 (ed. B. R. Suchla, *Corpus Dionysiacum* I. *De Divinis Nominibus,* Berlin: Walter de Gruyter, 1990, 188).

13. Cf., e.g., *Amb.* 7 (PG 91.1085A).

point to which creation is moving, is discerned through the invocation of the Spirit.

So, what do we learn from the Byzantine Fathers about the role of the Spirit in creation and re-creation? There is first a warning about translating our own hopes and expectations, as well as our fears, into a theological vein — a danger to which church bodies are all too prone. We are talking about something that can only be discerned as the result of prayer and discernment, itself only reached through a process of ascetic struggle, a struggle as real for the scientist who seeks to distance himself and his hopes and fears from his reflections by the acquisition of a kind of dispassion that is not all that remote from the *apatheia* of the Byzantine spiritual masters. It is, if you like, about acquiring a personal vision: personal, not in the sense of being individualist and arbitrary, but personal because it has been thoroughly assimilated in a personal life. For the Byzantine Fathers that is a process that required a synergy between the human and the divine: both rigorous and honest self-abnegation, which is directed towards reception of the Spirit, who both helps us to realize the purification that such ascetic struggle is directed towards, but also, as the One who comes in response to selfless invocation, requiring in us a capacity for openness that enables us to receive the Spirit. Along with this openness to the Spirit, there comes a respect for the created order itself; the *logoi* of creation that we seek to discern are God's creation and inviolable. What we learn, in short, is that the way to understanding the role of the Spirit in creation and re-creation is not to expect some kind of programme that we are simply to implement, but rather to seek for an attitude of humility and watchfulness — νῆψις in Greek — that will enable us to be responsive to the signs of the Spirit in the world that he created and is re-creating.

Justified in the Spirit: Implications on the Border of Theology and Science

Frank D. Macchia

Justification by grace through faith seems at first glance to be an odd lens through which to view the relationship between a pneumatological theology of creation and science. The classic Protestant understanding of that doctrine is based on Christ and not the Spirit and seems to many to be confined to well-worn and dated debates over works and grace. Yet, is not justification the critical lens through which Protestant theology has always sought to tear down layers of human presumption and ideology in order to open us up to life as a gift to be respected and embraced on its own terms within the overall purposes of God? What if we were to dig deeper into the biblical understanding of this doctrine to discover its vast pneumatological, relational, and even cosmic dimensions? How would a pneumatological doctrine of justification by faith in the light of the first article of the Creed (God as Creator) inform a science/theology conversation? We will start with a challenge that Luther himself bequeathed to us.

1. Luther's *Small Catechism:* The Challenge

At a time when medieval piety was centered on the process of human conversion to God's grace, Luther shifted the axis of salvation to the grace of God revealed in Christ by highlighting the Pauline doctrine of justification by grace through faith. The great Protestant insight into justification is thus in viewing it as a *theological* reality before all else, or as a *divine* judgment and action that reveals the *righteousness of God* in a world that has called it into question. *For Luther, reality is thus not of our making, it is rather a gift to be discovered and participated in.*

We will explore the significance of this insight for a pneumatological theology of creation at the border of theology and science. For now, it is important to note that Luther arrived at his accent on justification when faced with the demands of penance and the uncertainty of the human ability to meet them. The question Luther faced was, "Who could judge the sincerity or adequacy of one's own penance?" As Luther wrote, "no one is sure of the integrity of his own contrition."[1] Luther elaborates by way of a testimony:

> When I was a monk, I made a great effort to live according to the requirements of the monastic rule. I made a practice of confessing and reciting all my sins, but always with prior contrition; I went to confession frequently, and I performed the assigned penances faithfully. Nevertheless, my conscience could never achieve certainty but was always in doubt. . . .[2]

As he tried to do penance faithfully, he "transgressed them even more," making his conscience "the more uncertain, weak, and troubled."[3]

In fact, Luther came to hate the justice of God before he discovered the sufficiency of Christ for salvation. No matter how vigorously he made satisfaction through penance, he was never assured of the results. The harder he tried, the more frustrated he became. Then, in the legendary prayer tower, Luther fell upon Romans 1:17 that "the just by faith shall live." He remarked concerning this discovery: "Here I felt that I was altogether born again and had entered paradise itself through open gates. There a totally other face of the entire Scripture showed itself to me."[4] Justification by faith alone attained the heights of a hermeneutical principle that unlocked the whole of Scripture in a new light for Luther, revealing the grace of God behind all of God's dealings with humanity. As Luther wrote, "For if we lose the doctrine of justification, we lose simply everything. Hence the most necessary and important thing is that we teach and repeat this doctrine daily, as Moses says about his Law (Deut 6:7)."[5]

---

1. M. Luther, *"Disputation of Doctor Martin Luther on the Power and Efficacy of Indulgences (95 Theses) (1517),"* no. 30, in *Works of Martin Luther,* trans. and ed. A. Spaeth, L. D. Reed, and H. E. Jacobs (Philadelphia: A. J. Holman Company, 1915), 1:32.

2. M. Luther, *"Lectures on Galatians"* (1535), in *Luther's Works,* ed. J. Pelikan (St. Louis, MO: Concordia Publishing House, 1963), 27:13.

3. Ibid.

4. M. Luther, *"Preface to the Latin Writings,"* in *Luther's Works,* ed. L. Spitz (Philadelphia: Muhlenburg Press, 1955), 34:337.

5. M. Luther, *Lectures on Galatians* (1519), in *Luther's Works,* ed. J. Pelikan (St. Louis, MO: Concordia Publishing House, 1963), 27:26.

By placing the focus of attention on the sufficiency of God's redemptive work in Christ for our justification, Luther redefined justice in his reading of Romans 1:17 ("the just by faith shall live") as a passive justice, a gift given from Christ to faith.[6] Rather than serving as one virtue among others, faith became the all-encompassing posture of a believer wholly dependent throughout life on God's mercy revealed in Christ. Luther arrived at a notion of grace as the divine righteousness revealed in Christ and alien to us as sinful creatures, thus setting in motion a notion of justification that tended to focus on God's (and our) embrace by grace of that which is alien.

More recently, attention has been placed on the fact that Luther understood all articles of the Christian Creed in the light of justification by grace through faith. This includes the doctrine of creation. Martin Luther wrote in his *Small Catechism* of the first article of the Creed (creation),

> I believe that God has created me and all that exists; that he has given me and still sustains my body and soul, all my limbs and senses, my reason and all the faculties of my mind, together with food and clothing, house and home, family and property; that he provides me daily and abundantly with all the necessities of life, protects me from all danger, and preserves me from all evil. All this he does out of his pure, fatherly, divine goodness and mercy, without any merit or worthiness on my part.

Oswald Bayer rightly notes that Luther in this commentary on the first article of the Creed used language reserved in his writings for justification by faith. At the time the *Small Catechism* was written (1529), the term "merit" was used in the controversy over justification and "unworthy" in the issue over the sacrament. It is significant that Luther used these terms to describe the gift of natural life.[7] Implied is that the believer shares with all living beings the gift of life with all of its vitality and goodness "without merit or worthiness." Again, the cosmos is not of our making. We are stewards of creation under God's Lordship and in respect for creation as God has made it and sustains it. Creation is a gift from God to be discovered and embraced by *faith* or absolute dependence on (and trust in) God as the Giver and Sustainer of life.

6. M. Luther, *Preface to the Latin Writings,* in *Luther's Works,* ed. J. Pelikan (St. Louis, MO: Concordia Publishing House, 1963), 34:337.

7. O. Bayer, *Justification: Basis and Boundary of Theology,* in J. A. Burgess and M. Kolden (eds.), *By Faith Alone: Essays on Justification in Honor of Gerhard O. Forde* (Grand Rapids, MI: Eerdmans, 2004), 70.

Implied in the above quote is that Luther's understanding of justification is part of a broader theology of creation. Similarly, faith is also not only of salvific significance, but is *ontological* in the sense that it is essential to one's fundamental orientation to all of life.[8] Justification by faith seems to have significance analogically for what it means to be human in the broader context of life as a gift. As interesting as these seminal insights are, however, they require development if they are to aid in the conversation between theology and science.

Even in the light of the insights taken above from Luther about the depth and breadth of his understanding of justification in relation to creation, it still must be recognized that the doctrine of justification has historically suffered the reductionism of the medieval preoccupation with penance and personal conversion. Though Luther sought to base the doctrine of justification more forcefully on the divine action, especially the event of the cross and the eschatological reach of the judgment enacted there, justification still tended to be explicated too narrowly within the confines of individual faith in Christ.[9] The classic debate thus raged between Luther and the schoolmen over whether justification was to be understood as God's acceptance of the sinner by faith in Christ or within the dynamics of personal conversion. Even the recent "Joint Declaration on the Doctrine of Justification by Faith," for all of its worth, does not proceed very much beyond the limits of this individualistic focus.

Moreover, the classic bifurcation of justification as either Christological (Protestant) or pneumatological (Catholic) has forced the conversation to choose between two economies that are meant to be viewed perichoretically. If justification is a Trinitarian reality, one cannot play Christology over against pneumatology in this way. Furthermore, the Christ who justifies is the Spirit Baptizer, who imparts the Spirit upon all flesh. Surely, this identity, so key to the way in which all four Gospels introduce him (e.g., Matt. 3:11), must relate to all lenses through which his saving work may be viewed, including that of justification. Thus, even a doctrine of justification based on the work of Christ cannot neglect the righteous favor that is experienced in the embrace and inner witness of the Holy Spirit (Rom. 6:15-16).

8. Ibid., 69-70.

9. I realize that there are resources in Luther for applying justification to the Holy Spirit and to the concrete existence of the church. Concerning this, see my book, *Justified in the Spirit: Creation, Redemption, and the Triune God* (Grand Rapids, MI: Eerdmans, 2010).

Moreover, *the addition of pneumatology to our understanding of justifi-cation has the added benefit of making the doctrine much more robustly rela-tional in the richest sense of that term.* No doctrine of justification that has a pneumatological substance can be individualistic. Though personal, it will also be communal, interdependent, and open to the alien other. A pneumatological dimension to justification would also offer promise for discovering analogous connections to how we relate to all of creation as human beings, connections that offer interesting insights for a conversa-tion between theology and science.

Luther has pointed us in the direction of the basic challenge, namely, to connect justification to the first article of the Christian Creed. But he was too confined to the second article (Christology) to grant us the robust means for taking justification to the first article. Luther's challenge can thus best be fulfilled by expanding his justification doctrine to the third ar-ticle of the Creed (pneumatology). This move is not only more biblical, but also offers greater promise for a pneumatological (and ultimately Trin-itarian) theology of creation that touches on important themes of interest to both theology and science.

2. Recent Pneumatological Expansion of the Theology of Justification

Justification is not only Christological in focus but also pneumatological in breadth. There is no intention here to deny the relevance of justification for personal faith in Christ. There is no question but that within the Pau-line teaching on justification there is a definite focus on the individual who believes on Christ: "For it is with your heart that you believe and are justi-fied, and it is with your mouth that you confess and are saved" (Rom. 10:10). As more recent research has shown, however, Paul's concept of jus-tification is arguably more than mere pardon for the sins based on God's reconciliation with humanity on the cross. Justification involves a reality that is pneumatological and relational as well. We should note several of the more prominent trends.

First, Ernst Käsemann has shown that justification in Paul has vast apocalyptic implications.[10] The crucial issue in justification is thus "new

10. E. Käsemann, *Perspectives on Paul*, trans. M. Kohl (Mifflintown, PA: Sigler Press, 1996), 170-182.

creation" rather than the narrow and relatively peripheral concern over circumcision (Gal. 6:15). God's righteous favor is a force that overcomes evil and transforms those who participate. Justification is thus forensic in the Hebraic sense of the term, in which Yahweh's righteous judgments triumph over the opposition and inaugurate new beginnings. Second, the so-called "new perspective on Paul" has pointed to the ecclesial, even social, implications of justification in Paul, so that rightwising through the death and resurrection of Jesus initiates a new humanity reconciled by faith rather than by the works of the law (Eph. 2:11-22).[11] In the Gospels also, the sinners (or outcasts) convert despite the complaints of the righteous, so that the righteous are expected to convert as well by accepting the sinners. Both the sinners and those who presume to be righteous must convert both to God and to one another at the altar of worship or the banquet table of the Lord (Luke 15:11-41; 18:9-14). Third, there has been a revival of interest among Protestants in the nature of faith beyond confession or mental assent and in the direction of participation in the divine nature. Faith participates in that which it grasps. Justification by faith thus becomes a life-transforming experience that connects mainstream Protestant soteriology with the Eastern notion of *theosis*.[12] Justifying faith is expanded when placed within the reality of God's act of new creation both in Christ and in the reality of the Spirit.

All of these developments sound quite pneumatological, belonging definitely to the third article of the Creed. I have thus tried to integrate these streams through a pneumatological, and thus, fully Trinitarian, understanding of justification within the context of divine *koinonia*.[13] Justification is expansive and relational because it rests ultimately within the life and communion of the triune God. Nicholas Wolterstorff helped me to see that justice is fulfilled within the Trinitarian *koinonia,* since justice is not fundamentally a negative but rather a positive concept, namely, not retribution for a wrong committed but a quality of life in a just self-giving and reciprocity governed by love and mutual regard.[14] *Koinonia* is thus richer than terms like "rectification" for describing the creative and life-giving

11. See N. T. Wright, *What Paul Really Said: Was Paul of Tarsus the Real Founder of Christianity?* (Grand Rapids, MI: Wm. B. Eerdmans, 1997), 114-129.

12. See V.-M. Kärkkäinen, *One with God: Salvation as Justification and Deification* (Collegeville, MN: Liturgical Press, 2005).

13. See my *Justified in the Spirit.*

14. N. Wolterstorff, *Is There Justice in the Trinity?* in M. Volf and M. Welker (eds.), *God's Life in Trinity* (Minneapolis: Augsburg/Fortress, 2006), 177-190.

righteousness of God attained by divine grace. It is more robustly relational, and, therefore, more profoundly holistic and concrete, more explicitly pneumatological.

Justification is indeed a relational dynamic in Paul. One can make the case that the doctrine came to prominence in the Pauline letters due at least in significant part to his commitment to the new humanity formed in Christ consisting of a fellowship of Jew and Gentile. By calling uncircumcised Gentiles righteous, Paul was attaching a typically Jewish category to the Gentiles. By calling Jews sinners, he was attaching a typically Gentile category to Jews. The one body in Christ caused Paul to Judaize Gentiles and to Gentilize Jews. He did this in order to make sense of the new *Christoformed* community entered by the gift of the Spirit received through faith in Christ. In other words, the life of the Spirit of Christ caused an upsetting of the traditional religious categories and a new way of viewing the self-in-communion. The universality of sin in Paul was thus not an abstract category but a very specific one in which people were fundamentally changed in their self-perception by receiving Christ and that which was alien. In the process, one saw one's former self as an accepted alien too, both alien and righteous.

As implied above, Paul's pneumatological and relational understanding of justification has the advantage of connecting justification more profoundly with the Synoptic witness. As Moltmann has suggested, it would be fruitful to examine first the doctrine of justification in the Synoptics where the sinner is identified with the socially outcast. Gerald Sheppard has even suggested that the Gospels be viewed as foundational to the message of the New Testament canon, as the Pentateuch is for the Old Testament.[15]

In Luke, the publican is rightwised by the mercy of God while the privileged Pharisee is denied mercy in his implicit preoccupation with his own superiority over the outcast (Lk. 18:12-14). Justification is a social reality that takes in the alien. Justification in the light of the coming Kingdom of God is meant to change the perspective of both the privileged and the

---

15. "Justification by Faith: Hearing the Voice of the One God through Historically Dissimilar Traditions," in R. Heskett and B. Irwin (eds.), *Bible as Human Witness to Divine Revelation: Hearing the Word of God through Historically Dissimilar Traditions* (Forthcoming through T&T Clark). See also my *Justified in the Spirit: Creation, Redemption, and the Triune God* (Eerdmans). See also G. Sheppard, *Canonization: Hearing the Voice of the Same God through Historically Dissimilar Traditions,* in *Interpretation* (Jan. 1982): 30-32, and J. Moltmann, *"Was heißt heute 'evangelisch'?" Von der Rechtfertigungslehre zur Reich-Gottes-Theologie,* in *Evangelische Theologie* 57 (1997): 41-46.

outcast so that they may embrace each other within the reordering of life occurring through the new life of the Holy Spirit: the justice of the Kingdom of God and the larger reality of divine *koinonia.*

Justification in the Synoptics (as Moltmann has suggested) offers hope not only for the sinners but also for those who suffer most as victims of sin.[16] Jesus thus exhorted the Jewish leaders to invite the oppressed outcasts to their banquet table (Lk. 14:12-14), urging these leaders to show mercy and favor to those who cannot benefit them in any way. It seems that this charge to accept the unclean at the banquet table was criticized at least by some: "This man welcomes sinners and eats with them" (Lk. 15:2). This complaint is the setting in which Jesus then tells the parable of the lost sons in Luke 15. In this parable, justification implies conversion, not just for the outcast and the alien but for the so-called righteous as well. The conversion of the justified is highlighted, since, unlike the lost sheep or lost coin, the errant younger son who squanders his inheritance in a distant land has a change of heart and returns to the household of his father. Rather than receiving the wayward younger son as a household servant, however, the father receives him as a royal guest. When the "righteous" elder son complains about this assumed shameful display of compassion, the father invites him to be converted by this compassion to a higher form of righteousness, a righteousness dedicated to mercy and a respectful acceptance of the alien other based on God's will for the other rather than one's own understanding of what the other should be.

Not only is justification a new relationship with God through Christ and the embrace of the Spirit, it is also a new community that is there for others and that groans for the new creation yet to come. It would be most interesting in the light of this more richly pneumatological and relational understanding of justification to return to Luther's implicit connection of justification to the first article of the Creed to see what insights may be gained for a theology and science conversation.

3. Modalities of Grace: Justification, Pneumatology, and Science

If justification is a pneumatological and richly relational reality, it offers interesting possibilities for a pneumatological theology of creation that borders on interests common to both theology and science. First, we can re-

---

16. J. Moltmann, *"Was heißt heute 'evangelisch'?" Von der Rechtfertigungslehre zur Reich-Gottes-Theologie,* in *Evangelische Theologie* 57 (1997): 41-46.

address Luther's implication that all of reality is not of our making and does not gain its value from our schemes or purposes. It has its own value and worth from the Giver of life who nourishes and sustains life. In the presence of the Spirit, all of life "lives and moves and has its being" (Acts 17:28). Having its being in God's Spirit (as well as in Christ, Col. 1:17), life has its own inherent value that humanity cannot take away, since humanity has not given it. As all of God's gifts, creaturely life does not draw its value from us, nor can it be manipulated or distorted by subordination to our self-serving ideologies and agendas. The modality of what may be termed common grace implies that creation is a gift that must be respected on its own terms.

We should speak pneumatologically and, hence, more expansively about this element of transcendence beyond ideology. Applied analogously to a theology of creation, a pneumatological theology of justification points to a fundamental interdependence of all of life that requires mutual respect and gratitude. All of creation reaches for sociality or a communion that has its ultimate *raison d'être* in the communion of the Triune God. The fundamental interdependence and respect for life that is important to science resonates theologically within a pneumatological understanding of justification in relation to the first article of the Creed.

Sociality, of course, finds its deepest support theologically within the life of the Triune God in which the Spirit functions to enhance and to expand the bond of love enjoyed between the Father and the Son. The Spirit of life who provides the context for the mutual dependence and respect appropriate to all of life urges one to transcend inherent biases that close one off to the polyphony of life. Such an attitude to life can enhance one's theological vision and connect theology more meaningfully to science. As Joseph Sittler wrote:

> I am appealing for . . . an understanding of grace that has the magnitude of the doctrine of the Holy Trinity. The grace of God is not simply a holy hypodermic whereby my sins are forgiven. It is the whole giftedness of life, the wonder of life, which causes me to ask questions that transcend the moment. I am interested in the reality or the presence of the grace of God in the creation, because only the doctrine of grace will be adequate to change the spirit of our minds whereby we deal with timber and oil, fish and animals.[17]

---

17. J. Sittler, *Gravity and Grace: Reflections and Provocations* (Minneapolis: Augsburg Fortress, 2005), 3.

Second, in the light of a pneumatological theology of justification, respect for the communion of life is rooted more specifically in God's acceptance of the alien other by grace. This acceptance forms the basis of the justified community in which both Jew and Gentile reach across the boundary of alienation to embrace one another within the new reality of the Spirit of Christ. Analogously applied to creation, a theology of graced creaturely life sustained by God's favor implies a refusal to label and interpret the alien other in ways that are reducible to our purposes and expectations. This openness to the alien other is not only social within the human sphere of influence but also affects how we relate to the larger network of life, even in the area of scientific investigation. Bertrand Russell stated of the attitude important to both philosophy and science: "The enlargement of Self is not obtained when, taking the Self as it is, we try to show that the world is so similar to this Self that knowledge of it is possible without any admission of what seems *alien*."[18] For Russell, the Self that spins out a world reducible to fulfilling our wants and needs keeps the Self closed off to much of reality and confined within a narrow framework. The Self that opens up to the alien and unfamiliar is creatively challenged and expanded. Respect for the rich interdependence of life viewed on its own terms enlarges one's vision of life and of one's place within it.

Of course, this openness to the unique role of all of life within the framework provided by God as the Giver of life does not deny the presence of distortion and evil within the creation. Yet, that which is alien is not confined to such a privation of the good but extends also to the good intended by God and implied by the uniqueness of all forms of life as graced. All of life has its being in God and is embraced by the Giver of life with all of its distortion. Though precise discernment of the goodness of life is a valued part of one's appreciation of life, openness to that which is alien and unfamiliar is valued as well within the realm of human inquiry. Theologically, this acceptance of the alien other is basic to our understanding of life as graced as well as to the implicit yearning of life for the soteriological gift of righteousness willed by God for the entire creation as the dwelling place of God. Yet, the assumption that all of life is graced and embraced already by the Giver of life provides a fruitful common concern on the boundary of theology and science.

Lastly, the theological reality of faith is passive in the sense that it receives God's verdict and participates in the new reality of justice initiated

18. B. Russell, *The Problems of Philosophy* (Plain Label Books, n.d.), 156.

by God rather than a reality made by us out of our sense of want and need. Faith as a pneumatic reality is participatory and experiential, enjoying the divine presence in the here and now and anticipating the glory that is yet future. As a pneumatological reality, faith is not mere mental assent or confession but rather the means by which the reality of God's justice is grasped and experienced. Justification by faith is thus forensic in the richly Hebraic sense of a divine judgment that actively engages opposing forces in order to triumph over them so that grace becomes something active, creative, and transformative. Faith does not create this new reality though it does accept and participate in it. Note Tillich's admonition:

> It is thus important to stress that the phrase "justification by faith," is a shorthand for the more descriptive and accurate "justification by grace (the Holy Spirit) through faith." Grace as a turning of God to creation through the story of Jesus and the reality of the Spirit is the fundamental reality that justifies. Faith does not justify in the sense of creating the situation of divine favor. The world as favored by God is not of our making. Not faith but grace is the cause of justification, because God alone is the cause. Faith is the receiving act, and this act is itself a gift of grace. Therefore, one should dispense completely with the phrase "justification by faith" and replace it by the formula "justification by grace through faith."[19]

I thus agree with Albert Schweitzer that Paul's point of emphasis in his teachings on justification does not hinge on the issue of faith versus disbelief but rather on the contrast between the law and the eschatological life of the Spirit in Christ (Gal. 4–5). Paul's "by faith" slogan was a "linguistic and dialectic convenience" that allowed him to easily contrast his position with that of his opponents, who emphasized the *works* of the law.[20] The "by faith" principle yields the field to the life of the Spirit of God as the determinative factor in justification.

What faith does do is point to our yielding to a reality determined in its nature and purpose by God alone. Knowing yields to this reality and accepts it, participating in it in ways that respect its unique contribution to the communion of life. As Moltmann notes, knowing in relation to creation "does not transform the counterpart into the property of the

---

19. P. Tillich, *Systematic Theology,* Vol. 3, 224.

20. A. Schweitzer, *The Mysticism of Paul the Apostle* (reprint; New York: Seabury Press 1968), 206-207.

knower."[21] It is participatory and transformative, willing to accept the creation on its own terms as having its own purpose in God. Justification in the Spirit applied analogously to a theology of creation links the anthropological capacity for faith with scientific knowing.

Analogously connected to the first article of the Creed, justification in the Spirit fosters a mode of knowing respectful of that which is known and participatory in the reality being known. This epistemology is certainly the goal of science as well. Both theology and science converge at this understanding of knowing. There is no doubt a creative element to knowing by which we construct and are constructed. But this constructivism should not be taken to mean that there is no sense in which real self-disclosure and participation in the *other* is possible and even to be coveted. Otherwise, there is no possibility for *revelation.* Revelation respects the unique freedom, dignity, and worth of the thing known precisely within the process of knowing. This is true of God as well as of the life that God has brought into being and now sustains. Faith is the subjective (intersubjective) correlate of revelation. The work of the Spirit on both ends preserves the uniqueness of all things as sustained by the Giver of life so that what is known participates in the freedom of that which is known.

4. Concluding Reflection

Robert Jenson rightly notes in response to the overriding theme of justification, "Theology must be done for and in the name of the *ecumene* if it is to be theology and not ideology."[22] A pneumatological theology of justification in the light of the first article of the Creed dismantles all forms of self-serving or self-vindicating ideology and serves the vast *ecumene,* informing also common concerns between theology and science. Certainly, the resistance to ideology is an interest shared between theology and science. Both seek to respect nature on its own terms and to know the other in a way that is true to its own self-disclosure. Each of the two looks at its current state of knowledge and methods of inquiry with some suspicion in order to remain open to new encounters and insights. Each seeks to place all self-serving ideology under the glaring light of critical inquiry. Each

---

21. J. Moltmann, *Trinity and the Kingdom* (Minneapolis: Fortress, 1993), 9.

22. R. Jenson, *Triune Grace,* in N. H. Gregerson and T. Peters (eds.), *The Gift of Grace: The Future of Lutheran Theology* (Minneapolis: Augsburg Fortress, 2005), 17.

seeks a way of knowing that genuinely participates in the reality of nature. Both respect the reach of all things towards sociality and interdependence and see humanity as participants in this reality.

Of course, there are differences. A pneumatological theology of justification also proceeds to the second and third articles of the Creed as well as to the modality of sanctifying grace. It also awaits eschatological fulfillment and vindication in the new creation yet to come. My point in this essay is that a pneumatological theology of justification by grace through faith in the light of the first article of the Creed offers us a very specific means by which we can explore the points of common concern on the border of theology and science. A notion of justification in the Spirit offers us richer resources for this theology/science conversation than the classic Protestant understanding of justification that is confined to the second article. Justification in the Spirit clears away presumption and opens creation to that which God continues to offer us as a gift of grace.

Human Religious Evolution and Unfinished Creation

José Casanova

I am neither a theologian, nor a natural scientist working on evolution. I am a social scientist, specifically a sociologist of religion working on the interrelations between religion and globalization. As such, without claiming any expertise, my contribution to this particular interdisciplinary conversation can only be that of offering some speculative reflections on a few aspects of the interrelations between religion and socio-cultural development from the perspective of the contemporary global present.

But first I would like to introduce some methodological and disciplinary observations. Social scientists have been conspicuously absent from the recent acrimonious debates as well as from the more fruitful interdisciplinary conversations between natural scientists and theologians concerning cosmology, cosmogony, evolution, and creation, that is, the origin, nature, history, and meaning of the universe, its relation to the planet earth, geological history, biological evolution, and the role, place, and meaning of humanity in the whole scheme.[1] What is unquestionable is that today everybody, natural scientists as well as ordinary people, tends to view the *history* of the universe, the *history* of the solar system, the *history* of the earth, the *history* of the species, and human *history* as part and parcel of one single intrinsically related developmental process. In this sense, all methodological and cognitive distinctions notwithstanding, one can observe a clear convergence of natural science with theology.[2] After all, Christian

---

1. Cf. J. F. Haught, *God and the New Atheism: A Critical Response to Dawkins, Harris, and Hitchens* (Louisville: Westminster John Knox Press, 2008), and *Science and Religion: From Conflict to Conversation* (Mahwah, NJ: Paulist Press, 1995).

2. Cf. S. C. Morris, *Life's Solution: Inevitable Humans in a Lonely Universe* (Cambridge: Cambridge University Press, 2003).

theology has always viewed the mystery of creation, the mystery of human salvation, and the mystery of eschatology at the end of times as episodes of a single story. What is remarkable is that natural scientists themselves have adopted increasingly the form of narrative story-telling as they explain the unfolding of the universe in time and space.

This unification of cosmic, biological, and human "history" is the more remarkable if one considers the radical dichotomous methodological and disciplinary separation between the natural sciences and the humanities, particularly the one that emerged between the so-called *Natur-* and *Geistwissenschaften* during the German *Positivismusstreit* at the turn of the 20th century, that became institutionalized within the modern research university. Ironically, natural scientists feel increasingly comfortable telling evolutionary stories of the universe and of the human species, at the very same moment when postmodern debates within philosophy, history, and the social sciences have injected strong methodological suspicions upon all grand narratives, seemingly discrediting in the process all the philosophies of history derived from the Enlightenment.

But one gets the impression that the reticence of social scientists, other than socio-biologists, evolutionary cognitive psychologists, and physical anthropologists, to join natural scientists and theologians in contemporary contentious debates concerning creation, evolution, and the place of humanity in the whole process is not so much due to postmodern skepticism but rather to justifiable longstanding suspicions towards theological and natural scientist explanations of social developments. The reticence of the social sciences to develop theories of socio-cultural evolution has been in many ways affected not only by the misuse of "Social Darwinism" and theories of "the survival of the fittest" in ideological class struggles at home, in Western colonial and civilizing projects, and in the development of racial theories of Aryan superiority that culminated in the Holocaust, but by the justified discredit of "evolutionism" within anthropology and sociology in the 20th century.

Talcott Parsons, the most influential North American sociologist of the 20th century, began his classical work *The Structure of Social Action* somewhat ironically with the question "Who now reads Spencer?" His verdict was that both Spencer and his god, Evolution, were dead.[3] Not only the tone of the question but the response was ironic considering that Parsons himself thirty years later attempted to resurrect evolutionary think-

---

3. T. Parsons, *The Structure of Social Action*, Vol. I (New York: Free Press, 1969), pp. 3-4.

José Casanova

ing within the social sciences when he entertained his ambitious project of developing a "protonaturalist" theory of evolution which would show the fundamental continuity between general organic evolution and socio-cultural evolution.[4] Yet the life of the renewed evolutionary trend within sociology in the 1960's was even shorter and more circumscribed.

If the skepticism concerning the Spencerian version of social evolution was due, as Parsons indicates, to Spencer's extreme individualism, with its tendency to apply the principle of "survival of the fittest" not to the entire species but to individual and racial groups, the problem with Parsons' evolutionism was his inclination to apply it to particular societies. In Parsons' theory, "adaptation" through "differentiation" serves as the guiding principle of socio-cultural evolution, while what he calls "evolutionary universals" are stage-marks which serve to arrange societies within a developmental hierarchy. By selecting as the four evolutionary universals of modernity a bureaucratic administration, a complex market economy, a universalistic legal system, and a democratic polity, Parsons is able to construct the whole evolutionary movement as culminating in American society which shows the evolutionary future to all other societies. Moreover, Parsons is not merely content with reconstructing empirical trends. Implicitly at least he claims to be able to ascertain the "directional" logic of history, placing him in a position to judge which socio-historical developments are normal and which societies will need to change in the prescribed direction in order to adapt successfully and remain in the evolutionary struggle.[5]

The experience of how the application of evolutionary theory to the study of socio-cultural development has been contaminated ideologically again and again by methodological "individualism," by methodological "racism," by methodological "nationalism," indeed by the dominant social ideology of the time, offers a serious warning to any attempt to revive social evolutionism. Even those social scientists who may share the secularist bias of the radical neo-Darwinists concerning religion tend to be put off by cultural Darwinism, once they realize that the new neo-Darwinian evolu-

4. T. Parsons, *Evolutionary Universals in Society,* in *American Sociological Review* 29:3, 1964. This paper and a shortly revived evolutionary trend within sociology emerged out of a seminar on social evolution which Talcott Parsons held in the Spring of 1963 at Harvard University along with Robert Bellah and Shmuel N. Eisenstadt.

5. For a critical review see J. Casanova, *Legitimacy and the Sociology of Modernization,* in A. J. Vidich and R. M. Glassman (eds.), *Conflict and Control* (Beverly Hills, CA: Sage Publications, 1979).

tionary explanations of culture and society, such as Richard Dawkins' science of memetics, tend to be rather clumsy and reductionist.[6]

Yet, given the unquestionable triumph of evolutionary thinking, if professional social scientists continue to avoid entering the contemporary debates, the vacuum will be filled naturally not only by amateur social scientists but by the strident voices of the religious and secular fundamentalist camps. This is the context for my willingness to participate in this interdisciplinary conversation between natural scientists and theologians without claiming any authority or expertise in the field. Indeed, as a social scientist working on religion and globalization, I can only offer a few speculative reflections on the contemporary dilemmas facing humanity at the moment when it has become reflexively aware of:

1. Its natural evolutionary development as a species,
2. The history of human socio-cultural development that culminates in the contemporary phase of globalization, and
3. The radical moral and religious predicament we face as humans at a time when thanks to our cognitive scientific and technological achievements we have, on the one hand, the power to annihilate ourselves, to destroy our environment, or to usher into a new and uncharted phase of human evolution through demiurgic genetic and/or neurological intervention. Yet, on the other hand, we also have the serious responsibility to be receptive to the spirit of creation, to partake and be open to the process of unification and divinization of humanity, and to become intelligent collaborators in the unfinished work of creation.

1. From Natural-Biological to Socio-Cultural-Historical Evolution

Without further elaboration, in this presentation I am simply going to assume as a basic postulate that once the process of biological hominization was completed, socio-cultural evolution took over the reins from natural biological evolution, in the sense that the dynamic of developmental

---

6. Cf. R. Dawkins, *The Selfish Gene* (2nd ed.) (Oxford: Oxford U. P., 1989), *The Blind Watchmaker* (London: Longmans, 1986), and *The God Delusion* (Boston: Houghton Mifflin, 2006); and D. C. Dennett, *Darwin's Dangerous Idea* (New York: Simon & Schuster, 1995), and *Breaking the Spell: Religion as a Natural Phenomenon* (New York: Viking, 2006).

change has been primarily socio-cultural rather than biological; that humanity, while remaining a single human species, became irremediably plural, religiously and culturally. In this respect, in the strict sense of the term humanity has no common history, but multiple histories that converge into our age of globalization. Only now, from the perspective of the global present can we begin the task of constructing and writing the first global histories of humanity.

Much less can one speak of a single human religious evolution. We could at best attempt a narrative analytical history of world religion as a kind of collective biography of the human species, the kind which Robert Bellah is pursuing with his ambitious project on "religious evolution."[7] But such a project is no longer conceivable as a positivist history written from an external objective third-person perspective, but rather as a collective narrative written from the reflexive perspective of the contemporary global human present. As such, any narrative reconstruction that takes the form "we religious and secular humans" will necessarily have a plurality of authors and possibly a cacophony of voices and there is no guarantee that it may ever coalesce into a coherent narrative. The following narrative reconstruction is a modest and self-conscious contribution towards such a collective autobiography.

2. The Three Phases of Human Globalization

From the hermeneutic perspective of the global present, one can arbitrarily distinguish three axial turning points in the global history of humanity or three phases of human globalization:

(a) The original process of hominization, through the socio-cultural construction of language, kinship, and religion, reveals both the tremendous cultural diversity and the transcultural universality of structures which are clearly anchored in human biological, i.e. animal nature, and are thus a continuation of natural evolution. But this evolution undergoes a qualitative jump via the externalization of cognitive processes, i.e. "mind," outside of the brain through language and other cultural institutions and via the externalization of motor sensory processes outside the body through technology.

---

7. See R. Bellah, *Religious Evolution*, in *Beyond Belief* (New York: Harper & Row, 1970), for an early formulation of the ambitious project on which Bellah has now been working for several decades.

We can assume that before the emergence of human language proper hominids shared a phase of mimetic evolution in which biological-genetic evolution and socio-cultural developments were combined and in which forms of collective mimetic communication, proto-arts and rituals, began to emerge as socio-cultural learning processes.

In a certain sense, one could argue that the successive waves of migration of *Homo sapiens* out of Africa some 50,000 years ago and the subsequent settlements throughout the globe constitute the genuine point of departure of the modern process of globalization. But these migrations had no subjective dimension of reflexive consciousness and can only now be reconstructed objectively thanks to advances in DNA and other scientific technologies.

(b) Without any attempt to reconstruct the complex process of development of human consciousness, or the development from "primitive" to "archaic" societies and on to "ancient" civilizations, following Merlin Donald, one can analytically summarize such a development as the passage from "mimetic" to "mythical" to "theoretic" mind.[8] From such a developmental perspective one can also assert that the "Axial Age" constitutes a second turning point in the global history of humanity. It was so named by Karl Jaspers to signal the striking fact in world history that cosmological worldviews and world religions, based on some notion of "transcendence," emerged at approximately the same time, 600 to 200 BCE, throughout Eurasia.[9] These worldviews still serve as the foundations of the plural human civilizations which have remained influential globally till the present. This concept of axiality also sets the pluralistic thesis of the simultaneous historical origins of all Eurasian civilizations in contrast to the Eurocentric (i.e. Christocentric) fixation on Jerusalem and Athens. The concept of "axiality" is also central for contemporary formulations of the theory of multiple modernities in contradistinction to Western-centric theories of secular modernity.[10]

8. M. Donald, *Origins of the Modern Mind: Three Stages in the Evolution of Culture and Cognition* (Cambridge, MA: Harvard University Press, 1991), and *A Mind So Rare: The Evolution of Human Consciousness* (New York: W. W. Norton & Company, 2001).

9. K. Jaspers, *The Origin and Goal of History* (New Haven: Yale University Press, 1953).

10. Cf. J. P. Arnason, S. N. Eisenstadt, and B. Wittrock, *Axial Civilizations and World History* (Leiden: Brill, 2004); S. N. Eisenstadt (ed.), *Multiple Modernities* (New Brunswick, NJ: Transaction Books, 2002); E. Ben-Rafael and Y. Sternberg (eds.), *Comparing Modernities: Pluralism vs. Homogeneity: Essays in Homage to Shmuel N. Eisenstadt* (Leiden: Brill, 2005).

Any theory of "religious" evolution needs to make some distinction between the dyadic analytical categories sacred/profane, transcendent/immanent, and religious/secular. We have a tendency today to use those dyadic categories as if they were synonymous and interchangeable, when in fact they correspond to historically distinctive, somewhat overlapping but not synonymous or equivalent social systems of classification. The sacred tends to be immanent in pre-axial societies, transcendence is not necessarily religious in some axial civilizations, and much contemporary secular reality (the nation, citizenship, the person, inalienable rights to life and freedom) far from being profane, actually attains a sacred character in our modern secular age.

Sacred and profane, following Emile Durkheim, should be viewed as a general dichotomous classificatory scheme of all reality, characteristic of all pre-axial cultures, encompassing within one single order what later will be distinguished as three separate realms: the cosmic, the social, and the moral. All reality, gods and spirits, nature and cosmic forces, humans and other animal species, and the political, social, and moral orders are integrated into a single order of things according precisely to the dichotomous classificatory system of sacred and profane. The entire system, moreover, is an immanent "this worldly" one, if one is allowed to use anachronistically another dichotomous category that will only emerge precisely with the so-called "axial" revolutions.

What defines "axiality" is precisely the emergence of "transcendence," of an order, principle, or being, beyond this worldly reality, which now can serve as a transcendent principle to evaluate, regulate, and possibly transform this worldly reality. As in the case of the Platonic world of "ideas," or the Confucian reformulation of the Chinese *tao*, transcendence is not necessarily "religious," in the strict or modern sense of the term, nor does all "religion" need to become transcendent, if we are allowed once again to use anachronistically another dichotomous classificatory category, "religious/secular," that will first emerge within Medieval Christendom and will later expand into a central dynamic of secular modernity.

All axial breakthroughs introduce some form of transcendent path, individual and collective, of salvation, redemption, or moral perfection. In some cases, as in Buddhism, this transcendent path may entail a radical devaluation and rejection of all reality and a flight from this world, as analyzed by Max Weber. In the case of the radical transcendent monotheism introduced by the prophets in Ancient Israel, the axial revolution entails a desacralization of all cosmic, natural, and social reality, of all creatures, gods, and idols for the sake of the exclusive sacralization of Yahweh, the transcendent creator God.

Following Robert Bellah, one can view the various axial prophets, critics, or teachers as either radical world "renouncers" or radical world "denouncers."[11] Though not all axial paths entail some kind of refashioning or transformation of the world or the social order, as Charles Taylor has pointed out, all of them entail some refashioning of "the self," who is now "called" to live (or precisely to deny herself) according to some transcendent norm "beyond ordinary human flourishing."[12] In this respect, axiality constitutes also the point of departure of the process of disembedding of "self" from society and cosmos which culminates in modern individualism.

Transcendence serves also to anchor the ethical and logical universalism which permeates all axial worldviews. In this respect, it was in and through the axial breakthroughs that the subjective dimension of imagining a single humanity sharing the same global space (the earth) and the same global time (history) was first anticipated. Yet, these imaginary, and thus utopian or eschatological anticipations of the contemporary phase of globalization, while serving as preconditions for the civilizational expansion of the world religions, lacked a structural, i.e. objective and material global base. Until very recently, the civilizational *oikoumenē* of all world religions had very clear territorial limits, set by the very world regimes in which those religions were civilizationally and thus territorially embedded and by the geographically circumscribed limitations of the existing means of communication. The Bishop of Rome may have always claimed to speak *urbi et orbi,* to the city and to the globe. But in fact this became a reality first in the 20th century.

(c) The contemporary final phase of globalization is the one in which the subjective conditions of reflexive universal human consciousness and the objective conditions of a modern global civilization based on the world capitalist system, the international political system, and the modern scientific and technological revolutions have become aligned. In a sense the contemporary phase of globalization is a continuation of the series of world-historical processes initiated by the age of discoveries and the European global colonial expansion. But there is a qualitative break in so far as contemporary processes of globalization cannot be understood simply anymore as the global expansion of Western modernization, but need to

11. R. Bellah, "The Renouncers," in *The Immanent Frame,* http://blogs.ssrc.org/tif/2008/08/11/the-renouncers/.

12. C. Taylor, *A Secular Age* (Cambridge, MA: Harvard University Press, 2007), 17.

be recognized as a new dynamic of pluralization of multiple modernities which are in many ways related to the pluralization of civilizations which emerged out of the axial age.

From the perspective of religious evolution, what constitutes the truly novel aspect of the present global condition is precisely the fact that all religions can be reconstituted for the first time as de-territorialized global imagined communities, detached from the civilizational settings in which they have been traditionally embedded. Paraphrasing Arjun Appadurai's image of "modernity at large," one could say that the world religions, through the linking of electronic mass media and mass migration, are being reconstituted as de-territorialized global religions "at large."[13] What is characteristically novel of the present global condition is the emerging dissociation of world religions, civilizational identities, and geopolitical territories. Each world religion is being constituted on the global level through similar interrelated processes of particularistic differentiation, universalistic claims, and mutual recognition.

In this respect, as Roland Robertson has emphasized, universal particularism and particular universalism are intrinsically interrelated and inherent to processes of globalization.[14] Each "world religion" claims its universal right to be unique and different, thus its particularism, while at the same time presenting itself globally as a universal path for all of humanity. Global denominationalism emerges through a process of mutual recognition of the particular and universal claims. What is at stake, ultimately, is the recognition of the irremediable plurality of universalisms and the multiplicity of modernities, namely, that every universalism and every modernity is particularistic. One could say that we are moving from a condition of competing particularist universalisms to a new condition of global denominational contextualism.

3. Unfinished Creation and the Dilemmas of Intelligent Design

At the very same moment in which humanity becomes practically aware of its unity as a species and reflexively aware of sharing the same global his-

13. A. Appadurai, *Modernity at Large* (Minneapolis: University of Minnesota Press, 1996).

14. R. Robertson, *Globalization: Social Theory and Global Culture* (London: Sage, 1992); and R. Robertson and J. Chirico, *Humanity, Globalization, Worldwide Religious Resurgence: A Theoretical Explanation,* in *Sociological Analysis,* 46, 1985, pp. 219-42.

torical present, it is being forced to look simultaneously back into its past and forward into its future. It must both come to terms with its natural evolutionary development and with the complex dynamics of its socio-cultural development and at the same time contemplate its uncertain and radically contingent futures. The old moral and religious traditions appear at first to be woefully inadequate to confront the radically new challenges derived from the ever accelerating pace of techno-scientific developments. Yet, without a serious reflection upon its socio-cultural evolution, humanity may not find the moral resources needed to confront its radically new scientific and technological challenges. As Robert Bellah has pointed out:

> If, as I believe, we human beings are at least to some extent in charge of our own evolution, we are in a highly demanding situation. . . . Even if we can speak of societies with normatively lower and higher levels of social learning capacity, we can never assume that there is anything inevitable about attaining the higher levels. If we are going to talk about levels at all, as I am prepared to do, we must expect to find regress as well as progress and face the possibility that the human project may end in complete failure.[15]

Nuclear disaster has been ominously one of humanity's potential futures since the use of the atomic bomb at Hiroshima. A halt to nuclear proliferation appears geopolitically more out of control than ever. To this global apprehension one must add the increasing awareness that ecological disaster at a planetary scale has become an even more realistic threat due to global warming and the relentless exploitation of our natural environment. But, in principle at least, both catastrophes could be averted if global humanity finds the right combination of reflexive solidaristic consciousness, moral and political resolve, scientific-technological creativity, and a greater recognition of our irremediable cultural (and religious) diversity in order to make what appear to be the more intelligent and rational choices. Pragmatically, of course, we also know how difficult it is for individuals and groups to forgo their own particularistic self-interest for the sake of the common good, even when collective survival is at stake.

The ongoing sacralization of humanity which is part and parcel of the process of globalization is not enough.[16] Perhaps nothing short of a new

---

15. Bellah, *The Renouncers*, p. 1.

16. J. Casanova, *The Sacralization of the Humanum: A Theology for a Global Age*, in *International Journal of Politics, Culture, and Society*, 13:1, Fall 1999, pp. 21-40.

re-sacralization of nature and of the earth will be sufficient if we are to change our ways in order to face responsibly the impending ecological crisis. In this context, new *Gaia* and greener creationist theologies are going to be needed. But until now the Judeo-Christian tradition with its anthropocentric calling to subdue and master the earth and all living creatures has been more part of the problem than of the solution. All of humanity will need to draw on the religious resources of all the non-Western religious traditions if we are to develop a more reverential attitude towards animate nature. The *Gaia* principle should teach us that there is no such a thing as inanimate nature, that the spirit of creation dwells everywhere.

But perhaps the more difficult dilemma, in the long term, is going to be how we as a species learn to use morally, creatively, responsibly, and self-limitedly the tremendous demiurgic powers unleashed by the new breakthroughs in biogenetics and by the new cognitive sciences of the brain/mind. The tragic paradox of the new and vociferous scientistic materialist neo-Darwinism could be revealed in the humanist temptation or *hubris* to abandon the monotonous insistence on a blind, random, merciless, and meaningless process of natural selection for the sake of a model of rational scientific "intelligent design" at the moment when humans or "transhumans" can assume the role of creator's apprentice.

The no less ironic paradox of the creationist or "intelligent design" paradigm, by contrast, would be revealed in the loss of faith in the spirit of creation and the loss of hope in the promise of human theosis, at the very moment when humans could actually become active participants and collaborators in the process of unfinished creation and in a new emerging phase of human evolution.

But the greatest paradox of all, and possibly the greatest threat to our living environment and to any promise of human redemption within a renewed creation, could be revealed if "intelligent design" were to become the poignant metaphor of a new anthropomorphic post-Darwinian deism replacing the old post-Newtonian deist metaphor of the watchmaker. Man could again be tempted to eat of the tree of knowledge beyond good and evil.

Authors

DENIS ALEXANDER, Dr. phil., is a molecular biologist and Director of the Faraday Institute for Science and Religion, St. Edmund's College, Cambridge.

JOSÉ CASANOVA, Dr. phil., Dr. h.c., is professor of sociology at the Berkley Center for Religion, Peace, and World Affairs at Georgetown University.

SERGEY HORUJY, Dr. phil., is professor of philosophy at the Institute of Philosophy of the Russian Academy of Science (RAS) and Director of the Institute of Synergetic Anthropology (ISA) in Moscow.

CYRIL HOVORUN, Dr. phil., is Chair of the Department for External Church Relations, Ukrainian Orthodox Church. He is part of the staff of the Metropolis of Kiev and a lecturer at the faculty of the Theological Academy of Kiev.

VLADIMIR KATASONOV, Dr. phil., is professor and chair of philosophy of religion and religious aspects of culture at St. Tikhon's Orthodox University in Moscow. He taught mathematics at the Moscow Power Engineering Institute, a graduate school of the Mathematical Faculty of Moscow State University.

ANDREW LOUTH, Dr. phil., is professor of patristic and Byzantine studies and Orthodox chaplain at the University of Durham.

FRANK D. MACCHIA, Dr. theol., is professor of systematic theology and director of the graduate program at Vanguard University of Southern California.

Authors

JÜRGEN MOLTMANN, Dr. theol., Dr. h.c. mult., is professor emeritus of systematic theology and social ethics at Tübingen University.

FRIEDERIKE NÜSSEL, Dr. theol., is professor of systematic theology and Ecumenical Studies and head of the Ecumenical Institute at Heidelberg University.

RENOS K. PAPADOPOULOS, Dr. phil., is professor of analytical psychology at the Center for Psychoanalytic Studies at Essex University.

MARCUS PLESTED, Dr. phil., is an affiliated lecturer in the Faculty of Divinity and vice principal and academic director of the Institute of Orthodox Christian Studies (IOCS) at Cambridge University.

JOHN POLKINGHORNE, Dr. phil., Dr. rer. nat., Dr. h.c. mult., KBE, FRS, is professor emeritus of theoretical physics at Cambridge University. He is a Fellow of Queens' College as well as Canon Theologian of Liverpool.

JEFFREY SCHLOSS, Dr. rer. nat., is professor of biology at Westmont College in Santa Barbara, CA, and Director of Biological Programs for the Christian Environmental Association.

VLADIMIR SHMALIY, Dr. phil., is an associate professor of theology and vice rector for academic affairs at the Moscow Institute of Physics and Technology.

MICHAEL WELKER, Dr. theol., Dr. phil., Dr. h.c., is professor and chair of systematic theology and executive director of the Research Centre for International and Interdisciplinary Theology (FIIT) at Heidelberg University.